HE WHO DOES NOT HOWL WITH THE WOLF

WITH THE WOLF

The Wagner Legacy

A N A U T O B I O G R A P H Y

Design: David Houghton

Printed by: MPG Books, Bodmin

Published by: Sanctuary Publishing Limited, 82 Bishops Bridge
Road, London W2 6BB

Copyright: Verlag Kiepenheuer & Witsch, Köln, 1997

Preface: © Rabbi Julia Neuberger, 1998

Photographs: courtesy of the author except where credited. Cover
photo courtesy of the Lebrecht Collection, London

While the publishers have made every reasonable effort to trace the
copyright owners for any or all of the photographs in this book,
there may be some omissions of credits for which we apologise.

ISBN: 1-86074-228-9

HE WHO DOES NOT HOWL WITH THE WOLF

The Wagner Legacy

A N   A U T O B I O G R A P H Y

Gottfried Wagner

English translation by Della Couling

ACKNOWLEDGMENTS

My thanks to Eberhard Wagner, Karl Lubomiski, Dorothea Hug-Lauener, Michael Wieck, Ralph Giordano, Jan G Colijn, Michael Shapiro, Abraham Peck and Christian v Ditfurth.

I also thank my mother, Ellen Drexel-Wagner for allowing me to consult her diaries and photos.

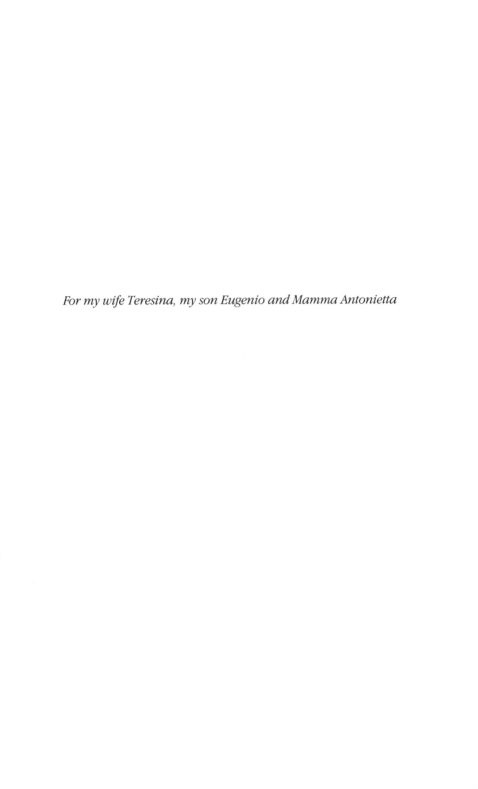

For my wife Teresina, my son Eugenio and Mamma Antonietta

CONTENTS

PREFACE

by Rabbi Julia Neuberger

For those, like me, who are convinced that something of Richard Wagner's antisemitism is to be found in his music, this volume of autobiography by his great-grandson brings comfort and hope. Gottfried Wagner was brought up in the overwhelming shadow of Bayreuth and Wagner-olatry. Life at home was wholly dominated by productions of Wagner operas by his father or uncle. His grandmother still talked of "Uncle Wolf", the family's pet-name for Hitler. There was no sense of guilt, no sense of apology, no sense of family warmth. They simply lived an unpleasant legend, with internecine quarrels within the family.

Meanwhile Gottfried began to doubt the legend, and then broke away entirely – or was dismissed from the "holy" presence of Wagner inspiration. He began to explore his family's role in the Holocaust, and the nature of antisemitism in Richard Wagner's own lifetime. It does not make a pretty tale. Gottfried tells the already well-known episode of Wagner's writing of 'The Jews In Music', and continues with an account of Wagner's gradual conviction that the racial theorising that became fashionable in the 1880s was right.

No one can argue that Wagner's deeply held prejudices and hatred led directly to the gas chambers. But the reluctance of his descendants in any way to condemn him for what he said, the desire to continue the great worship and the festival as if the man was somehow a hero because of the music he wrote, needs close examination.

Gottfried lived with this from his birth in 1947. He looked into the Wagner abyss and saw something horrible. He has made his life in dialogue and reconciliation, in recognition of human pain across ethnic divides. He has also made his way as a dramaturg in music insofar as he has been able. But his family has tried to prevent his success. This volume, published in English for the first time, will irritate and anger the Wagner clan more than ever. More than that, it will upset the very considerable number of anglophone Wagnerians, who have tried to close their eyes to the monster who was their musical hero, the fine artist and pig of a man who was able to put some of his more unpleasant ideas into his music.

One cannot say that one must judge the art by the man. But one can argue that the inclusion, in deliberate contrast to the noble Teuton, of figures such as Alberich and Mime in *Siegfried*, with the strong implication that they were Jews, is more than innocent art. It has a moral message and that message is a vile one.

In recent years, Israelis and other Jews have conducted at Bayreuth, including Daniel Barenboim and James Levine. Their own motives are left unexplored here. Yet many Jews are Wagnerians. My own grandfather was a keen enthusiast. Is it that they do not want to see? Or are they, as I sometimes am myself, so carried away by the animal appeal of the music that they will forgive its creator anything? Gottfried Wagner writes a tale that suggests that we should think again, and that those who continue the Wagner legend need to examine their consciences to see what they have contributed by their uncritical hero-worship.

Gottfried Wagner made his break, and tells his tale. He is a brave man, and to be congratulated for his courage and understanding. But he raises questions he then leaves in part unanswered, about the degree to which it is the duty of the artist to think how his work might be used, and the duty of the artist's descendants to ensure that the use to which the artist's work has been put is noble, or at the very least not damaging to others. His response is that empathy is the duty, the individual responsibility, of every single human being in their daily lives. Artists, such as the Wagners, cannot claim some superior status that exempts them from that duty as a result of their "high art". Gottfried Wagner's view is that in "the loss of empathy in our human existence [we can find]...the reason for all evil".

So far so good; but there is an additional point, about personal responsibility for what happened, as well as about a failure to recognise the duty of empathy – and here Gottfried Wagner leaves questions unanswered, though his sense that we are all responsible for one another, that we all have to sense what it might be like to be in each other's situations, each other's shoes, is a strong statement of his philosophical beliefs.

More compelling is what he does not so much spell out as live. The early chapters suggest a young man of a rebellious nature, rebelling against an impossible family whom he blamed – some of us would argue rightly – indirectly for some of what happened during the Holocaust. What he has grown into is someone who has taken on part of that responsibility, whilst failing to be recognised by that same family. By becoming involved in – indeed, helping to set up – his Post Holocaust Dialogue Group, we see someone trying to face his family's past, his nation's past, and struggling with it. He has accepted an indirect line, an indirect responsibility, though no one can be held accountable for what was done before their birth. But he has shown by his later actions a realisation that one can play a role in healing, in learning from "the other".

There is no doubt that Gottfried Wagner gets under the skin of his Wagner relatives. He does not believe the Wagner myth. He is not part of Wagner-olatry. He cannot sit breathless and silent through a Bayreuth *Ring*. His story tells us much about the family, much about the inability of many of its members to see where Richard Wagner's ideas would, could, lead. Yet Gottfried Wagner leaves us asking yet more questions about how far responsibility can be extended. Perhaps, as a man so curious about life and responsibility, it is only to be expected that he would.

INTRODUCTION

by Ralph Giordano

Classified Document "USA"

1.

H*e Who Does Not Howl With The Wolf* is an alternative account of official Bayreuth, its representatives, past and present, and the conventional history of the family and the *Festspiele*. It is written by a Wagner of our own times, who demands something that has hitherto been absent on the *Festspielhügel*: honesty.

It is an examination, with the essence of a feud and all the depth of a biography – and, compared to other such self-examinations, is in a dimension of its own.

Before me is a photo that anyone already familiar with the dramatic contents of this book can only view with emotion: taken in 1951 in Wahnfried Park in Bayreuth, it shows the four-year-old Gottfried, great-grandson of Richard Wagner and son of present head of the *Festspiele* Wolfgang Wagner, smartly dressed and leading Pupsi, a black Scotch terrier. It is a snapshot of a cute Wagner child, "in the sheltered ivory tower of the family Grail", as the subject was later to refer to the idyll. The image will not last, the first shadows fall early and soon find a name – "Bayreuth logic". Gottfried is forbidden to play with the other Wagner children – the fathers, Wolfgang and Wieland, have fallen out. And so he grows up with his father's contemptuous remarks about the brother, Gottfried's uncle.

Discord lies in the air, and has a powerful effect on the child's sensitive young mind.

But at that time, so soon after the end of the Second World War, control over family and *Festspiele* is exercised neither by Wieland nor Wolfgang, but by their mother Winifred Wagner, the wife of Richard Wagner's son Siegfried, who had died in 1930. The matriarch surpassed anyone's wildest conception of a Valkyrie; and the bosom friend she affectionately called "Wolf" was better known to the world at large as Adolf Hitler. Thus we identify the root of the conflict so personally described in this book, the initial spark, as it were, which was referred to in Winifred Wagner's era by a codeword that says much about the milieu: "USA" – which in this context did not mean the United States of America, however, but *"Unser Seliger Adolf"* – Our Blessed Adolf. The ardent allegiance to Hitler before 1945 took on a coded form afterwards, but remains the cornerstone in the mindset of the ruler of Bayreuth and leads to the continuation of a strictly observed repression: the copiously documented history of the Wagner family and National Socialism is still kept under lock and key.

2.

Of course Gottfried Wagner was not born with any knowledge of what was supposed to remain hidden. Rather he uncovered it layer by layer, all the time retaining a quality which would affect him all his life: the search and demand for honesty.

During the course of this discovery, it has taken on something of the nature of a political thriller.

At an early age Gottfried Wagner is fascinated by pictures from cinema newsreels, magazines, newspapers and school film screenings on the period of National Socialism showing hysterical, mass adulation for the "Führer", mass rallies, warlike parades, the victories of the Wehrmacht far beyond German borders and horrific images of mountains of corpses in the concentration camp of Buchenwald.

In horror, the child turns to his father: what is it all about, these pictures, accompanied as background music by his great-grandfather's own compositions? To which questions Wolfgang Wagner initially replies: "You are still too young to understand all that." Then, when the son refuses to accept this, the father shouts that he is to kindly go and play or, better still, "actually do some homework".

Intimidated, Gottfried Wagner withdraws, but even then, in 1956, as a child not yet ten years old a chord had been struck and a sensitive curiosity aroused, neither of which were to abate.

In the same year he finds the key to what was known as the painting room in the *Festspiele* building and, once inside, discovers a wealth of photos of his grandmother, Winifred, with Hitler, and countless handwritten letters – dusty and dirty, but legible – documenting devotion, admiration for and allegiance to the beloved friend "Wolf".

In 1963, now sixteen years old and his suspicions fully aroused, Gottfried breaks into a woodshed, where he finds two cardboard boxes containing a number of film cans. Held up against the light, the celluloid reveals a lively *tête-à-tête*: Winifred and other members of the family, right arms stiffly raised and beaming with joy, with the Führer. He obviously felt completely at home on the *Festspielhügel* – clearly scenes of an intimate gathering.

Why had this never been talked about in the family?

Now the clearer outlines of a feud become visible: a feud which later will lead one of the Bayreuth clan – the author of this book – to set off in an opposite direction, leaving the family forever.

Next step: Gottfried Wagner questions the cameraman – his own father. To ask his opinion without making him suspicious, the son, who has become distrustful after his initial experience, remains silent both about what he has found and his surprise that nothing is said about such gatherings. What is the truth behind the connection of the Wagner family and Hitler? Wolfgang Wagner's answers are quite spontaneous recollections of an insider, still-fascinated by "Uncle Wolf": the Führer's visit to his sickbed, cosy chats at the Führer's fireside, calling one another by the familiar *Du* form, words in praise of Hitler's "great services for the German people". To his son's question on the business with the Jews: that's a lot of gossip, anti-German agitation by left-wing intellectuals. But it was Hitler's only mistake: "If he had won over the Jews, then we would have won the war."

That set the lines of demarcation between father and son, although at that time their differences had not yet reached a point of open conflict.

A deceptive interim stage.

3.

The aversion to what he has seen and read sits deep in Gottfried Wagner. Not least is the effect Winifred Wagner's letters to Hitler have on him, especially as they were not the effusions of a flighty opportunist after the seizure of power on 30 January 1933, but were written at a time when the National Socialist Party was still a regional party based in Bavaria and no one could have believed that the muddleheaded author of an unread book with the title *Mein Kampf* would, ten years later, exercise total power over Germany.

As early as 14 November 1923 in the *Oberfränkische Zeitung*, a few days after Hitler's failed *putsch* attempt in front of the Munich Feldherrnhalle, Winifred Wagner ardently declares her allegiance to the supremo of the brown-shirted thugs as follows: "Bayreuth knows that we have friendly relations with Adolf Hitler." And at Christmas the same year Siegfried Wagner writes: "We got to know the splendid man here in the summer at the German rally…My wife is fighting like a lioness for Hitler – first-rate."

And Winifred Wagner remained true to this cause throughout her whole life, with unabashed incorrigibility, and full of contempt for the second German democracy, the Federal Republic, which was as little hers as the first one, the Weimar Republic.

Even after 1945 Gottfried Wagner's grandmother remained faithful to the Nazi bigshots: she received Edda Göring, Ilse Hess, the NPD chairman Adolf von Thadden, the British Fascist leader Oswald Mosley and many other ultra-reactionaries in Bayreuth and never made a secret of her unrepentant love for Hitler or her unflagging antisemitism. Later she liked introducing her wayward grandson Gottfried as the "friend of Bolsheviks and Jews", then, as he remembers with a shudder, "she would give a loud and manly laugh".

4.

'Antisemitism And Bayreuth' – that comes from deep down, from the cave of the "Grail", from Richard Wagner, the Master himself. It was continued by the anti-Jewish *ancien régime* of his wife Cosima, who died in 1930, having outlived her husband by forty-seven years, and by a labyrinthine clan, to which the Anglo-German racial ideologist Houston Stewart Chamberlain, husband of Richard Wagner's daughter Eva, belonged, and which was headed by Winifred Wagner.

"You still don't know the Jews," Gottfried Wagner quotes his grandmother as saying, "just wait. One day you'll understand me, and Hitler will be seen differently in world history." And when questioned about the Holocaust, she answers: "That's all just lies and slander by American Jews!" To which the grandson commented: "That reminded me of Father's reaction when I asked him about Hitler."

And it was Winifred Wagner too, more than all the others, who upheld the family's antisemitic tradition from almost the beginning of our century, until it was approaching its end.

When she died on 5 March 1980 at the age of eighty-two, there was no mention at all of this at her funeral five days later. Neither the lifelong hatred of Jews is mentioned, nor the name of her dear friend Wolf – Adolf Hitler, Chancellor and Führer of the greater German Reich who, although fallen, was still held in honour by Winifred Wagner to her dying day.

The farce was further heightened by the fact that even Bayreuth's mayor at the time, Mayor Wild, remained "diplomatically" silent on the National Socialism of the deceased, which had been internalised and openly propagated in equal measure.

Did the antisemitic era on the *Festspielhügel* die with the incorrigible Winifred? It is left to the readers of this book to gauge for themselves from statements such as that from the mouth of Wolfgang Wagner: "The Jews themselves have been the worst racists in history" and "Jews themselves made an essential contribution to the Nuremberg race laws". The head of the Bayreuth *Festspiele* is in fact saying that the Jews had contributed to their own disenfranchisement, which I regard as being tantamount to believing that the Jews are themselves the originators of antisemitism through their behaviour. Nothing is more infamous. The gulf between Wolfgang Wagner's autobiography, *Acts*, and this book cannot be bridged – nothing of the son's book resembles what he has criticised in his father's.

"I wanted to find answers to the question of why he represses his own and his family's past – as head of the Bayreuth *Festspiele*, as Wagner and as my father," the son writes bitterly. "But on reading *Acts*

19

I became painfully aware of how he had yielded to the contemporary mood in repressing his own past."

5.

It is no wonder that for Gottfried Wagner it became difficult, and ultimately impossible, to breathe in the stifling family air. No longer satisfied with sporadic questioning, he abandons such tactics. The more he probes the more it transpires that he is different from the rest of his family; something he even publicly announces. He refuses to allow himself to be intimidated by his father's defensiveness, which is at first distraught, then furious and finally hostile. What follows is that the disrespectful son – Gottfried – is expelled by the lord and master of Bayreuth.

What a Wagner dared here was sacrilege, blasphemy, the breaching of an unwritten Bayreuth Charter.

One who does not howl with the wolf.

And things have remained that way; that is the core of the matter. Gottfried Wagner is determined to reveal what a fossilised tradition still silences and conceals. How can there be a comprehensive and historically accurate picture of the family and the *Festspiele*, if the copious correspondence between the Wagners and Hitler, the film and photographic material from the Nazi era, are not made accessible to the public and to historians?

Even in the 1984 exhibition *Wagner And The Jews* there was as little to be seen of this evidence as there was to be read in the 1985 catalogue: not *one* line, not *one* picture! Or, to use the language of *Lohengrin*: the "Grail" remains as safely hidden as it ever was.

A rebel has emerged from the family that wants to draw a line under the whole business, countering the offended cultural might of Bayreuth.

What Gottfried Wagner is expressing in this autobiography is his inability to come to terms with the status quo: his refusal to remain silent about his family's murky collaboration with the prime perpetrator of the Holocaust, Winifred's beloved Wolf, a sympathy that extended far beyond the latter's cowardly end; the fact that the *Festspielhügel* will not allow its most treasured possession to be attacked; and to allow the living lie to go unpunished, that Bayreuth is cleansed of the swastika. The outcast speaks of a "Bayreuth connection" and gives some startling examples of its long arm, but he does not let this get him down.

It is Gottfried's incurable honesty, noted by everyone who comes into contact with him, that makes his life difficult. This "post-Auschwitz Wagner" who "would never be prepared to remain silent about, or offer unswerving loyalty to, a questionable family tradition for the sake of his career". And furthermore: "I have known since my childhood that by such behaviour I place myself outside the normal 'morals and tolerance' of a certain German establishment, which may repress its own past in an act of self-alienation."

Much of what is recounted in this book may be interpreted differently – why not? But, as anyone who knows him would understand, even where Gottfried Wagner appears to delude himself, it is the desire for truth that guides his pen.

6.

I am the godfather of this book.

The idea came to me at our very first meeting, which took place in 1988 via a friend from Bonn, Bettina Fehr. She had given Gottfried Wagner my book, *The Second Guilt or On The Burden Of Being German*, and after reading it he immediately asked to meet the author. Even if he had not been introduced to me as a Wagner, if we had encountered one another quite by chance in the street somewhere – I would still have guessed his identity. The similarity to his great-grandfather Richard Wagner is too striking, the unmistakable family features too noticeable – the emphatic profile, the aquiline nose, the prominent skull.

Until that day, now over nine years ago, I had no idea of his history, but immediately sensed the enormous pressure this man, then forty-one-years-old, was under, and I listened. Gottfried spoke for hours, it literally poured out of him, while I understood more and more of what I was witnessing.

What must it have been like for a man like him, to have to live with a cover-up, as artificial as it was energetically defended, with all its inevitable distortion of the truth? That physical punishment was also part of his father's method of education, as has now been revealed, does not really fit into the image of the long-time Bayreuth master of ceremonies which Wolfgang Wagner has presented in spoken and written word.

Naturally, I was curious about the connection between the great-grandson and Richard Wagner – and was soon to know.

In the same way that Gottfried Wagner seeks the truth about Bayreuth, he also wants to know the truth about his great-grandfather: a full picture, with nothing glossed over or concealed, a picture which has none of the falsifications and opportunism of Wagner marketing, still controlled by organised repression. The great-grandson wants to portray the complete person of Richard Wagner, with all his faults: the captivating charmer *and* the unspeakable antisemite, originator of the essay 'The Jews In Music', the universal genius Richard Wagner *and* the lamentable betrayer of friends, the everyday man fussing over trifles *and* the creator of new, previously unheard worlds of sound.

In his pursuit of clarification, the great-grandson's attitude towards his great-grandfather has become more radical. Asked whether or not Richard Wagner had contributed to the fatal development of antisemitism in Germany, Gottfried Wagner always answered in the positive, but added: "I maintain that the theory, based on his work and historical developments, that he is partly responsible for the Shoah, is not justifiable." He later modified this opinion, saying: "Richard Wagner himself has contributed to the inextricable link between Bayreuth, Theresienstadt and Auschwitz."

This theory is disputed by Bayreuth, which has long paraded maestros such as Daniel Barenboim (who Gottfried Wagner calls "alibi Jews") and at the same time leaves antisemitism undisturbed: in an untidy storeroom full of family and *Festspiele* history.

7

Gottfried Wagner is not satisfied with half measures. He builds a bridge to Israel, flies there and speaks publicly about "The Case Of Richard Wagner", as he had worked it out for himself, doggedly and exploring every detail, contradicting the presumption that a great artist must also have a great and noble nature. Anything else is an "alien image" of his great-grandfather, says the third-generation descendant. So he does not come as silent messenger or private individual, but as someone who wants to speak in plain terms: one

Wagner talking to Jews about another Wagner, who wrought evil against Jews.

A new, courageous chapter has opened, a bold undertaking in a land where for decades every note of Wagner's work has been taboo and where the people are more sensitive to things German than to anything else in the world. But what the great-grandson experiences there, in Tel Aviv, in Beer Sheva, in Jerusalem, is openness and a willingness to listen.

Israel has long become a feature of his biography.

Gottfried Wagner's work is also welcomed by Jewish voices in America. For example, by Elie Wiesel and Leonard Bernstein, who told him: "You have my full support for your work in Israel." The finest encouragement reaches Gottfried Wagner from Rabbi Steven L Jacobs from Huntsville, a wise man from Alabama: "You should not feel guilty for events which occurred before your birth, nor for the actions of ancestors, whom you could not choose for yourself. It is much more your own sensitivity, your concern, your capacity for pity, which make you what you are."

And so bonds developed which are enduring. In 1991, along with Rabbi Jacobs, Abraham Peck and the composer Michael Shapiro, Gottfried Wagner sets up the Post Holocaust Dialogue Group, officially registered in 1997 as a non-profit-making organisation. In sections 1 and 2 of its statutes the organisation declares:

"We, the children of the victims and the children of the victimisers, see the Shoah/Holocaust as a unique *rift* in Western and world civilisation and the starting point of a new morality in terms of thoughts, feelings and actions.

"We stand opposed to the repression or silencing of any and all discussion of the Shoah/Holocaust and the continuation of any and all prejudices and hatreds resulting from the activities of our parents and grandparents both now and in the future..."

Of the family clan, it is only Aunt Friedelind, Wolfgang Wagner's sister, who might have nodded in agreement. Of all his relations, she is the only one to have adopted a similarly pugnacious anti-Nazi stance, an attitude the nephew respects, without however condoning Friedelind's unswervingly uncritical attitude towards Richard Wagner's antisemitism.

Other than from his mother, Ellen Drexel-Wagner (whom Wolfgang

Wagner divorced in 1976 with devastating effect), Gottfried meets mainly with hostility from the clan – at best with indifference.

8.

This, the son's autobiography, is far more straightforward than that of the father: it has none of the pomp and carries nothing of the aura of a man recognised socially as successful. Rather, it portrays a life full of struggle, socially and financially insecure, full of pitfalls, obstacles, even ambushes, but – I think – of truly awe-inspiring consequences.

The once "cute little Wagner child" could have had it easy, his life could have taken quite a different course, if that child had not in fact been *this* Wagner.

I remember how deeply a phrase once impressed me which, unforgettably, speaks of the "casting down" of the human being on the earth, the organic crust of this lightless planet, only warmed by the sun. The image had such an effect on me that I further elaborated on it myself: man neither sought his own birth to his uncertain destiny, nor is responsible for it. No one, not even the most devout, is free from moments of desperate desolation in the search for meaning and a home here on earth.

From the first hour of my meeting with Gottfried Wagner I was reminded of that "casting down", an impression subsequently heightened even more by a remark of his that moved me more than any other: "I began painlessly to de-Germanise myself."

That was said way back in the seventies, when he left home, in search of himself, and came to the USA for the first time, with all the craving of a disappointed man to become "a liberal American", although it was perhaps meant ironically and was not a serious resolution. And yet the word has taken on lasting significance, for two reasons. Firstly (according to Margarete Mitscherlich), due to his aversion "to the German tendency not to respect others as others, but to despise them", and "to the German way of either idealising or devaluing their fellow men and themselves", both characteristics being for Gottfried Wagner two sides of the same coin: repression of the past.

The other reason is that the word "de-Germanise" has taken on more reality in the meantime – for today Gottfried Wagner's status is more that of an *emigré*, whose status by definition is not voluntary.

This Ahasuerus from Bayreuth must find it difficult to trace his identity back to his country of birth.

Therefore, in both respects, once again: "I began painlessly to de-Germanise myself."

Really? De-Germanise, in the sense quoted – possible, certainly. But *painlessly*?

Somewhere I still want to see a glimmer of hope – though the flame is weak – for a discussion with his father, in spite of everything; for a door that opens; for a sign that his course, so completely different from the one firmly taken by official Bayreuth, is nevertheless understood.

But Gottfried is equally as prepared for nothing to come of it.

For the "cast down" has – by some miracle – nevertheless found another home: *geographically* in the retreat of Cerro Maggiore, near Milan, and *emotionally* in the hearts of Teresina, Gottfried's Italian wife, and Eugenio, the son from Romania, who would have been destined for an early death there, but now shows the most radiant smile I have ever encountered. And of Teresina's mother, Mamma Antonietta, the pillar of the establishment – *tutta la famiglia*.

Each may read the relevant chapter towards the end of the book with his or her own feelings – it left me with a lump in my throat.

9.

Gottfried Wagner once compared his battle against Bayreuth with that of David against Goliath – illustrating the unequal forces confronting one another. But history teaches us on numerous occasions that the might of the stronger side can be deceptive and that a moment's lustre can all too quickly fade. And even someone not familiar with the Bible knows how the fight between David and Goliath ended – namely, with a hole in the forehead of the giant, who was stretched out on the ground, while the little man with the sling was still standing firmly on his feet.

It may be that the Bayreuth encrustation will only disappear in the generation of Richard Wagner's great-great-grandchildren and that the insubordinate great-grandson of our days will be deprived of that eventual satisfaction. I at least cannot believe that the current imbalance of forces between the adversaries has a chance of surviving.

This prophecy is not made lightly, but is founded on my unswerving confidence in the power of truth which ultimately, however long in coming, even when it comes too late, is nevertheless always the victor.

For after all our many encounters with repression, we know it does not work: those who try to stifle are fighting a lost cause and do not achieve their goal, however powerful they might appear for the moment. They are only pushing the mass of what is being repressed from one place to another, keeping alive that which they have not come to terms with from the past and maintaining it as part of the present, without losing one gram, a single molecule of the past.

The tragedy of Bayreuth continues, as does the drama of the family, including the issue of inheritance and succession – although Gottfried Wagner will remain untouched by either.

But what about the effect of this book? Will it increase the isolation of the author or break it? Intensify the inner unrest or appease it? Will light continue to come only from America and Israel and not from Germany? Or will even the old law "He who does not howl with the wolf" finally be refuted?

Through my inclination to write I have assumed a responsibility, out of concern for my friend, but with a clear conscience: irrespective of the consequences, the book is a blow for freedom.

Of greater personal significance than anything that could emerge from the *Festspielhügel* was his invitation from the Jewish community of Bayreuth to their New Year and Atonement Festivals, Rosh ha Shanah and Yom Kippur.

Auschwitz is my guiding principle. Gottfried Wagner, a non-Jew, says exactly the same of himself. I accept that.

What is to come now, we shall see.

Are the children responsible for the atrocities of their fathers? Yes, if they hold to the fatal way of their fathers. But do not all suffer from the atrocities of others? One stumbles by chance over the atrocities of others. Does that mean that all are made responsible for one another? Yes, there, where a man had the power in his hands to protest, and failed to do so.

Based on: *Sanhedrin, 27 b*

CHAPTER ONE

VILLA WAHNFRIED

From the moment I was born in Bayreuth, on 13 April 1947, it seemed I was predestined to follow Wagner family tradition. I was introduced to the world at large, via birth announcements, as Gottfried Helferich Wagner, son and heir of Wolfgang Wagner. The choice of my Christian names was already an indication of some future leading role in the family business. Gottfried is the name of Elsa's brother, the ruler of Brabant, in the opera *Lohengrin* by my great-grandfather Richard Wagner, and also the third Christian name of my uncle, Wieland Wagner. My other Christian name, Helferich, was the middle name of my grandfather, Siegfried Richard Wagner, a name Richard Wagner himself had invented for his only son.

This rather droll manner of giving names was typical of family tradition. In a letter to King Ludwig II, dated 9 February 1879, Richard Wagner wrote: "The son, now still so young, shall, when he has reached male maturity, know exactly who his father was. Nothing more. Then he may decide. This is also more or less the fashion in which we shall raise him. The boy will not be forced to do anything at all; we shall merely support and guide his inclinations quite freely. We are not at all aiming to turn him into an 'artist': I have only indicated one direction to him through the names which I have appended to his surname: two names mark him out as my son – Siegfried Richard – Wagner; but I have added 'Helferich', ie the 'helpful', to this."[1]

I was christened on Richard Wagner's birthday, 22 May. As godparents my father chose his mother, Winifred Wagner and Bodo

Lafferentz, my Aunt Verena's husband. Winifred Wagner, together with the staunch Nazi Heinz Tietjen, general intendant of the Prussian State Theatres, had run the Bayreuth *Festspiele* from 1930 until 1945. On orders from Hitler, Lafferentz, as a colleague of Robert Ley, head of the Labour Front, had safeguarded the organisation and material interests of the Bayreuth *Festspiele* from 1940 to 1944 through the National Socialist organisation "Kraft Durch Freude [Strength Through Joy]".

What looked, and was intended to look, from the outside like a peaceful family idyll, was in reality quite different. The main focus of interest for Wolfgang and Wieland Wagner was the Bayreuth *Festspiele*, which took place for the first time since the war in July 1951. In order to devote themselves undisturbed to preparations for this event, my parents took my elder sister Eva and me to the Etzerschlössl children's home in Berchtesgaden, a sort of upmarket boarding house for the children of well-to-do families. Before leaving us my father explained the reason for our sojourn: "The *Festspiele* will be starting soon now and it is very important. We must all make every sacrifice for the future and you, as a boy, will just have to grin and bear it. If you're good, you'll get some lovely presents."

I have never understood what was meant by the "sacrifices" our family was supposed to make for the *Festspiele*, except that in this, the first of the many places I was sent off to during my childhood and youth, I felt miserable. It created in me an aversion to the hectic activity of the *Festspiele* preparations and even to the "lovely presents" my parents bought to try to salve their guilty consciences.

Shortly before the solemn opening of the *Festspiele* my sister and I were brought back to Bayreuth where the public was to be presented with the image of a happy family. I longed not to be packed off to the children's home in Berchtesgaden any more, and decided that the most likely way to avoid it was through good behaviour. So I tried to be exactly what the grown-up world expected of a "genuine" shining example of a Wagner: I didn't answer back and didn't interrupt the adults' conversations. In recognition of the sacrifices my father was making for the great idea of the Richard Wagner Bayreuth *Festspiele*, I was not to bore or pester him with stories of the children's home, and showed nothing but gratitude and admiration for the genius of my illustrious ancestor. The work and the spiritual legacy of the great composer and founder of the *Festspiele* were portrayed as having global significance and I was permitted to live at its very centre.

My first image of the Wagner cult in Bayreuth was a photograph of the Wagner bust by Arno Breker, Hitler's favourite sculptor. It struck me at once as heroic and menacing. Another impression was made by Zdenko von Kraft, a devoted Wagnerian, who in 1951 wrote the following poem, 'Genius', for the *Festspiele* book on the opening of the new era:

> Many have passed on, many will come
> Yet ever faithful a new circle forms,
> What was once flame burns ever hotly
> The glow of the spirit shines undimmed
> For what the best of their time have perceived
> Is close to God, it endures and lasts.
> Who counts moons, thankfully counts death;
> The unforgettable knows naught of years,
> That are, that come and were before us,
> Are only leaves on the flourishing vine
> That winds about exalted beauty,
> That binds us together in a noble way.
> For this is the last word of art,
> What is common to all is its strength,
> What is valid to all creates its works,
> What is holy to all feeds its fruitfulness,
> And where it inflames a genius,
> He has announced himself for the whole world,
> Whether the paths of error or pain,
> Whether a cobbler's workshop or the trials of gods –
> Man's final word means death,
> But the seer says a redeeming "Grace!
> And so he refines the last things
> To a mysteriously beautiful Ring."[2]

I have never understood the New Bayreuth euphoria, but managed as a dutiful four-year-old to appear thrilled by Beethoven's *Ninth*

Symphony under the baton of the famous conductor Wilhelm Furtwängler, and by my uncle's *Parsifal*. I was taken aback by the tumultuous applause of the audience: I had not been at all prepared for such a spectacle in the *Festspielhaus* and didn't dare admit how frightened I was of Wieland Wagner's dark world of *Parsifal* and the Holy Grail.

I acknowledged with a smile the constant reminders of how much I looked like Richard Wagner, the "Master of Bayreuth", and the reassurances of what a great future I had before me. But however much I slipped into the role of the young Wagner, I could make little of the contrast between the devotion demanded within the family to Richard Wagner's art and the overwhelming, spontaneous display which the members of the Bayreuth artistic tribe seemed to find appropriate on public occasions. I felt at home neither in the monumental world of the *Festspielhügel* nor in the children's homes I was put into again and again as sacrifice for Richard Wagner's "art of mankind". I envied children allowed to grow up in normal families and in a normal environment.

During those first seven years, when I was not being packed off somewhere, I lived with my parents in what was known as the gardener's house in Wahnfried Park. We shared the first floor of the small brick house with the gardener Düret and his family. The nursery window in our small apartment looked over the front façade of the Villa Wahnfried. This particular section had not suffered war damage, and intact were its pictures of Wotan and Wagner's house motto: "Here where my fancies [*Wahnen*] found peace [*Frieden*], this house I name Wahnfried."

In front of the Villa Wahnfried on a high plinth was a bust of King Ludwig II, who had financed Richard Wagner's existence as a composer for many years. This statue was surrounded by a pine hedge where I liked to hide and watch undisturbed the many tourists passing in and out of the front part of Wahnfried Park. There too I waited for the right moment to start up a conversation with Uncle Wieland's family, or with American officers – that is once my father had left the Park. He had forbidden me to play with my cousins, or to enter the Siegfried Wagner House. From 1945 to 1957 the house was used as a casino for officers in the US Forces stationed in Bayreuth and overhead flew the American flag.

Exactly why I was not supposed to play with Iris, Nike, Daphne and Wolf-Siegfried, whom we all called Wummi, was never fully explained by my father. He just spoke disparagingly of his brother and his family, especially the children, referring to their bad manners: not the right company for my sister and me. I soon realised that these accusations were untrue. However, I was forbidden to play with strange children as well.

In a way I led a double life: with my parents I was the obedient son, but, given the opportunity, I broke the paternal laws. As soon as I saw that my father had left Wahnfried Park, I would leave my hiding place in the hedge around the Ludwig II monument, climb over the wall dividing the Villa Wahnfried and the gardener's house and enjoy wild games and what to me seemed boundless freedom with Wieland's children. As soon as my father returned, I would clamber back over the wall and scramble anxiously back into the hedge. Immediately my father had disappeared into the house, I slipped across the lawn next to the entrance drive, my allotted playground. Despite all my precautions my father caught me now and again during these escapades, which meant a sound beating. But these beatings only served to strengthen my resolve to leave the parental home and the Wagner bombast on the *Festspielhügel* as soon as possible.

It wasn't only in comparison with the free and easy hours spent with the "Wieland children" that our family life didn't only appear monotonous and regimented and I began to rebel. I was soon labelled the "little Russian", as my father recognised in me sinister characteristics which he believed were typical of "the Russians". My rebelliousness was worsened by the constant control my elder sister Eva tried to exercise over me, on our father's orders. If she caught me doing anything wrong, she reported it. As my mother also blindly subjected herself to her husband's will, I was alone in my own family.

There were a few bright spots, like my fifth birthday, when my father did allow me to play with Wieland's children. He had given me a bright blue car built of heavy iron with a moped motor and without prior explanation, sat me behind the steering wheel, put my sister on the back seat and started up the motor. The thing drove off, I tore round the fountain in the Wahnfried garden and lost control. The trip ended abruptly in the rhododendron bushes near Richard Wagner's grave. Swearing furiously, my father dragged me from the car and the afternoon of birthday games was over. I never got in the car again.

Even at that time, I already felt the tensions between my father and my uncle, primarily about who did what on the *Festspielhügel*. Their differences of opinion frequently exploded into noisy quarrels and, as even the children heard the mutual exchange of contemptuous remarks, family unity was gradually destroyed. The Wieland and the Wolfgang parties grew further and further apart. Eventually, they didn't even congregate at Christmas or Easter, either in Villa Wahnfried or in my grandmother, Winifred's, spacious house in the Fichtelgebirge.

During one of my own illicit visits to Villa Wahnfried, Christmas 1952, I was overawed by a gigantic Christmas tree standing in the hall, decorated only with red apples and beeswax candles. I suppose it was then that I wondered why the Wagner family did not stick together, especially at Christmas time, which as I had always been told in the Bayreuth kindergarten, was a festival of love and peace. I asked my father to pray with me at the time, but he refused, mockingly.

The family was now firmly divided into the "Wielands" and the "Wolfgangs". My father was denigrated by his brother as a simple-minded manager, whereas Wieland was generally regarded as an artist. It seemed there were "gifted" and "ungifted" Wagners, a label that was to remain for decades and even colour media reporting.

To escape at least occasionally from family tensions, my parents, my sister and I spent weekends in a small house near Neunkirchen, a few kilometres from Bayreuth, set in beautiful countryside. These weekends, together with the regular trips to children's homes, were at that time the only diversions. Their exertion on behalf of Wagner's work was mental stimulus enough for my parents. They also travelled on *Festspiele* business outside the season, but even when they were in Bayreuth they rarely told us children anything about it – their work claimed so much of their attention.

In order to escape from such enforced isolation, I disobeyed my father more and more frequently. I thought it ridiculous that I was forbidden to enter the Siegfried Wagner House. At the beginning of the 1950s, there were regular "big parties" at weekends, where American officers would celebrate noisily. They sang and danced, and there was always plenty to eat and drink. It was at these parties that I first heard dance bands, jazz and all the music of the 1940s from North America, which my father dismissed as "nigger music". I enjoyed the warm, lively atmosphere and instead of listening piously to homemade Holy Grail music, I sat in raptures in the Wahnfried garden in front of the Siegfried Wagner House music room window and tapped my feet to the boogie-woogie of the "uncultured Yanks", as they were called in my family. Once, one of the black employees noticed me. Suddenly remembering my father's objections, I went to make my escape but the big, powerfully built Afro-American saw I was afraid and approached me. With a broad smile and the words "have fun", he handed me a piece of wedding cake and an orange, at that time luxuries, and not just for me. Why should I be against "Yanks" and "Negroes"?

The year 1953 was to be important for me for two reasons: firstly my father staged his first production and also designed his first set for the *Festspielhaus*, and secondly I started school.

Father had chosen *Lohengrin* for his Bayreuth debut and, during his intense preparations, expected even more consideration and respect from us children than ever before for the great idea of the *Festspiele*. When he was working at home, we had to keep absolutely quiet, any noise disturbed him. Come rehearsals in June there was only one subject of conversation: his *Lohengrin*.

The sheer fascination of the preparatory work, first on the rehearsal stage, then on the main stage of the *Festspielhaus* compensated a little for the subjection of the whole family to the cause. The hectic life of rehearsals and in the workshops was exciting. But having constantly to pose for photographers – to illustrate the family enterprise – soon became annoying. I was placed in every conceivable pose next to the *papier mâché* swan prop and made to smile sweetly again and again.

My father categorically forbade me, without giving reasons, from sitting in on my uncle's *Rheingold* rehearsals, which were taking place at the same time. Such a ban seemed completely incomprehensible to me, but as I was thrilled just to take part in the theatrical work of the *Festspielhaus*, and not wanting to jeopardise this privilege, I didn't argue. At my insistence, my father briefly recounted to me the fairy tale of the good Lohengrin, who comes down to earth from the wonderful world of the Grail as a king's son, to free the good Elsa from the wicked Ortrud and Telramund. It struck me as odd that Lohengrin has to leave Elsa because she asks his name and where he comes from, but I didn't pester any further once my father answered my curiosity with: "The music explains everything anyway." I didn't understand that. I also suspected that something wonderful and unearthly was happening in the *Lohengrin* prelude, but I could not grasp why Elsa dies after Lohengrin's return to his father Parsifal in the Grail world, and why her brother Gottfried, after he had previously been turned into a swan by the wicked Ortrud, now had to go to war as "leader of Brabant" against the terrible "enemies in the east".

It was not so much whether I understood *Lohengrin* as the fact that it made me uneasy. And yet I assumed that I would take the non-speaking role of the boy Gottfried. It was a blow when I learned that my father had given this role to the son of the artist Weber, singing King Heinrich. The boy was only a little older than I. Father's explanation – "I don't want you to be given preference in getting a role, just because you are my son" – left me unconvinced: my cousin Wummi, four years older than me, was allowed to take part as one of the Nibelung dwarfs in *Rheingold*. But Father had decided and that remained unalterable.

After the *Lohengrin* premiere we sat with invited guests in the *Festspiele* restaurant and there I had my first dealings with the press. In contrast to my cousins, I had been excluded until then from public life, and I found unsettling the sudden overwhelming interest in me as a Wagner scion and in my opinion on *Lohengrin*. The questions of the tabloids in particular confused me. For example, they wanted to know how I had liked Father's *Lohengrin* and Wieland's *Rheingold*. It was natural for me to find my father's production good, in contrast to most of the critics, who preferred Wieland's directing. On the *Rheingold* I could only say that I hadn't seen it yet. Later I was alleged to have said that I didn't like it.

I was disappointed that my father would not let me sit at the same table with the Wieland children after the *Lohengrin* premiere. Since then at all such occasions there has been a "Wolfgang" and a "Wieland" table, and we children hardly spoke to one another. We were paraded as the "nice little Wagner children", instructed to greet particularly nicely those who were introduced to us as members of the "Society Of Friends Of Bayreuth" – that is, of the *Festspiele*. I didn't always manage this to my parents' satisfaction, tending to identify who I liked and who I did not with childlike naivety, whether these were influential sponsors or ordinary mortals.

I found my grandmother's behaviour on such occasions particularly unpleasant: she could not resist expounding in a very theatrical way on the theme – albeit with variations – of "family resemblance". At the core of this always highly elaborate tale were two sentences: "When you were in my house as a baby and I had guests, I would ask them if they wanted to see Richard Wagner as a baby. Of course they all wanted to see the infant Richard." Nothing could prevent her from parading this joke. Once when I cheekily countered with "Was I really that ugly?", "Omi" thought my retort droll and "typically Wagnerian".

After Father's great performance with *Lohengrin* my sister and I, in new clothes and loaded with new presents, were sent off to Berchtesgaden again. In September 1953 I started school in the nearby village of Maria Gern. This idyllic village school consisted of two classrooms; grades one to four were in one, in the other grades five to eight. Maria, a pretty peasant girl of around twelve, helped me learn to write, read and do arithmetic, and lessons were punctuated by long, happy walks in the countryside, during which the teacher Losch taught us the names of the plants. My new schoolfriends, who mostly came from farming families, were friendly and welcoming, and to better adapt to the new environment, I took up the local upper Bavarian accent. I enjoyed ringing the bell of the little village church with the other boys, jumping up and hanging on tight to the bellrope, swinging as the bell loudly tolled. In fact Maria Gern finally saw me play like other six-year-old boys, and I hardly missed my parents and Bayreuth.

But this carefree time was shortlived and in October I was entered in a second school, this time in Bayreuth. This was the start of a sixteen-year schooling period which was to be torture from the first day to the last. Towns, schools, tutors and teachers changed constantly and I had to repeat classes three times. The few highpoints were stimulating teachers and friendships with fellow pupils.

My very first school experiences in Bayreuth were nightmarish. It quickly became clear to me what it meant to be different from the other children: I was made fun of for my upper Bavarian accent and my traditional dress that I had so liked wearing in Maria Gern. And I was a long way behind in my knowledge too. My first teacher in Bayreuth, the kindly and sympathetic Frau Grohm, tried in vain to defend me: she got no help from my parents.

But what separated me most from my fellow pupils was the fact that I was a Wagner going to school in Bayreuth. Of course envy will have played its part in my isolation. First I tried to make the best out of the situation, and played the clown. But that didn't make any difference either. Gradually I began to withdraw into myself, which only made the other children more aggressive: I was once severely beaten up on the way home, and another time found written on the sandstone outer wall of the Wahnfried garden "Gottfried is stupid", which amused passers-by. My schoolwork deteriorated and as my parents had neither time nor inclination to help, they arranged extra tuition at home by nannies and private tutors. The number of tutors who strove in vain to improve my school marks grew steadily. I continued to stand out at school not only through bad marks, but also through frequent illness and absenteeism.

In 1954 my father revived his *Lohengrin*, an event which proved less exciting than the meeting with my aunt, Friedelind Wagner, my father's elder sister, who came to see the performance in the *Festspielhaus*. Strange stories circulated in the family about her, which made me curious to get to know her. My father made the most disparaging remarks about her, saying she had been a terribly naughty child and had eventually run away from home to America. When I met this "brazen American aunt" (known as "Maus" in the family) for the first time in the *Festspielhaus*, my immediate impression was quite different. She resembled us very closely bearing the "Wagner nose" and impressed me by her exotic dress and brash, assertive manner. She approached smiling and greeted me very affectionately, becoming the only one in the family who ever asked what my interests were and treating me like a boy of my age. "Call me Maus, not Aunt Friedelind," she said. She bore none of the Bayreuth affectation or "Wagner cult" ethic so fervently maintained by the rest of the family and I listened fascinated, as she told me how she had met some "Red Indians" in the American prairies. I could have talked to her for hours, but my father soon insisted on driving me home and *en route* forbade me any further contact with Aunt Friedelind. This time I didn't accept the edict; I protested and demanded reasons. I didn't get any, however, instead just stonewalling: "It's a long story, I'll tell you one day." I didn't give up and replied: "Tell me now." To which my father answered: "You wouldn't understand it anyway." Annoyed, he dropped me off at home. I began to suspect that there were a lot of secrets I was not to know about.

After our first meeting "Maus" and I only saw one another sporadically between 1959 to 1966, when she was working as director of her "Bayreuth *Festspiele* Master Classes" for music students from all over the world. These summer courses comprised discussions with the students on Wagner operas and productions and took place in a primitive shed, right next to my father's home. Father always made fun of Maus and rightly feared her cultural and intellectual standard, for she was fortunate to know not only the works of Richard Wagner, but among others also those of Franz Liszt and her father Siegfried Wagner, whom she was the only one in the family to promote. Whenever my father and I talked about her there was a row: I did not share his cutting opinion of my aunt.

After Wieland's death in 1966 the conflicts between Father and Maus over his style of directing reached such a violent level that in 1972 she finally left and settled in England. I missed her then: during the few conversations we were able to have together she was always frank with me and right until her death in 1991 she was always interested in my professional development, coming with a touching pride to the premieres of most of my productions. Maus helped my mother, too, after my parents' divorce in 1976, with great selflessness, which was typical of her plucky character – atypical of the family – and her ethical principles and yet she did not have much luck at all in her choice of friends, who often exploited her. I was particularly angry at my father when she died: not only because a funeral was held in Bayreuth when she had expressly forbidden any mourning ceremony for her there, but also because in his funeral oration on Maus he yet again ran down her 1944 book *The Royal Family Of Bayreuth* in front of the invited guests. In the book my aunt had recounted all those episodes regarding a subject which had been passed over or falsified in my father's autobiography of 1994, *Acts*, and by journalists close to Bayreuth: the intimate relations of the family with "Uncle Wolf", as they were permitted to call Adolf Hitler.

It still gives me great pleasure today to read my correspondence with Maus now and again. I recognise in it that we as Wagner descendants in opposition to the Wagner cult, and as family outsiders, actually always liked one another – in spite of all the obstacles, differences of opinion and Bayreuth intrigues. Maus was the only one in the family enthusiastically to applaud both my journey to Israel and the adoption of my son Eugenio. Today I believe I owe it to her to prevent her memory being dragged through the mud, for whatever reasons. Poor Maus, you don't deserve that!

In January 1955 we were able to leave the gardener's house and move into a villa on the *Festspielhügel*. "Finally we'll be able to live in peace and quiet," said my mother, who was worried about the precarious state of my health. Despite having a large room to myself, my situation did not improve: as our villa was only a few metres away from the *Festspielhaus* and my father now devoted himself day and night exclusively to the Wagner concern, the final vestiges of family life soon disappeared. Our new home turned into an annexe of the *Festspielhaus* and my father tolerated nothing but the cult of the Wagner legacy. He had the grounds enclosed by high walls, wooden fences and hedges, which I could only see over from the second-floor windows. The *Festspielhaus* was no longer visible from the garden in summer, but I often felt as though I were in a prison. I missed Villa Wahnfried with its big open garden, its proximity to the town and the forbidden games with the Wieland children.

Moving to another part of the town meant attending the Graser school. Here I was confronted with a very strict teacher, Herr

Schäfer, whom I found threatening. I impressed him only once, when I managed to sing without a single mistake a melody he had played on the violin. Of course, I was also fulfilling the school's expectations, which were that anything other than music would not interest a Wagner anyway. "You're not up to much in school, but at least you can sing," was Schäfer's only positive remark about me.

A more than welcome change from the dreary monotony of school was my first big trip abroad in April 1955. I flew with my parents to Barcelona, where the Bayreuth *Festspiele* were on tour with my uncle's productions of *Parsifal* and *Die Walküre*. This first experience of the Mediterranean had a profound and lasting effect on me. Not only the luxury hotels, big gardens, villas and the deep blue sea, but also the glittering society inside and outside the opera house. I found it all fascinating. The "Wolfgang" and "Wieland" children were made much of too. Grandmother Winifred declared at every conceivable opportunity "how decently and splendidly these Spaniards stood by us Germans against the Bolsheviks". Enthusiastically she recounted stories of Hitler, praised his Spanish ally, the Caudillo Francisco Franco, and wallowed in memories of the "glorious times" of the National Socialist dictatorship. The hosts applauded heartily, my father remained silent, and I started shouting with the others "Franco-Hitler! Franco-Hitler!". I didn't know what it meant.

In Barcelona everything seemed big and impressive. The reverence paid to all the Wagners went to my head and I now believed I had a great future in front of me. This burgeoning pride produced a direct effect when we returned to Bayreuth, where I completely lost interest in school, and my marks sank accordingly. I was only interested in the *Festspielhaus*, and I wanted to take part in everything that happened there. My parents made it unmistakably clear to me, however, that I was only to sit in on Father's rehearsals for the new production of *Der fliegende Holländer*. At the preparatory work for my uncle's *Tannhäuser*, on the other hand, I made sure I was not found out. I quickly discovered various hiding places in the *Festspielhaus*: over the auditorium, in the orchestra pit, in the prompter's box, under the stage, in the lighting towers, in the flies or on one of the many roofs. Now I could not only watch my uncle's rehearsals in peace, enthralled, but I was also witness to the ruthlessly waged conflict between my father and his brother and the latter's wife, Aunt Gertrud. Tyrannically, Wieland enforced his will in the interests of his work, and my father had to submit to him in front of everybody. Wieland's fits of violent rage, his cynicism and his damning remarks about people who did not agree with his ideas, alienated me just as much as his scornful remarks about my father's productions. Father suffered very much under this: he wanted to be his brother's equal as an artist. I did admire Wieland's directorial work and his sets, which appealed to me more than my father's stagings, but during this time I often felt sorry for my father.

My uncle's frank disparagement of my father's productions led to the formation of two rival factions in the *Festspielhaus* who worked and intrigued against one another. The climate became more poisonous, and the rift in the family deepened. During performances we children were no longer allowed to sit together in the family box. Only the "Wielands" sat there now, while the "Wolfgangs" sat on the left in the first row of the stalls. On official photos too the two families were no longer shown together.

Under these sorry conditions my father's production of *Der fliegende Holländer* was premiered. Wieland and the press closely allied with him rated it as badly as they already had the *Lohengrin*. My father, believing I was on his side, took the time to explain the story of *Der fliegende Holländer* to me. It had a similar effect on me as the story of *Lohengrin* had two years before: afraid of the ghostly ship, I could not understand what Senta's suicide at the end of the opera was about and why the Dutchman should then be "redeemed" by this.

Naturally, before these *Festspiele* events, my sister and I were once again packed off to a children's home, this time to the Renée home in Wyk on the island of Föhr in the North Sea, just off Schleswig Holstein. Saying goodbye to my parents and Bayreuth was easier for me than in former years. I didn't feel at home anywhere, a feeling which didn't change after we had got back to Bayreuth and I was ill more and more frequently.

That year, 1955, we spent the Christmas holidays in the Hotel

Wetterstein, Seefeld, in the Austrian Tirol. It was here that, for the first time, I met people who were proud of being German. I understood this just as little as the saying "We Germans are somebody again", which was often heard now.

Around this time the adults would heatedly argue about German rearmament. When I asked my father what the Federal Army, the National People's Army, the armed forces of the GDR were, he answered: "The Federal Army are our brave soldiers here, that would protect us from the wicked soldiers of the People's Army, if they attacked us." I couldn't understand this explanation. But the People's Army of the "Soviet zone" did not worry me in particular. What made the adults anxious in the intensifying cold war, I saw more as a cops and robbers story.

I was preoccupied now with National Socialists: seeing for the first time film news bulletins, newspapers and magazines. During one film presentation at school we saw excerpts from contemporary propaganda material on Nazi Germany, the Nuremberg Party congresses of the NSDAP and the world war unleashed by Hitler: goosestepping German soldiers, hysterical mass adulation of the Führer, the war crimes of the Wehrmacht, and all of it to a background of Richard Wagner's music. Shocked by the piles of corpses in the concentration camp of Buchenwald, I told my father about the awful films and especially about the music I had heard in them. "You are still too little to understand all that," he answered. But I refused to be satisfied with this and he shouted at me to go away and play, or better still to finally get down to my homework, instead of asking about things I could not understand anyway. If I had persisted any further with my questions I would have been beaten, so I shut up. But I resolved to get to the bottom of the matter.

My next attempt at finding out the truth was aimed at my grandmother, who answered my question of whether there really had been concentration camps in the Third Reich with: "That's all propaganda by the New York Jews who want to make us and the Germans out to be bad!"

At this time I had another experience which was to influence the course of my life: Wieland's *Meistersinger von Nürnberg* of 1956. I had already seen a few illustrations of sets of *Meistersinger* productions of earlier times, but hadn't found them very interesting. When the curtain went up in the 1956 *Festspiele* season though, I was stunned: before me was a magical set with constantly changing lighting effects in front of a simple and bright semicircular horizon, with just a few, but wonderful, changes in the different acts. At that time Wieland was my artistic ideal and I was determined to become a director. When I told my father of this he didn't say a word. I was dismayed when aggressive booing broke out as the curtain came down after the last act. Even my grandmother was among those who found Wieland's production a besmirching of the *Meistersinger*.

After these events, the end of the *Festspiele* was hard to take, as a great boredom then descended on the provincial town of Bayreuth. But this time autumn was to bring some diversions. Around then I also began to understand what Winifred meant at her celebrations on 20 April, Hitler's birthday, by "USA": "*unser seliger Adolf*" [our blessed Adolf] and now I started secretly investigating the family history.

My parents, as was usual after the *Festspiele* period, had gone on holiday, and so Gunda Lodes, who worked in the telephone exchange of the *Festspiele* administration, looked after my sister and me. Gunda had, through her warmhearted, loving nature become a substitute aunt for me, and I have her to thank that my childhood and youth in Bayreuth were not all nightmare. Gunda's father, the kindly Hans Lodes, had been the caretaker of the Bayreuth *Festspiele* for decades. "Grandpa Lodes", as I called him, guided the crowds of tourists through the *Festspielhaus* and explained in simple words everything essential about the history of the *Festspiele* and Richard Wagner. My first knowledge of the history of my family I owe to him. Of his wife Kunigunde I have equally good memories. She was small, round, good-natured and like her husband came from a Catholic farming family. What's more, "Grandma Lodes" made the most wonderful "Bayreuther Glees" – potato dumplings. At weekends the grandchildren Werner and Helmut turned up at the Lodes family home, and finally I could play like other children. Werner, who is six years older than I, became my favourite playmate. I admired him for his technical skills which for me, a Wagner in training to be an artist, were totally lacking. His powers of invention for a steady stream of new games in the garden and then more and more in the *Festspielhaus* as well, were limitless. Neighbouring children soon joined us, such as Matthias Röntgen, the son of a painter, who lived in a wooden hut on the other side of the *Festspielhügel*, and Hubert Franz, the son of the forester from the adjoining plot of land.

Of course, before my parents left on their holidays my father had strictly forbidden me to play in the *Festspielhaus*. Such prohibition was like a challenge for me to furtively slip the master key to the *Festspielhaus*, that Father had hidden in a secret place, into my trouser pocket and to begin my expeditions round the historic building. First I opened all the doors that had been locked to me until then, and behind which I suspected momentous secrets. My heart thumping I entered the rooms over the old set-painting workshop, where I found a large plaster model of the *Festspielhaus*, paintings depicting scenes from the *Ring des Nibelungen*, thick tomes on racial theory, *Festspiele* guides from the years 1933 to 1944, and photos of my grandmother, Uncle Wieland and my father with the Führer. I also found an enormous oil painting of Hitler with a menacing Alsatian dog. In boxes I found countless handwritten letters which, being partly written in the old German script, I had difficulty deciphering. Although these finds were lying around dusty, dirty, torn up in wild confusion or leant against the wall, I carefully picked up each one, piece by piece, and examined them.

The plaster model I thought particularly intriguing but the question was who would be the best person to answer my questions. I dared not turn to my father, as I was in forbidden territory here. Besides, his previous reaction to my questions on the Nazi films had shown me how loath he was to talk about the subject. Grandpa Lodes on the other hand seemed a suitable informant and so as not to give myself away, I invented an excuse which would enable me to return to the scene legally. I told him I had heard strange noises over the painting workshop and he immediately whistled up his powerful Alsatian Bodo, who terrified me and hurried with me in his wake to the painting workshop. I urged him to climb up the stairs into the lumber room. He contemplated the little footprints on the dusty stairs suspiciously and although when we entered the room I pretended I had never seen any of it before, he noted drily: "You've already been here." He wanted to know how I had got in and finally I told him the whole story, swore I would never do it again and started questioning him.

He answered my questions quite readily: "That's a plaster model of the *Festspielhaus*. After the Final Victory the Führer wanted to have the old *Festspielhaus* roofed over and only used for very special occasions by very special people. Next to the old *Festspielhaus* he wanted to have another built exactly like the old one, to be used for performances."

"This Führer, was he here often?" I wanted to know.

"The Führer loved Wagner and your family very much."

As Grandpa Lodes talked about the Führer in such a friendly way, I wondered where he was today.

"He's been dead a long time," answered Grandpa Lodes and firmly took my hand to draw me out of the room. Silently and with a serious expression he locked the doors and then said: "I don't want to see you here again without your dad, otherwise you won't be able to come and see us any more."

It was only much later that I learned how this plaster model was part of the "monumentalisation" of the *Festspielhaus* by the Nazi architect Emil-Rudolf Mewes in 1940.

I promised Grandpa Lodes to keep my mouth shut, for the sake of Werner, Helmut and the wonderful wild games, but I didn't promise that I would not go into the mysterious room again.

After my parents returned the family investigations ended, as did the carefree life with the Lodes family. Our school class got a new teacher called Herr Popp, who had apparently set himself the task of bringing me up to scratch. He enjoyed coming up very close when talking to me: "Now, *Wagnerchen*, let's just hear what you've been learning." This sentence was the prelude to his interrogations, which always ended in my having nothing left to say. With a malicious grin he would slowly curl the fingers of his right hand into a fist, and then belabour the back of my head with it in short, rhythmic blows. "The Wagnerian musical skull sounds hollow yet again," he would say, before finally pulling the hair over my right temple and to the delight of my classmates gleefully entering a six in his notebook. Another favourite pastime of Herr Popp was to recount his experiences as a soldier in the Second World War. "If we Germans had only had a bit more time, we would have been certain of the Final Victory. But the whole world was against us," he would moan.

After one of Popp's attacks I would have severe pains in my head. When I complained about his treatment at home, my father called me a "crybaby", but he did send my mother to talk to Popp, and from then on he only reminded me once a week that I had a hollow Wagnerian musical skull.

During this time my father was away more often than usual for the *Festspiele*, and with his production of *Tristan und Isolde* in the summer of 1957 he was scarcely approachable at all. He no longer gave me any introductory information on the works he was directing: I read the contents of the programme instead, understanding little of the story, but gripped by the *Tristan* music as never before. I attended every orchestral rehearsal and performance under Wolfgang Sawallisch that I could. Birgit Nilsson as Isolde and Wolfgang Windgassen as Tristan remain unforgettable.

My grandmother only had time for my father's productions and campaigned against Wieland's work. She constantly tried to play my father off against my uncle and so the tensions in the family continued to increase. I was not exposed to this strain for long, though: my grades were bad yet again that summer and because of an allegedly weak heart owing to growth problems, I was sent off to the Schliersee to stay with an elderly couple called Zankl. There were no playmates, but at least I was free of Popp.

In September I came back to the Graser school. My new classmates welcomed me by chanting: "Wagner, ploughed again, time-waster." Their ill-will was coupled with a growing pressure to do well, as I now had to prepare myself for the forthcoming entrance examination for the *Humanistisches Gymnasium* [classical grammar school]. My grandfather, my uncle and my father had all attended this school, and I was constantly reminded of their example. Frau Moritz, a teacher who appreciated my situation and encouraged me, provided a little relief. It also says much for Frau Moritz that she was obviously uneasy when we had to sing all three verses of the German national anthem. Since 1952 only the last verse was valid: "*Deutschland, Deutschland, über alles...*" Yet another reflection of the mental rearmament of the West Germans in the cold war.

Winifred, my grandmother, had returned to the Siegfried Wagner House in 1957, after the Americans had left. I visited her now and again and usually found her in the anteroom to the dining room on the ground floor, sitting at her desk. She would be chainsmoking her unfiltered North States, writing letters or gazing through the open window out to Wahnfried Park. That way she could keep a check on who came in and out. During one of my visits I told her of Frau Moritz's reservations about the first verse of the national anthem. She lost her temper and railed against the school where they were now apparently starting to tell the children a distorted version of German history.

In July 1958 I found out that I had passed the entrance exam for the *Humanistisches Gymnasium*, although at first I couldn't quite believe it. Buoyed up by my unexpected success, I sat in on the rehearsals of Wieland's first *Lohengrin* on the *Festspielhügel*. Just as his *Meistersinger* had, my uncle's new production enthralled me. Whenever I could I watched him at work. When Father noticed my enthusiasm he forbade me spending so much time in the *Festspielhaus*. But that had little effect on me. I would say I was going to the cinema or swimming and instead creep into the *Festspielhaus* via my secret routes. Wieland understood my situation but didn't comment on it. Once my father suddenly appeared during a lighting rehearsal. He had somehow found out that I hadn't gone swimming and angrily he asked my uncle if he had seen me. Wieland had spied me shortly before on the lighting bridge, but he played dumb. Scarcely had my father disappeared in fury when he winked at me with a grin and murmured: "The coast's clear."

This was not our only conspiracy. One day I crept secretly into Wahnfried Park again, waited until Wieland came out of the Villa and then told him how fantastic I thought his *Lohengrin*. Such naivety from the other family camp surprised my uncle. He went back into the Villa and returned very soon with an envelope which he pressed into my hand. I didn't dare open it in his presence. When he had got into his car I asked him for his autograph. "But I'm your uncle," he replied astonished. I replied: "But we can't ever talk to one another, so at least I'll have something from you," I explained. When I got home I opened the envelope and found a twenty-mark note in it. I had hoped for a more personal present, but I was still pleased. With the money I bought my first record, a Louis Armstrong LP – "nigger music", as my grandmother would say.

After my first exam success I was looking forward to secondary school. But my optimism was soon quenched. I became ill, and again private tutors had to visit me in Bayreuth and Berchtesgaden. It wasn't until April 1959 that I was able to attend the *Gymnasium*.

In the autumn of that year my father started preparations for his first production of the *Ring*, which he intended putting on in the coming season. My mother had to devote herself primarily to the great Wagnerian undertaking as well and as usual her children were an encumbrance. My father became more and more of a stranger to me: our holidays together in Braunwald in the Swiss Alps, were mainly for our exhausted parents to recover.

On our return from the winter holiday our enormous schnauzer, Froh, died after a painful death drawn out over months. He had been my companion for twelve years and I had loved him very much. My father had no sympathy for my tears.

As the 1960 *Festspiele* approached, my sister and I were once again sent off to Berchtesgaden again, this time to the elegant Hotel Geiger. I viewed the *Festspiele* by this time solely as a threat to domestic peace. A visit to the ruins of Hitler's "*Berghof*" on the Obersalzberg left me feeling very oppressed. When I told my father about it, he replied with a positive observation on the architecture of Hitler's Alpine home.

The family was in reality suffering because my father was overstretched and constantly under the pressure of competition from my uncle. It lay like a shadow over my parents' marriage and at that point my childhood ended. I found the intrigues of the hostile camps sickening, and yet I was being pulled into them more and more. I tried to be loyal to my father, but his productions excited me far less than those of Uncle Wieland.

In the summer of 1961 I opposed my father openly for the first time, protesting against his constant reprimanding of my mother. It ended in a beating for me and an almighty row between my parents. And the conflict had a sequel. My father threatened that he would put me into the strictest school in Germany, to finally make a man of me, little wimp that I was. I answered back defiantly: "Go on then, do it." Promptly a chauffeur delivered me to the boarding school in Stein, near Traunstein. The drive was agony for me as I was very worried about my mother. She was undergoing a difficult crisis at the time and again and again referred to the *Festspiele* as "suicidal". Yet in spite of all the family strain, life in the boarding school proved to be far from punishment. I now reaped the benefits of the Bayreuth training; for I was ahead of my new classmates and found myself in the unaccustomed position of being one of the best in the class. Instead of swotting I did everything I was not supposed to do: I smoked, secretly visited girls at night, drank beer, annoyed the teachers and preferred going swimming to attending class. My only worry was having to go back to Bayreuth.

One day I was surprised by the news that my cousin Wummi was joining the Stein boarding school as well. The everlasting family battle had proved incapable of weakening my affection for Wummi, much to the annoyance of my father, who had kept on running Wummi down. We had many things in common: he too had grown up practically parentless, had changed schools and tutors frequently and had acquired the reputation in Bayreuth of being stupid and lazy. I hadn't seen him for a long time and was keen to meet him again. He just said: "Hallo, Gottfriedla", and immediately the feeling of belonging together was re-awakened. At that time we were convinced that we would one day take over our quarrelling fathers' "shop". We hardly spoke about our parents and Bayreuth, finding these subjects awkward. But I did confess to him how much I admired his father's work. Wummi was always generous to me and treated me affectionately like a younger brother. It was a pleasant time, but it ended abruptly, in fact as soon as my father learned that Wummi was there. Immediately I was brought back to Bayreuth, although I continued to meet Wummi secretly.

My sudden departure from Stein did have one advantage, however, in that I was able to enjoy Wieland's *Tannhäuser* rehearsals. There was a commotion in the *Festspielhaus*: the beautiful young black singer Grace Bumbry was singing Venus, and Maurice Béjart created a provocatively erotic choreography for the *Tannhäuser* bacchanal in the Venusberg scene in Act One. The Wagnerian old guard were horrified and declared: "Thank God she's not singing Elisabeth. That's all we'll have needed, a negress singing a Wagner heroine in Bayreuth."

But that wasn't the only reason for the uproar. Wieland had joined up with the "left", although the Ulbricht regime in the GDR had built a wall that summer right through Berlin, to prevent the country from "haemorrhaging" by a mass exodus. The anti-Communist hysteria affected the Society Of Friends Of Bayreuth too; there was even talk of war. Quite beside herself, my grandmother raged publicly: "How on earth could Wieland join up with those left-wing Jews Bloch and Schadewaldt of all things. And then the Bumbry on top of everything else! Bayreuth is turning into a whorehouse." My father said nothing. At that time I only had vague ideas of what "left", "Jew" and "Negro" meant, but as a secret Wielandian I was angry at my grandmother's intrigue and my father's silence.

After so much freedom in Stein and the excitements on the *Festspielhügel*, going back to the Bayreuth *Gymnasium* became torture. When a ruptured appendix had me bedbound, my schoolmates accused me of shirking. I was often ill after that and became once again the outsider in my class, especially as my best friend at the time, Tyll Schönemann, had moved to Munich. I developed an aversion to the opinion forming by bully tactics in my class, and was unwilling to appreciate certain teachers just because the majority said so. One of the most popular teachers was called Herr Och. On one occasion before Christmas he decided to tell us about his experiences as a soldier in Russia. Sparing us no detail he raved about the courage of the Nazi army. I dared to criticise Och in front of other classmates, for which they gave me a thorough beating one day.

In April 1962, after a year's preparatory instruction, I was confirmed by the witty Reverend Flotow. In his precise and critical way he opened my eyes to the splendours of the Bible as a history book. My family only ever talked about "stupid priests" and "the bloody church". Sometimes my parents enthused about Albert Schweitzer, but this was mainly because the man from Lambaréné had had contacts with my grandfather Siegfried and such a connection was good for the family image. My grandmother, on the other hand, considered Schweitzer's commitment "pointless efforts for niggers" and expressed her opinions more and more openly against this form of Christianity. My father meanwhile called us Wagners "pious heathen" in Goethe's sense of the phrase, which I didn't understand and I owe an awakening interest in ethical questions to the Reverend Flotow. In other ways too, step by step I departed from the well-trodden family path. For example, I listened enraptured again and again to Johann Sebastian Bach's *Brandenburg Concertos*, in the Pablo Casals recording, whereas in my family only Richard Wagner mattered.

In the summer of 1962 Wieland staged an epoch-making new production of *Tristan und Isolde*. The set was strongly influenced by the English sculptor Henry Moore, with a lighting design clearer and more penetrating than ever before. This production in particular illustrated just how wide the artistic gulf was between Wieland and Wolfgang, and my admiration for the creative work of my uncle reached a new pinnacle. Not so my school career unfortunately: in 1962 I had to repeat the fourth-grade *Gymnasium* year.

The summer of 1963 was devoted to the 150th anniversary of Richard Wagner. The slogan was "A life for the theatre" and Wagner was yet again presented unpolitically as a "European genius of the theatre" – something of a nonsense, as Wieland had already moved further to the left politically through his contacts with Ernst Bloch, which provoked some very sarcastic comments during rehearsals. He continued to criticise the CDU and CSU, although this did not prevent him paying court to the ultra-conservative Friends Of Bayreuth and accepting their finance. The more Wieland played the armchair socialist, the more conservative my father acted. It was only logical that my grandmother regarded him as the true heir of the Wagnerian legacy.

Wieland's second *Meistersinger* production of 1963 was marked by elements of the Shakespearean stage, comprising a basic set that remained the same throughout, with only minor changes. This concept coincided, of course, with several anti-illusionist elements of the Brechtian stage, such as clearly visible scene changes and mobile screens. There was something else too: in 1960 the very young Anja Silja had made her debut in Bayreuth as Senta in *Der fliegende Holländer*. For Wieland she embodied the ideal of the modern singer-actor. For him she meant, as he so wonderfully and provocatively put it, the end of the "bourgeois singing cow". So it was no surprise that he cast her as Eva in the *Meistersinger* – and fell in love with her! Whether he got divorced for that reason is something one can only speculate about, since in November 1966 he died suddenly at the age of forty-nine. My father moralised heavily against Anja, who had loosened up the internal climate of the Bayreuth *Festspiele* with her cheeky Berlin ways and unconventional remarks.

As usual, we were sent away before the *Festspiele*, but this autumn two important turning-points took place in my life. Firstly, my sister, having now finished secondary school, was sent to a domestic science college for young ladies, freeing me from her constant supervision, so I spent much of my time with the warmhearted and cultured Bayreuth family Grossmann, who together with Gunda had kept an eye on me for years. I used my new freedom most of all, when Father and Mother were on holiday, to hold parties on and over the *Festspielhaus* stage, which was empty outside the season. I waited for the weekends, when nobody was working in the administration building, and using Father's master key I let my party guests in through the office area, up to a giddy height over the flies into a large room over the circle, which we turned into a dancehall. From there Elvis Presley's 'Jailhouse Rock' boomed out so loudly that passers by alerted the police to the noise in the "Woogna Deooda" (Wagner Theatre). Grandpa Lodes turned up with the police, we hid, and scarcely was the place "fuzz-free" when we rocked on.

The beginning of my friendship with Eckart Grebner and Reiner Heller also dates from this time. Together we kept an eye out for pretty girls and played at dares, one of which was to smear red paint over Arno Breker's populist Richard Wagner bust that had stood in the *Festspielpark* since 1955. I looked on with relish, while the fire brigade cleaned up the menacing monster. My school grades went rapidly downhill at that time.

The other turning-point of autumn 1963 that was to have a long-lasting effect occurred when my parents were on holiday, recovering from their *Festspiele* exertions. I took the chance to explore a wooden shed next to the garage, where Father's heavy BMW motor cycle and sidecar were housed. In the sidecar, in two cardboard boxes I found a large number of round, aluminium cans of various sizes. They were so rusted that I could not open them with my bare hands, so I secretly conveyed them to my room, got rid of the rust and prized them open carefully with a screwdriver. In each can there was a reel of film. I took out one of the larger reels and inspected it with a magnifying glass. What I discovered left me stunned. I saw my aunts, Uncle Wieland and my grandmother, Winifred, together with Hitler, who was dressed in an elegant double-breasted suit, laughing as they strolled in Wahnfried Park. Happy Führer, happy Wagner children, happy Grandmother Winifred! Then pictures of the Führer in the *Festspielhaus*. All arms were outstretched in "Heil Hitler" salute. Wagner's art and the Führer's power. Strutting members of the master race and laughing victors, in premature celebration of the Final Victory. Uncle Wolf and the Wagners belonged together – such was the message behind the film. And my father had been the cameraman throughout.

He and Wieland, like the rest of the adult world, suddenly became sinister to me. I remembered pictures of Buchenwald from the cinema newsreels I had seen in 1956 and it became clear to me that I had to keep the films and prevent my father hiding them again or even destroying them, so I hid them away in my wardrobe, covered the empty cans with dirt again and put them back in the two cardboard boxes in the sidecar. I decided not to tell my parents anything about my find but to question them persistently about Hitler.

The first opportunity presented itself during the winter holidays in Arosa, in Switzerland in December of that year, on one of the long walks with my parents and my sister. I didn't want to put my father on the defensive as that would have brought the conversation to an abrupt end. So I emphasised, against my convictions, that I was interested more or less "for purely historical reasons" in the connection between my family and the Führer. I asked Father what impression Hitler had made on him as a human being. He made no secret of the fact that Uncle Wolf had fascinated him and described his meetings with him with restrained affection. Later he told me proudly again and again of how the Führer had visited him in the Charité hospital in Berlin where the famous surgeon Ernst Ferdinand Sauerbruch himself had treated Father after he had been wounded in the Polish campaign. "Your uncle was exempted from war service by Hitler, I alone had to serve the Fatherland," he added and in detail and with enthusiasm he talked of community service and military training, where a unique camaraderie had developed. He recounted how the only friend in his life, Emil, had been killed in a village by "crafty Polacks" as the "brave German army" had conquered Poland.

And Hitler, again and again! After the National Socialists' seizure of power a "Führer annexe" had been specially constructed on the Siegfried Wagner House, and inside the annexe was built the "Führer fireplace". After a performance of *Götterdämmerung* in the *Festspielhaus* my uncle and father accepted Hitler's invitation to a lengthy nighttime discussion at the "Führer's fireplace" on the future of German art in the spirit of Richard Wagner, as an expression of the renewal of the world through National Socialism. I had some difficulty in understanding my father's torrent of words, but didn't interrupt for fear of provoking him to break off and he continued his story. "We were sitting round the fireplace, and Hitler sketched out for us his cultural visions of the future. 'Once we have rid the world of the Bolshevik-Jewish conspirators, then you, Wieland, will run the theatre of the West and you, Wolfgang, the theatre of the East.'" Quietly I asked Father who he meant by "Bolshevik-Jewish conspirators". My interruption annoyed him and I was worried he might end the conversation, but instead he launched into German history. It had all started with the "shameful Versailles treaty", which was then followed by mass unemployment in the chaotic Weimar Republic with the incompetent Left and the "bloody liberals". And so he came to the "great achievements of Hitler up to 1939". I wanted to know about this in detail and Father did not let me down, answering: "Hitler cured unemployment and restored worldwide respect for the German economy, he freed our people from a moral crisis and united all decent forces. We Wagners have him to thank for the idealistic rescue of the Bayreuth *Festspiele*."

"But what about the Jews, Father?"

He replied: "There's a lot of talk about that, and there are a lot of malicious lies told about us Germans by left-wing intellectuals about how many and so on. But that was the only real mistake Hitler made. If he had won over the Jews to his side we would have won the war. After the war things would not have got as bad as the Allies' propaganda machine makes out."

We continued side by side in silence for the rest of the walk, until my mother started talking about Christmas presents.

CHAPTER TWO

NEW DIRECTIONS

I t was after our return to Bayreuth in January 1964 that I met
Maria Kröll, my first great love. In her were combined the
qualities of *joie de vivre*, mental alertness and femininity that
I found so fascinating, and she wrested me from my isolation in
the golden *Festspielhaus* cage. Because of her I drove regularly to
Creussen, thirteen kilometres south of Bayreuth, where she was
living with her parents and her younger sister Dorle, who was in
my class. Her father, Professor Joachim Kröll, was extraordinarily
gifted in many fields. He taught German, history and geography at
the German *Gymnasium* and was popular with his pupils, having
a quite unconventional manner and teaching methods. Maria's
mother Ursula was a kindly, intelligent and cultured woman.

Maria helped me to be more self-confident and I owe to her
parents – active liberal socialists – some essential influences for
my intellectual development. The Krölls were keen readers of
books on every conceivable subject. I quickly felt at home with
these friendly and open people, and woke from my provincial
Festspielhügel sleep. Joachim Kröll, the first person to explain
German Jewish history to me, also stimulated me to read Heinrich
Böll, Günter Grass and other committed writers. I was full of
enthusiasm for my new reading matter.

After such influence I found my parental home, *Festspiele*
business and its audience unbearable. My father could not fail to
notice that I was becoming critical and that my interest in German

history and politics was growing, not least because I found myself continuing at home the discussions I'd had at the Krölls'. For example, I applauded the existence of two German states at a time when my father regarded Franz Josef Strauss as the only decent politician: he reacted to my remarks with fury. The discussion on the GDR's right to exist ended like many previous discussions with my father forbidding any further word on the subject, and cursing Joachim Kröll as a "dirty Leftie" who was having a bad influence on me. Furious, I stormed out of the dining room, slamming the door behind me. My father tried to catch me up on the stairs but I was faster than him, ran to my room and locked the door behind me. Hammering on the door, he ordered me to open it. I had no such intention. "The only answer you've got is giving me a hiding!" I shouted at him. Then I climbed down a rope ladder from the first floor into the garden and sped off on my moped, cigarette in mouth, to Maria in Creussen.

My father couldn't come to terms with my new-found attitude and, unbeknown to me, visited Joachim Kröll to demand that the relationship between Maria and me be broken off. And furthermore, that the Kröll family stopped influencing me. Maria later described the clash between the two fathers. Joachim Kröll was not at all prepared to share my father's views on politics and love relationships.

After this episode I threatened to disappear for good if my father interfered in my life or beat me ever again. In fact, one year before this I had disappeared during the night because of another unhappy love affair, and that occasion had become the subject of Bayreuth scandal. This time my father thought up an alternative means of punishing me for my rebellion. At the end of April 1965, against my will, I was taken once again to Stein, to separate me from Maria and her family.

My cousin Wummi had passed his *Abitur* [A-Levels] in Stein and the new headmaster, Olf Ziegler, was the son of a friend of my grandmother's; thus my father thought the school would be a suitable place for me again. The pain of parting from the Krölls and in particular from Maria was enormous. And adapting to a life with a lot of people in a small space was difficult. But gradually I made friends with some of my fellow pupils who – like me – turned their backs on the main body of pupils, which comprised the arrogant sons and daughters of "good" and not so "good" homes. The majority of the pupils came from "economic miracle" families, whose parents either had no time for them, or were divorced, or knew their spoiled offspring were bone idle, ungifted and would probably never have got their *Abitur* in a normal school. Two descendants of the Bismarck family behaved with particular arrogance. Constant quarrelling with such insufferable show-offs strengthened my urge to read left-wing literature. A fellow pupil Henry Hohenemser helped me to come to terms with my family history, and drew my attention to forms of open and concealed antisemitism. It was an important time for me. I started reading the works of Ernst Bloch, Sigmund Freud, Theodor Adorno, Hannah Arendt, Max Horkheimer and Bruno Bettelheim.

In the 1965 summer vacation I sat in on rehearsals of Wieland's new *Ring*. Although I found the vision of the atomic mushroom at the end of the *Götterdämmerung* effective, its style contradicted that of the set, which was orientated towards the world of Henry Moore and Richard Wagner's music, which certainly does not end in nothingness.

The contrast between the sponsors, the Friends Of Bayreuth, and festival guests such as Ernst Bloch or Hans Mayer, the distinguished literary historian, became even clearer to me. And even my uncle's halo started to fade. Wieland hardly knew where to draw the line in his relations with his colleagues. Once during a rehearsal he clouted the electrician of the *Festspielhaus*, his former playmate, round the head, in front of everybody, because he allegedly or actually had not meticulously carried out Wieland's imperious demands. This, coupled with other events, led me to believe that Wieland had not really overcome his own past, tacking back and forth between Krupp and Siemens on the one hand, and Bloch and Mayer on the other. In my eyes he became more and more opportunistic, leaning to the left because he vaguely realised that the balance of power in the culture business was tending in that direction.

I returned to the Stein boarding school after the summer vacation and absorbed myself in the early writings of Karl Marx, in particular his essay 'On The Jewish Question'. Later, when I brought up my reading matter in a discussion with my father, he resorted as usual to a monologue, starting off with the 1935 race laws, which the Jews had themselves to blame for, as they had been "the worst racists in history". I ventured to counter this by saying that you couldn't confuse the Nuremberg race laws with orthodox Jewish traditions. Angrily my father retorted that Jews had themselves made an essential contribution to the Nuremberg race laws: "Marx himself was an antisemite and wanted to emancipate society from Judaism." "But scarcely the final solution," I answered. That ended the discussion.

In the 1966 local elections in Bayreuth, when the Neo-Nazis won three of the forty-two city council seats, my grandmother's hopes for a "Final Victory" were reawakened. Aunt Friedelind was furious when my grandmother slowly started to emerge again as First Lady and received as guests political friends such as Edda Göring, Ilse Hess, the then NPD chairman Adolf von Thadden, Gerdy Troost, the wife of the Nazi architect and Hitler-friend Paul Ludwig Troost, the British fascist leader Oswald Mosley, the Nazi film director Karl Ritter (related to the Wagners) and the racist author and former senator for culture under the Reich, Hans Severus Ziegler. At her receptions one could "finally" talk openly about the Führer again, after having referred to him in code as "USA". Rightly, in a *Spiegel* interview in December 1967, Friedelind criticised the return of "fascist demons".

In July 1966, shortly before the *Festspiele* season, Wieland was admitted to the hospital in Kulmbach and was later transferred to the University Clinic in Munich. My father did not inform me of my uncle's state of health but like others I suspected that the matter was serious. Now open warfare broke out between the Wieland and the Wolfgang camps – the latter believing his hour had come. In the Wieland camp the first cracks appeared. Some toyed with the idea of changing sides, and my father enjoyed a sudden sycophancy. Quite unexpectedly he was now the sole director of the *Festspiele*, at least for that year. Even I was now greeted with friendly words by people who had ignored me until then. The Wolfgangs were "in", the Wielands were "out" and I found the new situation just as repugnant as the old one. Bayreuth, the *Festspielhügel*, the family and the whole shebang just made me feel sick. I toyed with the idea of leaving Germany. But how, without money and without a profession?

On 17 October, while I was watching the film *The Spy Who Came In From The Cold*, I was informed that my uncle was dying. I hitchhiked to Munich and there my father embraced me for the first and last time in his life. Not a word was spoken. Mother informed me of Wieland's death with tears in her eyes.

I shall never forget the funeral ceremony. Held in the *Festspielhaus* on 21 October 1966, it was a demonstration of superlative hypocrisy: Grandmother Winifred burst into tears, for her poor Wolfgang – "Wolf" – who would now have to bear the responsibility for the Bayreuth *Festspiele* all on his own. Meanwhile, high society suddenly discovered its love for Wieland. The only bright spot was Ernst Bloch's address.

Flash-lights popped and cameras whirred as the long procession moved off to the cemetery and almost immediately, the power relations began vying for position, of which my father, my grandmother and my sister Eva held the best cards.

In the following winter holidays together in Arosa the discussion came round to an open letter Günter Grass had written, warning against the formation of a grand coalition – "that bad marriage" – in Bonn, "which will see the youth of our country entrenched into left and right positions". My father was horrified by my "lurch to the left" and attributed it, not without reason, to my reading matter of the time – Bertrand Russell, Erich Fromm and Karl Jaspers. He complained bitterly about my ungratefulness for all the sacrifices he had made for my education in a boarding school such as Stein. Were it not for my mother, I would have packed my bags; but it was Christmas after all.

I also refrained from telling him about my grandmother's reaction to my choice of Christmas present. I had asked her to give me Bloch's book *The Principle Of Hope*. She replied: "I'm not giving you any of that left-wing Jewish trash." I answered that from now on she could strike me off her Christmas present list: her Nazi attitude was incompatible with my principles. I was to get a few more "paybacks" for that comment.

CHAPTER THREE

"THE WILL TO POWER" I

In 1967 my father began to alter beyond recognition. Where the *Festspiele* had been the central focus of family life, it now became an obsession for him. He began by eliminating the Wielandians, except for those who vowed allegiance to him. Wieland's productions were from now on distorted and my father made strenuous efforts to destroy his brother's superego. Realising that the pressure of sole responsibility for the *Festspiele* and the stress of the final battle on the *Festspielhügel* was threatening to damage our relationship even further, he allowed me to attend the school in Stein as a day pupil.

During this time my friendship began with Dietrich Hahn: a man with an unusual literary gift, who is interested in contemporary art, painting, and who had originally wanted to be an actor. Grandson of the famous radiochemist and Nobel prizewinner Otto Hahn, he had suffered greatly from losing both parents in a traffic accident after which he was fostered by the Kalkhoff-Roses, a family of industrialists who supported Helmut Kohl. He felt ill at ease in their home and vacations were always something of a problem for him. I sometimes invited him to Bayreuth. Having worked in the theatre for only a short time, he was soon, like me, disgusted by its superficiality and hierarchy. He then started, as a journalist specialising in the history of science, working through his grandfather's considerable posthumous works and making these universally available. What particularly drew us together was an interest in humanitarian activities and German-Jewish history. Both of us now view our boarding school time in Stein without any rosy glow.

It was while we were both day pupils that another life opened up for me. Forbidden reading matter was followed by forbidden activities: namely disrupting NPD meetings in Upper Bavaria with my friends Norbert and Henry. Norbert and I carefully planned our escape routes before turning up at Neo-Nazi meetings disguised as Charlie Chaplin's "Great Dictator". It sufficed to walk silently through the beerhalls to goad the mob, then we would run off like hunted hares via previously reconnoitred routes and leap into Henry's ancient VW "Beetle" waiting for us with the engine running. At that time I was no longer capable of integration in the Stein school, despite a regime which was almost liberal by Bavarian standards, and so I left. The chorus master of the Bayreuth *Festspiele*, Wilhelm Pitz, interceded for me in June with Charles Spencer, the chairman of the renowned New Philharmonic Chorus in London. It was to be a stay which was to steer my life in a decisive direction.

The Spencer family gave me a warm welcome. I took full advantage of what was on offer in concerts and opera that season and attended a language school daily to improve my English. I was thrilled to be living right near The Beatles' studio. Charles Spencer, a successful choir manager and businessman, was a keen music-lover and discerning Wagnerian and we often conversed jokingly in Wagner quotations. This idyll was abruptly broken off by a political event of world importance: the six-day war between Israel and the Arab countries in June 1967. More violently than ever before I was confronted by Jewish history. Anxiously we sat in front of the television.

Day and night we had passionately discussed the events, during which I discovered that Charles's parents had been Viennese Jews. In 1938, after the *Anschluss* of Austria to Hitler's Germany, they fell victim to the Nazi terror. Charles and his sister escaped. Charles's daughter Diana told me further shocking details while we were looking at family photos. There was I as a child of criminals living like a son in a family that had suffered terribly under Nazi barbarism: Charles noticed my embarrassment and shame. I confessed how oppressive I found the Bayreuth legacy with its antisemitism, and told him about my grandmother's fanatical racism. He said: "Only after the generations of the perpetrators will there perhaps be hope for a new beginning between Jews and Germans, which will not prevent the possibility of friendships between individual Germans and Jews. Don't feel guilty but learn from your family's mistakes." This wise advice from my "elective relation" was to be a motto for life.

Charles had an exemplary influence on me. Despite tragedy, he lived without enmity and hatred and with quiet modesty he helped people in need as he went about his daily life. During my stay I watched a television programme with contributions from many countries, including a report from Germany on the opening of the 1967 *Festspiele* with *Lohengrin* in my father's new staging. I felt remote from everything connected with Bayreuth and Wagner, and was relieved when, after the usual boring excerpts from the Bayreuth stage, there came a Beatles song. During a telephone call, I told my mother that I did not intend returning to Germany for some time: she understood, and Charles supported me when I decided to live in France for a while.

But before that I visited Bayreuth briefly. With amazement I noted how my father was acting as the man holding the reins, and my sister, who had just finished training as a kindergarten teacher, was playing the lady boss. My father only tolerated yes men around him, and any form of criticism, especially of his *Lohengrin* production, made him aggressive – tacitly Wieland's epoch-making *Lohengrin* of 1958 was the yardstick. Contrary to my convictions I did not voice an opinion on the new *Festspielhügel* dictatorship for fear of damaging my relationship with my father even further. Grandmother Winifred and the chorus of right-wing old Wagnerians rejoiced at the beginning of a new era. I was glad when I could finally leave for Paris.

I was overcome by Paris just as I had been by London. Overnight I changed from an "Englishman" into a "Frenchman". I would love to have denied my German roots, but I gave myself away by my accent, which I was often reminded of with a certain arrogance. Much of my time I spent in the Sorbonne and at the Alliance Française on language courses, although I didn't actually learn much there as I mostly spoke in English with my fellow students. In the sixth *arrondissement*, where I lived near the Jardin du Luxembourg, I often went walking, visiting museums and at night the lively and disreputable Les Halles. My Aunt Blandine de Prévaux, a great-granddaughter of Franz Liszt, took touching care of her *"cousin allemand"*. She lived in an elegant apartment on the Seine, with portraits of her great-grandfather, the future father-in-law of Richard Wagner, hanging on the walls. I knew hardly anything about the Austro-Hungarian composer, piano virtuoso and promoter of Wagner's music. My father rated him just as little as Uncle Wieland.

Aunt Blandine told me that the Nazis had murdered her husband, a resistance fighter. She did so without reproach. After that our talks became open, and we overcame the generation gap between the barely twenty-year-old nephew and the seventy-three-year-old aunt. I owe to her not only initial critical introductions to Liszt's work and biography, but also the stimulus to learn something of French painting and literature. She only mentioned her cousin Winifred in passing, but made fun of the latter's lack of education in subtle hints.

In the middle of July Blandine's daughter Daniela invited me to Lessey in Normandy, where she lived in a castle. There I got to know her daughter Blandine who, my age, fascinated me by her open opposition to the world of her parents. After a brief exchange of civilities we recognised at once that in all essential matters we had similar views and that in the few points we didn't agree on we found the difference an enrichment. Cousin Blandine told me a lot about her contact with the film director Jean-Luc Godard – *A Bout De Souffle* – and of the radical democratic circles she frequented. For whole nights we discussed how our depraved world order could be changed. She argued passionately, fought social injustice, had courage and formulated her socio-political ideas in an admirably creative yet concrete way. This close intellectual relationship, which still continues today, is only peripherally to do with Wagner and Liszt.

How musty the Wagner cult on the *Festspielhügel* seemed compared with all this, but it once again got me in its grip as school beckoned. I avoided conflict with my father, knowing his insecurity. He was still far from comfortable with his role as sole ruler and often suffered from severe criticism by the media. In the autumn of 1967 I had to repeat twelfth grade because of my long absence. I wanted to get school over with now as quickly as possible, and in a bearable way. I assured the headmaster at Stein that I would keep up an acceptable standard of achievement if, in exchange, he agreed to allow me to organise my presence in the classroom "more freely". That meant, among other things, that I went to Prague and Budapest with Henry Hohenemser, where we sent postcards to the teachers whose lessons we had bunked. But the excursions were not just tourist jaunts. When we crossed the heavily guarded border between East and West we felt the breath of world politics. The Vietnam war and the student unrest in West Berlin and Paris preoccupied our thoughts and dominated our discussions. At home I defended the students' positions, to the horror of my father and of my sister as well, who was looking for her niche on the side of the establishment.

In the hot political summer of 1968 my father had the premiere of his *Meistersinger* production, which, after Wieland's stagings of 1956 and 1963 I found unbearably conventional. My grandmother and the majority of the mostly uncultured bourgeois sponsors were thrilled that the *Meistersinger von Nürnberg* were finally being staged again as they were in the "good old times". I restrained myself from commenting on my father's artistic achievement, but reacted passionately to any glorification of the Nazi past, after which my grandmother introduced me to her "terribly decent circles" with the phrase: "This is Gottfried, the friend of Bolsheviks and Jews". Then she would give a loud and manly laugh.

Before the opening of the *Festspiele* a police contingent arrived, armed as if prepared to counter terrorists intending to blow up the *Festspielhaus* and its first-night audience. In fact it was just a few harmless students protesting against the West German industrialists among the *Festspiele* guests. When I saw the police using violence against the protesters I swore at them as "pigs" and it was only the fact that I was the son of the boss that saved me from arrest. After the premiere there was the usual reception in the Neues Schloss. Demonstrators had gathered there as well. Although I wasn't welcome at the reception, I sat down at Willy Brandt's table. At that time I considered the SPD Foreign Minister and Vice Chancellor of the grand coalition in Bonn the only credible German politician. In an effort to boost their careers, Bayreuth SPD bigwigs fawned over their chairman and grew nervous when some members of the ballet openly sympathised with the protesting students. Alarm grew when they started asking Brandt uncomfortable questions on contemporary world politics, on Vietnam and Rudi Dutschke, the leader of the Socialist German Student

Federations (SDS). Brandt, on the other hand, remained unflappable: he invited the protesters to his table and debated with them, to the horror of the Bayreuth establishment and the invited guests, including sponsors, who like my grandmother, referred among themselves to the SPD head only as a "socialist pig" or "Willy Weinbrand [cognac]". My father voiced no opinion on this. I took that as acquiescence.

Although I didn't want to go to Arosa that winter with the rest of the family for the Christmas holidays, I finally obliged for my mother's sake, since she missed me now that I was mostly at school. My father complained bitterly about my alleged communist worldview: he criticised my political opinions as infantile, and reminded me of the great sacrifices of his youth, the things he had had to do without during and after the war and his struggle to build up the *Festspiele*. He said he had put a lot of money into my education and now had to put up with his own son demonstrating as a "parlour pink" against the very people who financed the Bayreuth *Festspiele* and consequently his own life. My answer was heartfelt and uncontrolled: "You and your bloody ideals from the past! I'm talking here about the criminal war in Vietnam. It's about time you finally took part in a demo instead of serving as supplier of luxuries to an inhuman international bourgeoisie."

At the beginning of 1969 I finally understood that the *Abitur* was my key to personal freedom and began intensively studying for the final exams. I was particularly interested in German-Jewish authors of the Weimar Republic, so to the consternation of my German teacher Herr Grütter I chose Arnold Zweig's novel *Der Streit um den Sergeanten Grischa* [The Conflict Concerning Sergeant Grischa] as the subject for an essay. With the background of the Vietnam war at that time, what interested me in the book was the antiwar theme and Zweig's way of revealing the bourgeois capitalist society as the cause of the war. In the *Weltbühne* in 1930 Zweig wrote about his novel: "How, I ask, does one refute a system, a social order and the war, which is difficult to conceive as not being connected with it? By letting off steam with passionate counter-actions and producing caricatures? In my opinion one refutes a system by showing what its level best might perpetuate, how it forces the average decent person to act indecently...We don't want to expose villains like our friend Schiller, but systems."[3] Just to provoke, I told first my grandmother and then my father of my decision. Grandmother was indignant: "Left-wing Jews – how can you do this to us!" Father's reaction was once again eloquent silence.

Around this time I heard talk at family meetings of some planned "*Festspielhaus* foundation statutes". I wanted to know more about it. Father kept emphasising that this was all in my interest as well and was for the sake of my future too. He mentioned one article of these statutes that set down the regulations for my succession if I could provide evidence of the appropriate qualifications. I found this vague information worrying, especially as I was wondering how I could attain my chosen profession once I had completed my *Abitur* and left secondary school. I wanted to work in the theatre as assistant director: but my father had quite different plans. He wanted me to study law so that one day I could join the *Festspiele* business as manager.

Only my mother came to the *Abitur* graduation ceremony in Stein; my father claimed he was indispensable on the *Festspielhügel*. When I got back to Bayreuth I found much had changed. The troop of yes men had grown bigger and their servility, even to me, the son of the boss, was disgusting. Opportunism ruled. And a lot of them had an eye out for signs of the times, picking up on longlasting changes in the political and cultural climate. The 1968 revolts had broken down many outdated structures. The socialist-liberal coalition under Willy Brandt was just around the corner; it was soon to prove courageously democratic and turn to our Eastern neighbours. But already in the time of the grand coalition there had been clear signals that the mood in the country was altering. Times were changing and gradually the ideological spectrum was shifting to the left in the cultural world too. If you didn't want to find yourself an outsider, you had to shift your ideas. In particular the head of the press department of the *Festspiele*, Herbert Barth, tried in an adroit and cautious way to convince my father that a moderate move to the left was now necessary.

But my father was not yet ready. In 1969 he allocated the first post-Wieland production outside the family to August Everding, now general intendant of Munich's theatres. But after Wieland's, Everding's staging of *Der fliegende Holländer* was a depressing continuation of the series of prosaic premieres. Only the eager gossip was new. Father, along with his servile flock of directorial assistants had buried Wieland a second time, in the interests of reviving Old Bayreuth. Everding was a valuable element in this.

What in my eyes was monotonous opera aroused enthusiasm among the major part of the Bayreuth sponsors and Wagner Societies. My grandmother had abandoned all restraint since Wieland's death, a demonstration of which I witnessed. The American conductor Lorin Maazel, had been responsible for musical direction of Wieland's 1968 and 1969 *Ring* and was booked for the next *Ring* in my father's staging in 1970. At one of her receptions in the Siegfried Wagner House my Grandmother Winifred declared, to the amusement of her guests: "Although Maazel is a Jew he does seem to be quite gifted. So in spite of everything Wolf will engage him again next year." I was sitting next to Lorin Maazel and his wife and wanted to die of shame. Maazel appeared not to have heard this remark, or perhaps he didn't want to hear it. In 1970 he cancelled because of illness.

The official press reports of the 1970 season were manipulated, but even in these there was a lot of criticism. The media scene, in particular the arts pages, had gone too far to the left for the Bayreuth sclerosis to be publicly applauded outside the faithful Wagner community. The world was talking a different language. My father was forced gradually to realise this too, as ultimately it was a matter of securing the *Festspiele* and his own existence at a material level.

In the autumn of 1969 I yielded to pressure from my father and started law studies at the University of Munich. But I also used the time to attend lectures in the humanities, which interested me very much. In the semester break in October I visited my parents in Bayreuth. At that time they were reading Albert Speer's *Memoirs*. Speer had been Hitler's architect who, together with the Führer had designed bombastic buildings which were to be constructed after the Final Victory. During the war, Hitler had appointed him head of war production and it was in this capacity that Speer saw to it, among other things, that Nazi Germany was able to prolong the war and therefore the system of terror. In the Nuremberg war crimes trials he was sentenced to twenty years' imprisonment, which he served in Berlin Spandau, using the time to write his book of justification. Speer died in 1981.

Father quite openly expressed his sympathy for Speer, and as did those who were once big in Nazi circles, he repeatedly voiced his admiration for Hitler. This provoked a fresh quarrel between us, which continued throughout the winter holidays in Arosa. As always, when we were not of the same opinion, I was forced to hear how I was too immature to understand the tragic and martyred history of Germany. The atmosphere was worsened when I applauded the change of government in Bonn (Brandt had become Federal Chancellor), which was unbearable for my father, who consequently suspected left-wing plots everywhere.

As it was, Father was in *Götterdämmerung* mood. The reviews of his 1970 *Ring*, discussions on the future course of the *Festspiele* and on the projected Foundation, had all worn him down. I advised him to just drop the whole bloody *Festspiele* and finally make a decent life for himself, without his band of toadies, and without playing the entertainer of German high society. My suggestion was not destined to improve the atmosphere.

My sister found such discussions pointless. Quite coolly she started to get friendly with Everding and to safeguard her future in Bayreuth, supported by her "grandma" Winifred. She was soon the darling of influential sponsors and industrialists and was of one mind with Father, regarding everything I suggested as worthless, and integrating herself fully in the *Festspiele* business. From time to time she was allowed to play directorial assistant to Everding and Otto Schenk and by these means discovered that the international opera business was destined to be her profession, and her future, the intendant's seat in Bayreuth. Anyone who did not keep in with her had a difficult or a short life on the *Festspielhügel* until 1975. The maxim advocated by Wieland that "After Cosima and Winifred, never again a female dictatorship", no longer applied.

Father and Eva found my way of life quite unreasonable: a left-wing idealist, absorbed in contemporary philosophy, psychology and politics, in other words totally unworldly things which were a waste of time. Eva shared our grandmother's opinion that there was no place on the *Festspielhügel* for Marxist crackpots like me, a label I was never to lose. Even at that time she knew that it would earn her the applause of the Society Of Friends Of Bayreuth.

My father's 1970 Bayreuth *Ring*, which was only technically improved, like his 1960 *Ring*, contributed nothing new and relied solely on Rüdiger Tamschick's projections. Herbert Barth was able to use this to his, and his internal and external chorus of yes men's, advantage through his adroit manipulation of the press, and also by exploiting my father's increasing reluctance to listen to criticism of any kind. The manipulation of media opinion at this time was one of the great master strokes of Bayreuth power politics. Its culmination was the discovery of a left-wing Wagner in preparation for the coming gold rush years: the *Festspiele*'s centenary was just around the corner.

Even then, the only people tolerated on the *Festspielhügel* were those who submitted to my father's authoritarian rule, which was sold to the outside world as liberal. The heyday of the toadies had begun and anyone who praised the artist Wolfgang Wagner earned privileges. I noticed with some unease how the marketing of Bayreuth for the 1976 centenary celebrations had had a left-wing image grafted on. The architects of this shift were Herbert Barth, the head of the press department, the writer and Wagner devotee Martin Gregor-Dellin, appointed together with Dietrich Mack as editors of the Cosima Wagner diaries, Egon Voss, later the editor of the new critical *Richard Wagner* complete edition, and Dorothea Glatt-Behr; later also Oswald Georg Bauer, today general secretary of the Bavarian Academy of Fine Arts.

A typical example of this deliberate shift to the left was the essay 'The Tragedy Of Power', a miscellany on Father's and Dietrich Mack's *Ring* interpretation in the *Rheingold* programme of the 1970 Bayreuth *Festspiele*. There among other things I read to my amazement: "Does this mean afterwards [at the end of the *Götterdämmerung*] an apotheosis, a salvation of the world, a certainty of salvation or does it mean an apocalypse, a total annihilation; an optimistic tragedy or total tragedy [*Pantragismus*]?...[It is rather] not a handing on of the legacy, not a continuous transition from one generation to the next, but a radical break, *tabula rasa*, smoking ruins. So it is the apocalypse? Yes, but as example, not as end in itself; for two things have been added. People, who...have been demagogically abused with alcohol and drugs to become a dull and stupid mass, experience this inferno. They fall prey to lamentation and horror [sic]. Enlightenment must be brutal, the world must burn from one end to the other. One funeral pyre alone is not enough to achieve a cathartic effect. Knowledge of this terrible end must be attested to and the realisation handed on, so that perhaps a way can be found out of this void."[4]

No trace of all these atrocities was to be seen on the stage though. What Father meant by the break between generations, I only understood later: unconsciously he had woven his own family problem into his directorial concept. (I shall be returning to this again in my interpretation of the statutes of the Richard Wagner Foundation, being drawn up at that time, and signed in March 1973.)

Under these circumstances I had no intention of becoming Father's assistant, especially as Eva was making it more and more clear that my presence on the *Festspielhügel* was a nuisance. To avoid such tensions and intrigues I moved to Mainz in the autumn of 1970, where I finally began studying what interested me: musicology, psychology and German literature. My father was against these new studies and could only be placated by my promising not to give up my law studies completely. He asked the musicologist Professor Gernot Gruber to keep a discreet eye on me, and tried to find out from him whether I even had the prerequisites for this study. Gruber told me of my father's reservations and relations between my father and myself were jeopardised once again.

In Mainz I took piano lessons in addition to my other studies. In the summer semester of 1971 I studied piano, counterpoint and harmony in Graz, Austria, and then in the Bayreuth *Festspielhaus* with Maximilian Kojetinsky. I went about this thoroughly and astounded my father, who would never have believed that I could pursue my self-chosen studies with such dedication.

The rumour arose that I would soon be taken on board in the *Festspiele* business. Eva vehemently denied this. Rather defiantly, I declared that, on the basis of my progress with Kojetinsky I would continue studying musicology. Gernot Gruber supported me in this resolve, and finally my father agreed to my giving up the loathsome law studies.

In the summer of 1971 I learned from Mother that one of Wieland's closest collaborators, Gerhard Helwig, had been sacked. On 7 August 1971 Helwig handed over to my father all the documentation he possessed from the Wieland period. Father voiced doubts on the completeness of these documents. Such events increasingly aroused my interest in my family history and at the same time a mistrust of the official methods in dealing with family documents.

In the winter semester of 1971-2 I continued my studies in Erlangen and started looking for openings as an assistant director. The university there disappointed me; I found the music teaching too conservative, especially as some professors wore their political opinions so openly on their sleeve, while students and professors alike treated me like a museum piece that might prove useful for making a few contacts. The teaching of the psychology lecturers dealt solely in formal analyses. I felt equally uncomfortable in the theatre studies department. Although I could get along with the heads, I found a lot of the students ideologically too fixated – stragglers of the 1968 generation. Anyone who was not as "progressively Marxist" as they were was quickly branded a reactionary. As Bertolt Brecht already fascinated me at that time, I attended a course on his theatre work and so initially was ranked among the "progressive forces". When the student guardians of pure left doctrine found out who I was, though, they wouldn't believe my interest in Brecht: how could the "reactionary Wagner" be compatible with the "progressive Brecht"? So yet again I was relegated to outsider. But I regarded Erlangen merely as a stopgap, a place to get the necessary papers in order then to continue my nomadic life elsewhere.

The urge to do practical theatre work continued to grow and, in the autumn of 1971, I contacted Hans Peter Lehmann, chief director of the Nuremberg Opera House. Lehmann had been one of Wieland's assistant directors, and my father had appointed him to preserve some of my uncle's still existent productions for the Bayreuth programme. However, he was somewhat torn: on the one hand he was very affectionately attached to Wieland's legacy; on the other hand he followed my father, who was in favour of modifying Wieland's works, for example by making the lighting brighter. Either way, for Lehmann it was certainly of advantage to foster the connection with Bayreuth.

I believed at the time that he was interested in my professional development as an opera director. At first everything went as I wanted it to and in February 1972 I was finally able to begin my first assistant directorship with Lehmann, in Wuppertal on his *Tannhäuser* production. I threw myself into the work with great enthusiasm: keeping the prompt-book, looking after rehearsals with the second cast, planning rehearsals, making arrangements with soloists, chorus, orchestra, technicians and administration and, last but not least, with the media. I realised how difficult it must have been to have been Wieland Wagner's assistant. After his death the shadow of his great example lay over any Wagner production. No wonder Lehmann's *Tannhäuser* in Wuppertal was also strongly influenced by Wieland. New in this production was the first music theatre choreography of the revolutionary Pina Bausch.

After the premiere Lehmann attested in writing that I had done good work. Despite this I didn't get any further engagement from him when I was in difficulties and looking for work.

It was not far from Erlangen to Bayreuth, and I visited my parents at weekends now and again. For the *Tannhäuser* of the 1972 *Festspiele* my father had engaged the opera director Götz Friedrich. He had been Walter Felsenstein's assistant at the Komische Oper in East Berlin and had earned an excellent reputation. So there were no grounds for argument where content was concerned. I hoped that the Everding incident with the 1969 *Dutchman* had been a one-off mistake and that my father would give up his own directing efforts. I wanted him instead to attract distinguished people from other houses to Bayreuth. Unfortunately my wishes were not fulfilled.

The peace between my father and me lasted only a short time. It ended when the talk turned to Willy Brandt's *Ostpolitik*. I didn't see any alternative to this, whereas my father described the policy of détente as a sell-out of German interests.

I also visited my grandmother during these weekends, mainly to learn more about her and her years with the Führer. Although she knew my "radical left" attitude, most of the time she answered my questions quite frankly, describing such things as Hitler's wonderful, bright, hypnotic eyes, his gentleness, his good manners, his charm, his love for Father and Wieland, his plans for the boys in the future of a "better Germany", his profound knowledge of Wagner's works, his love of nature and of mankind.

Here I interrupted the flow and asked her what about love of mankind in the case of the Jews. She replied: "You still don't know the Jews, just wait. One day you'll understand me, and Hitler will be seen differently in world history." Her reaction was reminiscent of Father's.

At first in these discussions I made the mistake of reacting to her monstrous statements: "How can you say things like that! Six million Jews don't seem to be enough for you to stop kidding yourself." But she constantly defended herself with the same sentence: "That's just lies and slander from American Jews!"

What I had more or less uncritically accepted as a nine-year-old, who didn't understand, I now, at twenty-five, wanted to know in detail. My grandmother's antisemitism was shockingly brutal: I asked her about the fate of Jewish singers who had performed in Bayreuth before the Nazi takeover and later had to emigrate or were murdered in concentration camps, such as Henriette Gottlieb, Ottilie Metzger-Lattermann, Margarethe Matzenauer, Hermann Weil, Alexander Kipnis, Eva Liebenberg, Friedrich Schorr and Emanuel List. At such moments she found herself caught out in her lying and became particularly aggressive. "You can't understand that. That wasn't Hitler at all, it was Schleicher and the other criminals who betrayed National Socialism. I always tried to help the Jews who sang in Bayreuth!" she screamed. I countered: "So you and the family did know about Auschwitz!"

This ended the discussion. Anyway she had not shrunk from a blatant distortion of the historical truth in order to maintain her view of history: General Kurt von Schleicher had been murdered by the Nazis in 1934 and so he could not have had anything to do with the Holocaust. But my grandmother meant Julius Streicher, the founder of the antisemitic inflammatory paper *Der Stürmer*.

No longer satisfied with this type of information, I decided to change my tactics and, remaining calm, acted as though I were a historian without personal involvement. It worked. Grandmother answered my questions and more importantly instructed her confidante, Gertrud Strobel, a militant antisemite, to give me historical material without my father's knowledge. Gertrud Strobel who, amazingly, did not see through my intentions, now regarded me as the only thoroughly decent Wagner and provided me with a wealth of documents. This included all the *Bayreuther Blätter*, *Festspiele* guides and other documents from the period from 1850 to 1944. I was particularly fascinated by the correspondence between Hitler, my grandmother, Wieland and Father. The more I read, the more horrified I became: I could never have suspected the scale of my family's involvement in the Nazi tyranny.

CHAPTER FOUR

THE ANTISEMITISM OF THE WAGNER FAMILY (1850-1945)

The starting point for discussion on Richard Wagner's antisemitism is a pamphlet published in 1859, entitled 'The Jews In Music'. Predominantly ideological, it is based on Wagner's pathological idea of the Jews as the enemy. This is for him the negative keystone to his future political and artistic concept, that lies at the basis of the idea of the *Festspiele* and its realisation in Bayreuth. In order to defame the imaginary Jewish enemy and develop his counter-concept, Wagner resorts in 'The Jews In Music' to disgusting abuse: "The Jew is repulsive...he rules and will continue to rule as long as money remains the power before which all deeds and actions must needs pale into insignificance...In ordinary life the Jew, who, as we know, has a God unto himself, strikes us first and foremost by his outward appearance which, no matter which European nationality he belongs to, has something about it which is foreign to that nationality and which we find insuperably unpleasant...The Jew, incapable in himself of communicating artistically with us by means of his outward appearance or language, and least of all through his singing, has none the less come to dominate public taste in the most widely disseminated of modern artistic genres, music...The Jew has never had an art of his own, and therefore never led a life that was capable of sustaining art...we are bound to describe the period of Judaism in modern music as one of total uncreativity and degenerate anti-progressiveness."[5]

After a denigration of Felix Mendelssohn, Wagner concludes his diatribe with an appeal that sounds like a heralding of what was to begin scarcely ninety years later: "Join unreservedly in this self-destructive and bloody battle, and we shall all be united and indivisible! But bear in mind that one thing alone can redeem you from the curse that weighs upon you, the redemption of Ahasuerus: Destruction!"

Wagner's outbursts against his "enemies" Felix Mendelssohn and Giacomo Meyerbeer, without whose efforts Wagner's stage works are unthinkable, display disgraceful aggressiveness. He owed to his one-time supporter Meyerbeer essential elements of the musical dramaturgy of his early works and to Mendelssohn a decisive influence on melody and instrumentation. In 'The Jews In Music' Wagner wilfully blurs essential foreign influences on his artistic development. Herein lies a central motive for his pathological antisemitism, which runs like a red thread through all the composer's writings up to 1882.

'The Jews In Music' is by no means the end, as was later asserted in Bayreuth, but the beginning of Wagner's antisemitism in the sense of a politico-cultural concept. He repeats the ideas of his first antisemitic pamphlet, scarcely altered, in his key work on the theory of art of 1851, 'Opera And Drama'. Later Wagner relativised his revolutionary art theory in order not to distance himself too much from the taste of the bourgeoisie. But his antisemitism remained and was expressed in particular in the writings 'On State And Religion' (1864), 'What Is German?' (1865/78), 'German Art And Politics' (1867), right up to the regeneration pieces (1879-81). Under the influence of the racist philosopher Arthur Gobineau, Wagner's antisemitism increased to the fateful biological racism of the late Bayreuth period, as it also continued to develop after Wagner's death (1883) until 1945. At the end of the regeneration essay 'Know Yourself' of 1881 Wagner formulated ideas that today read like a horrifying anticipation of Hitler's Final Solution, invoking a Germany free of Jews as the "great solution": "And the very stimulus of the present movement – conceivable among ourselves alone – might bring this great solution within reach of us Germans, rather than of any other nation, if only we would boldly take that 'know thyself' and apply it to the inmost quick of our existence. That we have nought to fear from ultimate knowledge, if we but conquer all false shame and quarry deep enough, we hope the anxious may have called from the above."[6]

Wagner's attitude towards the Jews kept changing, for obvious reasons. He even claimed to be philosemitic if he considered it useful for carrying through his ideological-political and artistic goals. But from 1850 on, every enemy of his art, irrespective of birth, was "an artistic Jew".

Wagner's essay on 'The Jews In Music' provoked strong protests which also influenced many later reviewers of Wagner's operas and writings. His antisemitic writings read like a constant exchange of attack and counter-attack between himself and the music critics of his time. Here Wagner loses sight of the development of European Jewry in the second half of the nineteenth century and therefore increasingly too his sense of reality and humanity. So Wagner's art, in spite of all the brilliant innovations, as manifested in his first works staged in the Bayreuth *Festspielhaus* – the *Ring* and *Parsifal* – also became anti-Jewish, or anti-art, and the *Festspielhaus* an anti-Jewish anti-culture establishment, completely in tune with the 'Report On The *Festspielhaus* In Bayreuth' of 1873. In it Wagner compares his German "new European theatre, taste and morals...to a Parisian whore or a successful stock market speculator" – an allusion to Meyerbeer's operas. So he tacitly refers back to his essay 'What Is German?' and the second edition of 'The Jews In Music' which appeared in 1869. The circle closes here that Wagner had already begun to forge in 1850: the idea of the *Festspiele* was realised as the "Bayreuth *Festspiele*", which very soon had a propaganda effect all over Germany. Added to this were the Wagner Societies springing up everywhere, that appeared in the German-nationalistic *Bayreuther Blätter*. From the beginning of the *Festspiele*, then, antisemitism and racism belonged to the ingredients of the Bayreuth opera undertaking, whether implicit or explicit. Wagner's antisemitism was closely connected to this.

Some of Wagner's writings – in particular 'Modern' of 1878, 'Public And Popularity' of 1879 and the reprint of 'What Is German?' of 1878 – encouraged other antisemitic, chauvinist authors in their efforts to align German culture according to the standards of the Bayreuth shrine. How much the thinking of the bourgeois Richard Wagner influenced his art is shown in the stage works he realised in his Bayreuth *Festspiele* from 1876 to 1882 as director and theatre impresario. Who is portrayed by Alberich and Mime, the dwarfish exploiters, and Hagen in the *Ring*, Beckmesser in the *Meistersinger* and Klingsor and Kundry, the female Ahasuerus figure in *Parsifal*? If we look at Kundry's baptism in Act Three of *Parsifal* in connection with the regeneration writings, we understand how serious Wagner was with the conversion of the Jews to Christianity already demanded in 'The Jews In Music'. The above-mentioned "great solution" of 1881, on the other hand, is realised on stage in the dramaturgically superfluous and therefore ideologically eloquent death of Kundry at the end of *Parsifal*.

Just as Wagner in his works of art admits different interpretations, he seduces his followers in his regeneration writings to "his" new Christianity. This is a confused blend of antisemitism, antifeminism and Buddhist ideas, mixed with elements of Schopenhauer's philosophy of renunciation. In other words: "In regard of knowledge of truths, the artist possesses a weaker morality than the thinker; he does not wish to be deprived of the glittering, profound interpretations of life and guards against simple and sober methods and results. He appears to be fighting on behalf of the greater dignity and significance of man; in reality he refuses to give up the presuppositions which are most efficacious for his art, that is to say the fantastic, mythical, uncertain, extreme, the sense for the symbolical, the over-estimation of the person, the belief in something miraculous in genius: he thus considers the perpetuation of his mode of creation more important than scientific devotion to the true in any form, however plainly this may appear." So perceptively writes Nietzsche in his *Human, All Too Human* of 1878 to the background of his experiences with Wagner and his works.[7]

Cosima, Liszt's daughter, Richard Wagner's second wife and director of the *Festspiele* until 1907, was no less antisemitic than her husband. Evidence of this is offered *inter alia* by an entry in her diary of 18 December 1881, in which she records a conversation she had with Richard:

"Then he tells me about a recent performance of *Nathan* [*Der Weise*] at which, when the line asserting that Christ was also a Jew was spoken, an Israelite in the audience cried: 'Bravo!' He reproaches Lessing for this piece of insipidity and when I reply that the play seems to me to contain a peculiarly German kind of humanity, he says: 'But not a trace of profundity.'…One adds fuel to these fellows' arrogance by having anything at all to do with them, and we, for example, do not talk of our feelings about those Jews in the theatre in front of Rub[instein], 400 unbaptised and probably 500 baptised ones."[8]

The attitude of Richard and Cosima Wagner expressed in such remarks was to have its effect far beyond their death. This quotation from Cosima's diaries sums up in a few sentences what was to form the Bayreuth tradition until 1945. This is shown, for example, in the writings of Cosima's son-in-law, the English racial theoretician Houston Stewart Chamberlain, one of Adolf Hitler's mentors. A quotation from Chamberlain's 1895 biography of Richard Wagner substantiates the enduring effect of Wagner's antisemitism:

"At the beginning of his *Judenthum In Der Musik* ['The Jews In Music'] Wagner tells us that his purpose is: 'to explain the unconscious feeling which in the people takes the form of a deep-rooted antipathy to the Jewish nature, to express therefore in plain language something really existing, not at all by force of imagination to infuse life into a thing unreal in itself.' And how was this really existing thing to be removed? How was the baneful yawning abyss to be bridged over? Wagner points to the regeneration of the human race, and to the Jews he says: 'Bear your share undauntedly in this work of redemption, gaining new birth by self-immolation; we shall then be one and undivided! But remember that there can only be release from the curse which rests upon you: the release of Ahasuerus – destruction.' What he means by destruction is evident from an earlier sentence: 'to become men in common with us is, for the Jews, primarily the same thing as to cease to be Jews.'"[9]

A direct line runs from Chamberlain to Hitler, whom he revered from the very beginning. On 7 October 1923, Chamberlain writes to the future Führer: "Dear Herr Hitler…You are not at all, as you have been described to me, a fanatic, rather I would like to describe you as the direct opposite of a fanatic. The fanatic heats heads, you warm hearts. The fanatic wants to persuade, you want to convince, only convince – and that is why you are successful; yes, I would likewise define you as the opposite of a politician…for the axis of all politics is membership of a party, whereas in your case all parties disappear, consumed in the fire of love for the fatherland…You have tasks requiring tremendous force before you, but in spite of your strength of will I do not consider you a man of force. You know Goethe's distinction between force and force! There is a force that originates from chaos and leads to chaos, and there is a force whose essence it is to form the cosmos, and of the latter he said: 'Ruling, it takes on any shape – and even in the great it is not force.' I mean it in this cosmos-building sense when I say I want you to be listed among the ranks of the uplifting, not the forceful men…My belief in Germanness has not wavered for a moment, but my hopes – I admit it – had reached a low ebb. At a stroke you have transformed the state of my soul. That Germany in the hour of its deepest need has borne a Hitler, that attests to its vitality; likewise the effects emanating from him; for these two things – personality and its effect – belong together. That the great Ludendorff openly allies himself with you and joins the movement emanating from you: what a splendid confirmation! I could calmly fall asleep and would not even need to wake up again. May God protect you!"[10]

In 1915 Richard Wagner's son Siegfried, my grandfather, married Winifred Williams. She held Hitler in just as high esteem as her brother-in-law Chamberlain, as documented, for example, in her "Open Letter" of 14 November 1923 in the *Bayreuth Oberfränkische Zeitung*, that is, only a few days after Hitler's attempted *putsch* in Munich: "The whole of Bayreuth knows that we have a friendly relationship with Adolf Hitler. We happened to be in Munich in those momentous days and were the first ones to come back from there. Understandably, Hitler's followers turned to us for information from eye witnesses…For years we have been following with the greatest inner sympathy and approval the uplifting work of Adolf Hitler, this German man who, filled with ardent love for his fatherland, is sacrificing his life for his idea of a purified, united, national greater Germany, who has set himself the hazardous task of opening the eyes of the working class to the enemy within and to Marxism and its consequences, who as no other has managed to bring people together in brotherly reconciliation, has been able to do away with the almost insuperable class hatred, who has restored to thousands upon thousands of despairing people the joyous hope of a reviving, dignified fatherland and a firm belief in it. His personality has made on us too, as on anyone who comes into contact with him, a deep, moving impression, and we have understood how such a simple, physically delicate man is capable of exercising such power. This power is founded on the moral strength and purity of this man, who without ceasing stands up for an idea he has seen to be right, which he is trying with the fervour and humility of divine vocation to realise. Such a man, who is standing up so directly for good, must inspire, electrify people, animate them with selfless love and devotion for his person. I freely admit that we too are under the spell of this personality, that we too, who stood by him in happy days, will remain faithful to him now too in his hour of need."[11]

From 1907 to 1930 Siegfried Wagner ran the Bayreuth *Festspiele*. He too corresponded with Hitler. But Siegfried Wagner's antisemitism was not as extreme as his wife Winifred's, or Cosima's. On 6 June 1921, for example, still quite uninfluenced by the later pro-Hitler atmosphere in Bayreuth, he wrote to an antisemitic editor of the *Deutsche Zeitung* in Berlin: "Among the Jews we have very many faithful, honest and selfless supporters who have given us countless proofs of their friendship. You want us to close our doors to all these people, to rebuff them for the sole reason that they are Jews. Is that humane? Is that Christian? Is that German? No!...On our *Festspielhügel* we want to produce positive, not negative work. Whether a person is Chinese, Negro, American, Indian or Jew is totally immaterial to us. But we could learn from the Jews how to stick together and help one another."[12]

This letter was used after the Nazi period as a pseudo-liberal alibi for the Bayreuth *Festspiele* in order to be able to present the period from 1907 to 1930 in the light of the pure art of Richard Wagner. The (still) extant documents of the period from 1925 to Siegfried Wagner's death show, however, that even in the 1920s Richard Wagner's work was serving politico-cultural ends on the *Festspielhügel*. In his letter of Christmas 1923, only a few weeks after Hitler's failed November *putsch* in Munich, Siegfried Wagner wrote to Rosa Eidam: "We got to know that splendid man [Hitler] here in the summer at the German Rally and remain true to him even if it should mean our going to prison. We were never timeservers here in Wahnfried. [Alluding to the political unrest in the 1920s in Bavaria.] The situation in Bavaria is appalling. The times of the Spanish Inquisition have returned. Perjury and betrayal are sanctified, and Jew and Jesuit are working hand in glove to exterminate Germanness! But perhaps Satan has miscalculated this time. Should the German cause really succumb, then I'll believe in Jehova, the god of revenge and hatred. My wife is fighting like a lioness for Hitler – first-rate!"[13]

It is in the light of this that Hitler's letter to Siegfried Wagner of 5 May 1924 becomes clear too. Writing in memory of his official visit to Bayreuth on the occasion of the *Deutsche Tage* [German Rally] on 30 September 1923 aimed at a future electoral victory, and regarding the Wagner family's open support of him, among other things, Hitler says: "I was filled with proud joy when I saw the people's victory in the very city in which, first through the Master [Richard Wagner] and then through Chamberlain, the spiritual sword was forged with which we are fighting today."[14] Comparing Richard Wagner's and Chamberlain's inflammatory antisemitic writings with Hitler's racist politico-cultural ravings in *Mein Kampf* leaves no doubt of their historical connection.

The fact that Siegfried Wagner, his wife and sisters took over the honorary presidency of the national Bavarian Federation Of German Youth (BBdJ) on 1 August 1923, further enhances the historical connection. The BBdJ set itself as future objectives "to convey the ideas of Bayreuth, the artistic works and politico-cultural ideals of Richard Wagner, to the whole of the German people; to reveal the profound sense of the direct bond between the great German memoir [*Mein Kampf*] of Adolf Hitler and his cultural will and the work of Bayreuth".[15]

Closely connected with the national stock of ideas and the Bayreuth *Festspiele* were the *Deutsche Festspiele* in Weimar from July 1926, in which operas by Siegfried Wagner were performed and national poetry published, among others by Hans von Wolzogen, editor of the antisemitic and chauvinist *Bayreuther Blätter* from 1878 to 1938. The Weimar *Festspiele* were, like the Bayreuth *Festspiele*, an aggressive politico-cultural counter-concept to the avant-garde art of the Weimar Republic. With the foundation of the National Socialist Society For German Culture in 1927 and the Militant League For German Culture [*Kampfbund Für Deutsche Kultur*] in 1928 by Alfred Rosenberg, the semi-official National Socialist philosopher and author of the propaganda work *The Myth Of The Twentieth Century*, the leading Nazis Hans Frank, Baldur von Schirach, Wilhelm Frick, Hans Severus Ziegler, Hans Schemm and Adolf Bartels among others were won over to the Bayreuth cause. As son of the Master and cultural inspiration for Hitler as much as through his wife Winifred's party membership since 1923 – confirmed by the Canadian Wagner scholar Philip Wults – Siegfried Wagner could play outwardly the role of the non-partisan artist, but enjoy all the advantages of the national, pre-National Socialist movement.

Shortly before his death in June 1930, Siegfried Wagner had appointed Arturo Toscanini to Bayreuth. Toscanini was a man who throughout his life had doggedly only seen the artist in Wagner and his appointment was quoted repeatedly after 1945 as exonerative proof that Siegfried Wagner had opened up to other cultural trends. Quite how Siegfried Wagner would have survived in the Third Reich is pure speculation today: his homosexuality rendered him decadent in the eyes of Hitler and his propaganda minister, Joseph Goebbels.

After Siegfried Wagner, my grandmother, Winifred, ran the *Festspiele* until 1944. Her belief in Hitler's Final Victory is evident from a contribution by her to the *Meistersinger* programme of the wartime *Festspiele* of 1943: "If during the wartime *Festspiele* in 1943 the *Meistersinger von Nürnberg* are chosen, then that has a deep and symbolic meaning. For this work shows us in the most impressive way the creative German man in his nationally conditioned will to create, which the Master gave immortal form to in the figure of the Nuremberg shoemaker and national poet Hans Sachs and which, in the present struggle of the Western cultural world against the destructive spirit of the plutocratic-bolshevist world conspiracy, gives our soldiers invincible fighting strength and a fanatical belief in the victory of our arms."[16]

CHAPTER FIVE

"THE WILL TO POWER" II

Investigation into my family's Nazi past in February 1972 was interrupted by my first stint as assistant director in Wuppertal. After my experiences there I was keen to see how Götz Friedrich would direct *Tannhäuser* for the *Festspiele*, so in April 1972, a few months before his debut in Bayreuth, I visited him in East Berlin. He explained his concept to me and I was thrilled. Afterwards Friedrich invited me to a performance of the Berliner Ensemble's *Coriolanus* which turned out to be disappointing: sterile in its perfection and robotic acting.

I used the time after Berlin to continue conversations with my grandmother and Gertrud Strobel. My father didn't like this at all. Grandmother had faithfully reported to him my great interest in Bayreuth's political past, my numerous questions and note-taking. Father was particularly on edge during these months regarding anything to do with the *Festspiele*, Hitler and the Wagner family: he wanted to carry through his Foundation statutes and avoid any irritation that could prejudice this great undertaking. Consequently I had to be even more careful in my investigations. Frau Strobel informed me with horror of the left-wing musicologists of the Thyssen Foundation, who were constantly pestering her concerning the great 1976 jubilee. I later learned she meant Egon Voss, Dietrich Mack and Michael Karbaum, of whom I was to have personal experience. The Thyssen Foundation supported these and other authors financially, and they were now working on the project: *The Festspiele Centenary*.

In July 1972 the dress rehearsal for Götz Friedrich's *Tannhäuser* took place in Bayreuth. Friedrich had not raised my expectations in East Berlin in vain. I was fascinated in particular with how he handled the soloists and the chorus in Act Two. I expected an uproar at the premiere when the Wartburg company clothed in dinner jackets and evening dress greeted the Landgraf with raised arm and "Heil Hitler" and later tried to evict Tannhäuser from the Wartburg Nazi style. Grandmother Winifred put pressure on my father to prevent this production from being performed unaltered, but I urged my father to let Friedrich work in peace. It says much for my father that he exercised restraint.

As it happened there was indeed a furore at the premiere, not in reaction to Act Two, but because of the epilogue, which I had found rather tame. The chorus, dressed in out-of-place leisure clothing, announced as a message for universal rejoicing, that Tannhäuser was now redeemed. The majority of the audience misunderstood the final scene as "worker and peasant greeting" of the GDR director Friedrich. They screamed out their hatred as fanatically as their predecessors a few decades before had cheered the Führer. The cause of such hysterical aggression was clear: Friedrich had held up a mirror to the audience and quite unconsciously, many of the ladies and gentlemen from the land of the economic miracle had recognised themselves in the Wartburg society. The fascistoid behaviour acted out on stage by the singers was repeated after the premiere in real life in the auditorium.

I too got mixed up in one of these violent scenes as Friedrich came to take his bow in front of the curtain. One of the gentlemen standing next to me, a member of the Society Of Friends Of Bayreuth, shouted: "Go back to your dirty communists in the GDR, we don't need you here!" The members of the audience around us agreed enthusiastically. I asked the heckler his name, but he didn't want to tell me. "Who are you, anyway, to ask me my name here in the *Festspielhaus*?" he asked. Furious, I retorted: "You coward hiding here in a group! Have the courage of your convictions. Who are you?"

Scarcely had I said this when he grabbed me roughly by the neck.

He evidently wanted to tear off my bow tie and would probably have beaten me up. Realising that it may be to my advantage to introduce myself, I said: "My name is Gottfried Wagner. I am the son of the director of the *Festspiele*, who fully backed this splendid production. You are still on the private property of my family, and I shall take you to court for disturbance of the peace and bodily harm. Now come to the police with me." I had hardly finished speaking when the Wagner friend fled from the theatre. My behaviour was to have repercussions a few days later, when one of the audience wrote to my father to complain about my "left-wing radicalism".

There was more controversy after the premiere. Ewald Hilger, president of the Society Of Friends Of Bayreuth, together with his retinue, was outraged by Friedrich's production. Hilger, who had succeeded his father – an influential gentleman of West German society and a patron of Arno Breker, Hitler's favourite sculptor – to this office, advised the *Festspiele* administration and on that evening lost control of himself, attacking my father for having engaged Friedrich. Father scarcely defended himself. As Hilger's attacks got cruder, my mother and I intervened. She jumped up, pointed to the door and shouted so loudly that the whole room fell silent: "Now that's enough! Stop insulting my husband like that. The Friends Of Bayreuth have no right to dictate their opinions to my husband and us." She continued to stand pointing her finger until Hilger, deeply offended, rushed from the room, not before threatening: "This will have consequences!" It had no consequences. Father and he were soon bosom pals again.

I was thrilled by Mother's action. But all around us the atmosphere was icy, a foretaste of what my mother and I were later to experience frequently. Even the "left-wing vanguard" around Herbert Barth, the press spokesman of the *Festspiele*, cautiously drew back. Only a handful of people came to say a few words of appreciation to Mother: my sister and my father remained awkwardly silent, but seldom had Mother and I been so close as we were on that evening. The next morning my father asked for more restraint. Such an opinion made me very concerned, as I was convinced that Mother and I were fighting for the right cause. All these lies and later too the opportunistic changes in the

Tannhäuser production disgusted me.

My father found himself so much under fire that he started questioning the final scene of Act Three. That sparked off a violent quarrel between us, as I was against any change and sacrifice of artistic freedom, just because the sponsors had set their minds on not being able to live with Friedrich's production. I told Father of the incident in the auditorium and he seemed to want to reconsider his decision yet again. But he finally gave in, and the second performance had to make do without the alleged "worker and peasant greeting". This lame compromise satisfied the Society Of Friends Of Bayreuth, but I felt it to be a cowardly concession.

The reaction of bourgeois society, especially of Franz Josef Strauss, who had publicly pronounced himself vehemently against Götz Friedrich's staging and was negotiating with my father on the Foundation statutes, hurt my father and probably contributed to him distancing himself from Friedrich's final scene. The liberal and left-wing press, which at first had only applauded, now voiced some doubts as well. The new and the old endings were passionately discussed. Bayreuth had overnight not only been "retheatralised" [*retheatralisiert*], as Friedrich put it, but publicly repoliticised. The fronts between right, liberal and left, blurred since 1951 by Wieland's apolitical, psychoanalytical stagings, became clear again.

The era of the "left-wing Richard Wagner" had now well and truly dawned. The fanatical majority of the premiere audience was made insecure by such public debate and before expressing any further opinions waited for the reviews of Joachim Kaiser and other well-known Wagner experts, in order then to repeat their remarks, even if these strongly diverged from opinions they had held in the auditorium shortly before. It was imperative to remain "in". Many Wagner friends who were in a quandary about what to think went to my grandmother for comfort and advice. She declared: "I think the *Tannhäuser* of this communist Friedrich repulsive as well, but think of my son. He can make mistakes too and he's already started altering the worst scenes. Our Bayreuth is still our Bayreuth! It just makes Wolf's great artistic gifts even more obvious!" A short time later the same ladies and gentlemen who had found Winifred's judgment so wise, were to be in close cahoots with "wicked" Friedrich. "Fine friends," commented Grandmother, disappointed.

Father continued to be publicly abused. At the annual meeting of the Society Of Friends Of Bayreuth the members objected to being limited to supporting the *Festspiele* financially, they also wanted a say over the content as well. The attitude of the majority of the sponsors regarding the *Tannhäuser* premiere in July 1972 reminded me of Friedrich Nietzsche's comments in the epilogue to his essay 'The Case Of Wagner':

"One pays heavily for being one of Wagner's disciples. Let us take the measure of this discipleship by considering its cultural effects. Whom did this movement bring to the fore? What did it breed and multiply? Above all, the presumption of the layman, the art-idiot. That kind now organises associations, wants its 'taste' to prevail, wants to play the judge in *rebus musicis et musicantibus*. Secondly, an ever growing indifference against all severe, noble, conscientious training in the service of art; all this is to be replaced by faith in genius or, to speak plainly, by impudent dilettantism (the formula for this is to be found in the *Meistersinger*). Thirdly, and worst of all: *theatrocracy* – the nonsense of a faith in the precedence of the theatre, in the right of the theatre to lord it over the arts, over art.

"But one should tell the Wagnerians 100 times to their faces *what* the theatre is: always beneath art, always only something secondary, something made cruder, something twisted tendentiously, mendaciously, for the sake of the masses. Wagner, too, did not change anything in this respect. Bayreuth is large-scale opera – and not even *good* opera. The theatre is a form of demolatry in matters of taste; the theatre is a revolt of the masses, a plebiscite against good taste. This is precisely proved by the case of Wagner: he won the crowd, he corrupted taste, he spoiled even our taste for opera!"[17]

In the winter semester 1972-3 in Erlangen I suddenly became popular in the theatre studies department. The Institute had organised a "Richard Wagner Music Theatre Seminar", and I had invited my lecturers and fellow students to the dress rehearsal of *Tannhäuser*. Wagner was mistakenly identified as a pioneer of socialism in 1848, analogous to the assessment of Wagner in GDR musicology, with Werner Wolf in the forefront, although he could not quite manage without the old Wagnerian Gertrud Strobel in the Bayreuth archives department. Authors such as Bloch, Gregor-Dellin, Hans Mayer and Walter Jens were quite indiscriminately numbered among left-wing Wagner interpreters in the Erlangen seminars. At my instigation, the dramaturg of the Bayreuth *Festspiele*, and at that time close adviser of my father, Dietrich Mack, was invited.

Around the same time I was almost swamped by disinterested friends. On my flying visits to Bayreuth I was careful not to say anything about my researches into the Nazi past of our family, and I also still kept secret from my father my meetings with Gertrud Strobel. Claiming that I had to prepare for a Wagner seminar at the university, I now stepped up my investigations in the Siegfried Wagner House. I can still clearly remember hearing my father complaining during one of my visits that "the situation" with Gertrud Strobel could no longer be tolerated: she persisted in passing on material that only concerned the family and that especially now, so soon before the signing of the Foundation charter, should not be made public.

Cautiously, I asked Father what material he meant: "All those private letters between Hitler and Grandmother and other things that have nothing to do with politics and the family. If the lefties from the Thyssen Foundation get hold of them there'll be hell to pay!"

I retorted calmly, albeit not very diplomatically: "Everything should come out in the open, otherwise there will never be a fresh beginning!" My unreasonable demands infuriated Father. I remained silent, afraid that he might possibly remember his films from the Nazi period which I had hidden. In fact, for fear of being discovered I occasionally checked to see whether he had taken the empty film cans out of the sidecar.

In May 1973 I took a job as assistant director with Götz Friedrich in Amsterdam and now had to combine practical theatre work and studies while ensuring that my exam deadlines were not missed. I followed everything that was happening in music theatre with the greatest attention. Hence my trip in mid April with Dietrich Mack, at the invitation of the city of Leipzig, to the premiere of *Rheingold*, directed by Joachim Herz and with set designs by Rudolf Heinrich.

The staging was based on Bernard Shaw, who had interpreted the *Ring* in connection with the early capitalism of the nineteenth century. Alberich and Wotan were swindling bourgeois businessmen locked in a deadly competitive struggle for world domination. After having seen so much noncommittal abstraction in my father's stagings, I was thrilled by such a strong narration and interpretation. Herz and Heinrich created a model staging on which many directors were later to base their own, including Patrice Chéreau in his 1976 *Ring*.

But what a contrast to this epoch-making *Rheingold* staging was Leipzig itself, Richard Wagner's birthplace! The bleakness of the grey daily routine and the omnipresence of the security police depressed me. I wanted to know more about life in the GDR, but real discussion on social or political questions never got going. Instead, people took refuge in hints or bitter jokes which I could not find funny. For example: "Honecker spoke in our theatre. Then the set fell down and killed him." Scarcely had Rudolf Heinrich's father finished the last sentence when they all burst out laughing while I waited in vain for the punch line. I was compensated a little by finds in secondhand bookshops: I discovered wonderful first editions of books from the "bad old" feudal and bourgeois days. They were dirt cheap, compared with prices at home. I didn't just buy valuable old tomes, such as the famous Gotha peerage guide of 1860, but also, just as cheaply, GDR literature on Brecht and Weill.

On the way back, Dietrich Mack and I discussed the GDR. Like many left-wingers of the time, he defended the social achievements of the system, which I on the other hand rejected as too high a price to pay for the loss of autonomy. When we reached the border my opinion was confirmed: with German thoroughness a GDR border guard searched my VW "Beetle" and, of course, he found the Gotha.

"Why did you buy this book?" he asked.

I replied: "I'm interested in German history."

"Why are you interested in German history?"

"Because I'm a German."

I almost started laughing, which annoyed the guard. In the end I got fed up and introduced myself, informed the good man of my invitation by the city of Leipzig and said I was going to be making a report of this journey as a journalist. At this, the dour man in uniform turned into a thoroughly polite human being who let us pass through the border without further ado.

Scarcely had we reached the Bavarian side when the game started all over again, this time on behalf of the West Germans. The border guard discovered the GDR literature during his inspection and found it offensive. This time I cut the procedure short and repeated what I had told his GDR colleague. Here too I experienced a wonderful transformation within seconds. The border guard begged for *Festspiele* tickets. Naturally he didn't get any. It was really quite exciting travelling from Germany to Germany as a Wagner.

After such trips I felt ill at ease with my German nationality, so I was glad when in May 1973 I was able to go to Amsterdam to work as assistant director under Götz Friedrich on a production of *Aida* at the Théâtre Carré. Friedrich narrated Giuseppe Verdi's opera as a violent political thriller, in which love comes into mortal conflict with the State. Unfortunately the compelling concept was realised on a rather *kitschig* set, so that I was only enthusiastic about the directing. I worked like a slave twelve hours a day: my feet bled from the sheer amount of rushing between stage and auditorium, which Friedrich, who tended to be a bit of a tyrant, found quite in order.

More important however was the fact that I learned much from him about my chosen profession. His keen intellect was coupled with wide-ranging imagination, his directing of the chorus and principals was of great intensity, and his theoretical passion gave me ideas for my own theatre work. But I subsequently refused further invitations to work with him, as I didn't want to become the eternal student of one master.

Two events remain particularly memorable from that hectic period. Friedrich was used to behaving in an authoritarian way, a hangover from his background in the GDR, and dealt with the chorus like a German army sergeant would deal with his troops. One day the representative of the chorus came to Friedrich and me and said: "We are familiar with this tone from the time of the German occupation and we are not prepared to put up with it." Friedrich dismissed this out of hand, and the atmosphere abruptly worsened. I urged him to give in, which he finally did.

The next day I had the first rehearsal on my own. My enviable task was to select twenty slave girls for *Aida* out of eighty auditionees – beautiful dark-skinned girls from the former Dutch colonies – and to rehearse with them the scene from Act One in Amneris' apartments. So there I stood, poor fool, surrounded by all these splendid flower girls, feeling like Parsifal in Klingsor's magic garden. I would have loved to have engaged them all. However, after I had made the choice I had to instruct the chosen beauties in their tasks in Amneris' chamber. They were only supposed to serve as decorative framework for Amneris and if need be comb her hair, adorn her, wave palm fronds or just lie seductively on cushions. I insisted on frequent rehearsals with my slave girls.

Then I had to go and fall in love with the conductor's sister! Edo de Waart had generously offered me accommodation in his spacious home, and it was here that I got to know Manja. She had a finely formed oval face and an irresistibly sunny smile. We floated hand in hand through nocturnal Amsterdam, visiting the notorious area around the railway station and all the important museums. She taught me, with a combination of charm and knowledge, everything one ought to know about Dutch history, in particular the German occupation in the last war, and about Dutch painting and music. A gifted viola player, she was by no means only interested in the world of the arts. After a visit to the Anne Frank House I felt ashamed to be German, but Manja brought me back to the present, saying in her attractive Dutch accent: "Our generation has to make it better!" She was right. It was difficult for me to say goodbye to her when the time came to return to Germany.

In summer 1973 I informed my father that, as a result of my studies in Erlangen, I intended to write my thesis on the contemporary music theatre of Kurt Weill and Bertolt Brecht. Brecht and Weill were the most notable opponents of Wagner and his Bayreuth shrine, and when Father realised that my choice was not for purely musicological reasons, his comment was cutting: "Can't you think of anything better than this honky-tonk music?" I was furious: "The pirate Jenny song is a thousand times preferable to the whole phoney bourgeois Wagnerian redemption shit!" It would probably have been better if I had kept silent, as Father had one of his fits of blind temper and left the dining room. With a certain relish I also brought the ill tidings to my grandmother. She reacted calmly and bluntly as I had expected her to: "So you're getting mixed up with the Jews, even with the left-wingers! That your father has to do it in these Jew-ridden times I can understand to a certain extent, but you? The wheel of history will turn for us again, I'm sure!" I interrupted her with: "Maybe Wieland was right after all: you still believe in the Final Victory."

The only person to encourage me in sticking with the Weill-Brecht subject matter was my friend Eberhard Wagner, editor of the *East Franconian Dictionary* at the Bavarian Academy of Sciences, a committed dialect poet, playwright and novelist, today the second chairman of the Bayreuth Studio Theatre. I had got to know him in Erlangen and he always proved one of my few genuine friends in Bayreuth. Later he was always there for me during personal crises.

The Wagner family in 1881
on the steps of Villa
Wahnfried, photographed
by Adolf von Gross

Top: Blandine von Bülow,
Heinrich von Stein,
Cosima and Richard
Wagner

Middle: Daniela von
Bülow, Paul von Joukowsky

Bottom: Isolde von Bülow,
Eva and Siegfried Wagner

Richard Wagner, photographed by Joseph
Albert, in Munich 1880

A caricature of Richard Wagner which
appeared in the magazine *Puck*, Leipzig on
3 September 1876, referring to the opening
of the Bayreuth *Festspiele* in the same year

Richard Wagner's home in Bayreuth. L-r: Cosima, Richard, Franz Liszt and Hans von Wolzogen, the editor of the racist journal, *Bayreuther Blätter*. Oil painting by W Beckmann, 1882

Cosima and Richard in Vienna, 1872. Photographed by Fritz Luckhardt

L-r: Cosima, Siegfried and Richard, in Bayreuth 1873, photographed by Adolf von Gross

1872. Richard Wagner's children.
L-r: Eva, Siegfried and Isolde Wagner,
Daniela and Blandine von Bülow

Cosima, in the 1890s

"A week in the life of Wagner" – a cartoon featured in *Der Floh* (*The Flea*) at the opening of the *Festspiele* in 1876

A design by Fantin-Latour in 1883, following Richard Wagner's death in the same year

Richard Wagner as Siegfried. "I will take away the shining treasure." Published in *Schalk,* Leipzig on 5 January 1879

A cartoon published in *Kikeriki* on 18 February 1883 (five days after Richard Wagner died). "My dear angels! The reception is rather nice, but without the timpani and trumpets, you never will have an effect"

French caricature published by *L'Eclipse*, 18 April 1869

"The Jews In Music": their opinion of *Parsifal*, Wagner's last work, was that it had been a "firm, solemn stagework". Published in *Kikeriki* on 13 August 1882

How a Leipzig Jew slowly became Richard Wagner. Published in *Der Floh*, Vienna

Richard Wagner surrounded by Jewish children, one of whom presents him with the day's movement of the Stock Exchange. *Der Floh*, Vienna

A sketch by George Grosz showing his feelings against the Wagner cult. Published in the newspaper, *Simplizisimus* in 1921

Caricature of Richard Wagner by Olaf Gulbranson entitled 'It can't go higher' to commemorate his 100th Anniversary on 22 May 1913

Left and right:
Thora Nissen-
Drexel. Gottfried's
grandmother,
born 6 March 1891
and died 22
October 1953

The Berlin Wagner monument erected on
1 October 1903 by Professor Gustav Eberlein
and presented to the public on 3 October 1903

Siegfried Wagner with his dogs in
Wahnfried Park, Bayreuth 1909

CHAPTER SIX

THE RICHARD WAGNER FOUNDATION

In May 1973 the founding charter of the Richard Wagner Foundation of Bayreuth was signed. Representing the family were my grandmother, my aunts Friedelind and Verena, my father and the children of Uncle Wieland. I was indignant at the time that I had not been informed of the content of the document before the signing and that I was not invited to be one of the signatories. Although I had insisted on learning more, I only discovered the content of the founding charter from a superficial account of it by Martin Gregor-Dellin in the *Meistersinger* programme of the 1973 *Festspiele*. It wasn't until four years later that I received the complete text of the Foundation document from the lawyer of the Wieland children. Of its fourteen paragraphs the second, sixth and eighth concern me particularly. In paragraph six the Foundation council is defined. According to this, the members' votes were distributed – before the deaths of my grandmother and Aunt Friedelind – as follows: Federal Republic of Germany, five votes; Free State of Bavaria, five votes; Wagner family, five votes; City of Bayreuth, two votes; Society Of Friends Of Bayreuth, one vote; Upper Franconia Foundation, two votes; Region of Upper Franconia, two votes; Bavarian Land Foundation, two votes.[18]

Paragraph eight entrusted to this heterogeneous Foundation council, which was only partially capable of making judgments in artistic and cultural matters, decisions on the artistic suitability of a potential successor as director of the *Festspiele*. This would appear to satisfy certain minimum democratic requirements, were it not for the second and third clauses in paragraph eight, which state: "The *Festspielhaus* shall in principle be let to a member, if applicable several members of the Wagner family or to another entrepreneur, should a member, if applicable several members of the Wagner family run the *Festspiele*. This shall not apply only if other, more suitable applicants come forward. With the majority of their votes in the Foundation council the descendants of Richard Wagner may make proposals. As soon as it is determined that the contract with a *Festspiele* entrepreneur has ended or will end, the Foundation shall indicate to the representatives of the Wagner family in the Foundation council the possibility of making a proposal...Should the Foundation council entertain doubts on whether or not a member of the Wagner family is better than, or just as qualified for the position of *Festspiele* entrepreneur as any other applicant, then the Foundation council shall seek a decision of a three-person committee of experts. This committee shall consist of the intendants of opera houses from German-speaking regions, whereby the intendants shall be consulted in the order of the hereinafter named opera houses: Deutsche Oper Berlin, Bayerische Staatsoper Munich, Staatsoper Vienna, Staatsoper Hamburg, Staatsoper Stuttgart, Städtische Oper Frankfurt/Main, Städtische Oper Cologne."[19]

This also sounded sensible, but in practice is difficult to realise. So it is not much more than a question of taste, whether or to what extent a member of the family, or another applicant, is suitable to run the *Festspiele*. Furthermore, in view of the historical development of the family, one cannot automatically assume that they will agree on one or more candidates. This should have become sufficiently clear from what I have already related. It is also a question, of how far the members of the two boards – the Foundation council and, subordinately, the committee of experts – are able and willing to judge objectively. Nevertheless, for the intendants in the committee it is at least a question possibly even of non-family applicants for the post of director of the *Festspiele*.

Yet if all this, which sounds so sensible, is examined *in toto*, it becomes clear that it leaves the door wide open to despotism.

Unwearyingly, my father has for years publicly written off every member of the family (excluding himself, of course) as unsuitable. So much for the matter of "agreement".

I consider paragraph two equally dubious. In it, in connection with the joint will and testament of Siegfried and Winifred Wagner of 8 March 1929, the following four points are named as being the purpose of the Foundation: "1. To preserve the artistic legacy of Richard Wagner in perpetuity for the public good; 2. To maintain the Bayreuth *Festspielhaus* in perpetuity for the public good and make it accessible and constantly subservient to the purposes for which its founder intended, that is, solely for the solemn performance of the works of Richard Wagner; 3. To promote Richard Wagner research; 4. To promote understanding of the works of Richard Wagner in particular among young people and the younger generation of artists."[20]

In this regard, the following comments should be made: Richard Wagner's legacy should be understood basically not only as purely artistic, but also as a politico-cultural legacy. Out of the tragic history of the Bayreuth *Festspiele* a special responsibility has arisen in dealing with this legacy. In other words the present purpose of the Foundation denies and represses the possibility of dealing in future with questions such as "Wagner–Hitler and the consequences" in a critical and unbiased way. One could counter this by saying that the Wagner research mentioned in point three would guarantee this. However, as in point one, only the "artistic legacy" is mentioned, the "generosity" of point three is eyewash. From the legal point of view there are certainly no objections to point two, but it does indicate how little the compilers of the statutes have learned from history. For the *Festspiele* as an event to focus solely on Richard Wagner precludes any end to the Wagner cult, the horrifying consequences of which have already been shown in the past. In order to counteract a monoculture focused solely on Wagner, the existing concept of the *Festspiele* should be broadened:

1. All Wagner's works, including his early operas, symphonies, chamber music and *Lieder*, should be performed in the *Festspielhaus*, as they would make the various artistic influences on Wagner clear and capable of being materially experienced.

2. The works of those artists who had a particularly long-lasting effect on Wagner, should be offered within the framework of the *Festspiele*. This would bring about a considerable broadening of the artistic horizon.

3. All his life Richard Wagner emphasised the open, provisional nature of his concept of the *Festspiele*. In this sense contemporary representatives of all forms of art – with emphasis changing from year to year – should receive a regular opportunity to present themselves to the public.

These three points would also lead to the long overdue alteration in the structure of the audiences. Or, to put it another way, the *Festspiele* would then, in the spirit of Richard Wagner, exist not only for the "upper ten thousand", but would have a broad, democratic effect in keeping with the modern world.

Such a programme is rendered impossible however by paragraph two, which makes me and my proposals, as a cosmopolitan interested in the multiplicity of human culture, sound like an unworldly Utopian. I could live with that, if the Foundation statutes did not, according to their own logic, force me into a dual role: on the one hand I belong through membership of my family to the "circle of candidates" for the succession; on the other hand I could only conform to the demands of paragraph two of the statutes if I were prepared, in everything I do, to comply with the monocultural claims of the statutes. My personal involvement in the succession discussion is fictitious, yet it has nevertheless proved a serious obstacle for the development of my careers as a director and music journalist. Apparently a Wagner should only be able to be a trustee of Richard Wagner if he keeps strictly to the Foundation statutes. The dilemma I face is that by suggesting any changes I lay myself open to charges of personal ambition – no matter how ludicrous those charges are within the context of my life.

CHAPTER SEVEN

"THE WILL TO POWER" III

In the autumn of 1973 I enrolled at the University of Vienna, where I had Professor Otmar Wessely as doctoral supervisor and Professor Gernot Gruber to oversee my dissertation. They both helped me a great deal with my doctoral thesis on Weill and Brecht and I was pleased to have escaped the intrigues of Bayreuth. The university library was rich in materials, both for my studies and for my research into the history of the Bayreuth *Festspiele* in the Nazi period. I also spent a lot of time in the music publishing house, Universal Edition, where my passionate interest in Weill and Brecht caused much head-shaking. I was addressed in Austrian fashion as "Herr Doktor Wagner", which I found amusing. If the subject of Kurl Weill came up, again and again a covert antisemitism came to light. Many Viennese claimed they had had nothing to do with the Nazis – in their eyes the Germans had annexed Austria by force. So there was nothing to come to terms with. "But Herr Doktor, why go poking around in the past, and about Weill and all that. Wagner's music is much more wonderful!" was one of the many "good" suggestions preferred.

On holiday together, in the winter of 1973, I wanted to talk to Father about paragraph eight of the Foundation statutes, which in my view acted as a muzzle. On a long walk, I explained to him my concerns: "Isn't it absurd to assume that our family would agree on a candidate from the family? And who decides on which criteria the better, more suitable candidate would meet? And what interests do the intendants from Munich, Vienna, Hamburg, Stuttgart, Frankfurt or Cologne represent? Surely first of all their own, and they would surely *a priori* be against a Wagner family in conflict! Anyone from the family who wants to get in there, must get on with everyone, including the politicians, industrialists and members of the Society Of Friends Of Bayreuth. I don't understand that."

Father replied: "If you stand the test according to the Foundation statutes, then you have a good chance of making the running."

A quarrel erupted. It was also during these Christmas holidays that an argument broke out over the inclusion of the Federal Republic and the GDR in the United Nations Organisation. I considered the universal recognition of the GDR as a sensible and logical continuation of Brandt's and Genscher's *Ostpolitik*. Father didn't: "That means the end of the unification of Germany, and not only that, it means the communists will be rewarded for the division of Germany."

Early in 1974 my father had Peter Stein and Patrice Chéreau compete against one another to direct a new production of the *Ring*, scheduled for 1976, the centenary of the Bayreuth *Festspiele*. Pierre Boulez had already agreed to be the conductor, but the negotiations with the directors made no progress. Father considered directing the *Ring* himself, although I advised him strongly against this, because it would have meant interrupting the beginnings of a trend towards modern if not avant-garde interpretations of Richard Wagner. Because of my knowledge of French I was occasionally called in to the negotiations. Whether Father dangled the tasty morsel of directing the *Ring* under Chéreau's nose, or under Stein's, depended entirely on their remarks on the opera, and whether such remarks conformed with his own, especially in relation to the so-called reception history and the subject of art and power from 1850 to 1945. Father wanted an ambiguous, apolitical interpretation. Such competition did not exactly create a good atmosphere. The process reminded me of a poker game with marked aces. Once, when I picked up Peter Stein at Nuremberg airport, he said: "Your father's constant patronage reminds me of the old times." Chéreau finally won.

At the end of the summer semester, in July 1974, I returned to Bayreuth. But in the *Festspielhaus* I only saw *Tristan* under Carlos Kleiber's fascinating musical direction. August Everding's staging pleased the old Wagnerians and the circles around my grandmother. My sister knew about Everding's growing influence in the German opera and theatre scene and waxed enthusiastic about him. I, on the other hand, talked to him about the weather; we had nothing else to say to one another. Socially he tried to please everybody and, because of his conservative attitude, he was also a welcome guest of my grandmother, who together with Eva was taking over more and more representative duties in the Siegfried Wagner House, although this did not quite fit in with the new left-wing image of my father's chorus of yes men.

On 1 August 1974 I married Beatrix Kraus, who had been my partner for a long time, and unexpectedly introduced her as my wife to my astonished family. They had cold-shouldered her for years, as she manifested a refreshing lack of respect for the Wagner cult. She was equipped with a razor-sharp wit, social confidence and was able to defend herself with aplomb in the *Festspiele* snakepit. This did not improve her popularity, especially among the women on the *Festspielhügel*. I moved with her to an apartment in the villa of the Feustel family on the outskirts of Bayreuth, surrounded by a beautiful garden. People from the *Festspielhügel* were not among our many guests, nor was Richard Wagner generally a topic of conversation.

After my marriage the next most important event in these months was Ernst Bloch's visit to our home. I collected him and his wife Karola from Tübingen. Bloch gave me some important tips for my doctoral thesis and provided me with contacts, such as, for example, with the Austrian-American actress and singer Lotte Lenya. And it was because of him I got involved in a controversy with Bayreuth's SPD mayor Hans Walter Wild. I had suggested appointing Ernst Bloch an honorary citizen of the city of Bayreuth.

Hitler had been granted honorary citizenship in 1933, and nobody objected when, in 1974, a street was still named after the Nazi admirer and Wagner worshipper Chamberlain. In a letter dated 25 April 1974, the mayor wrote how he could see no grounds for my proposal and cited the names of other honorary citizens, among them that of my grandmother.

Ernst Bloch attracted me at that time mainly because of his passionate interest in all things cultural. I found his accounts of the Weimar Republic, and his time with Otto Klemperer at the Kroll Opera in Berlin, fascinating. Most of all I liked listening to him when he talked about the devil: he created images in my mind from the Old Testament that I shall never forget. When my father and Herbert Barth, together with the Macks, invited him and Karola to the centenary production of the *Ring* in 1976, he talked about Wagner as he understood him, in other words, about the revolutionary.

Bloch made something of a *faux pas*, however, when he told my father that my doctoral thesis on Weill and Brecht was a revolutionary gesture. On the return drive to Tübingen I had to explain to Bloch that Father was not at all in favour of my work.

In that *Festspiele* summer of 1974 our guests included the set designer Roland Aeschlimann and his wife Andrea, and the literary scholar Hans Mayer who brought with him a publisher's proposal for us to write a book on the history of the Bayreuth *Festspiele* together. At the time I regarded Mayer's interpretation of Wagner stimulating and what's more, saw an opportunity of making myself financially independent of my father. So, I agreed to the proposal and set to, filling in the gaps in my material on Wagner and the *Festspielhügel*.

In autumn 1974 I moved with Beatrix to Vienna to concentrate on my doctoral thesis and continue my research for the book with Hans Mayer. I was also able to gather further experience as an assistant director when Joachim Herz and Rudolf Heinrich invited me to work with them in the State Opera on a production of Mozart's *Die Zauberflöte*. Herz, a pupil of Walter Felsenstein, taught me a lot of things, both theoretical and practical, and he made it clear to me what a great, but still underestimated influence Meyerbeer had had on Richard Wagner's musical dramaturgy.

On a day to day level, working together was often difficult: Herz was always on edge and expected me to be prepared to work day and night. I went along with it, as the results said a lot for him. Equally stimulating for me in these weeks were talks with the brilliant set and costume designer Rudolf Heinrich, who with Felsenstein had brought world recognition to the Komische Oper in Berlin, which was also known as the "Anti-Bayreuth". The assistants attached to the opera house, who were mostly close to the clique of the influential director Otto Schenk and the singer Eberhard Wächter, found it disgusting that the Saxon Herz was daring to stage Mozart's *Zauberflöte* in Vienna in such a critical way. The usual intrigues – how could it be otherwise in the Vienna State Opera – were soon reflected in the media. A devastatingly critical reception was systematically prepared. The whole thing nauseated me, and I prepared my first interview as journalist for the Vienna newspaper *Die Presse* in order, out of solidarity with Herz's exemplary staging of *Die Zauberflöte*, to create a platform for his conception. Unfortunately it didn't help much.

At the beginning of December Roland Aeschlimann, Gernot Gruber, Eberhard Wagner and I had a meeting with Father. We were supposed to discuss *Parsifal* with him on the basis of a set model by Aeschlimann and we hoped to be able to give Father some ideas for his first staging of *Parsifal*, which was planned for 1975, and had to measure up to Wieland's 1951 production. In 1974 I had got Aeschlimann into the *Festspielhaus*, where he worked as lighting technician. He had worked out a set based on the work of the avant-garde set designer Adolphe François Appia, who died in 1928, a set that Cosima Wagner had violently rejected at the time. We all supported Aeschlimann's model enthusiastically, however, although my father acted as though he were interested, and paid noncommittal compliments, it amounted to a rejection. I committed a big mistake when I tried to talk to him about Kundry and Jewry – key word "female Ahasuerus". He said gruffly: "What on earth has Kundry to do with the Jews?" Since then I have given up discussing Richard

Wagner's art with my father, given his insistence in this area on absolute obedience. The set that he finally used for *Parsifal* in 1975 reminded some critics, not without reason, of the architecture of Albert Speer, Hitler's favourite architect.

CHAPTER EIGHT

WINIFRED'S FILM

On 20 January 1975 my sister wrote to tell me that the film director Hans Jürgen Syberberg wanted my collaboration on a film about our grandmother. The idea appealed and I accepted Syberberg's invitation to Vienna, where he was presenting his film about Karl May, which I actually found rather boring. In a conversation after the premiere Syberberg informed me that Ernst Bloch, Hans Mayer and Walter Jens had also reacted positively to the idea of his new film and he registered my interest in German-Jewish history and the work of Kurt Weill with obvious attention and seemed enthusiastic at my courage in tackling taboo subjects, such as the involvement of my own family in National Socialism. At this first meeting I noticed that he didn't know much about this area, or about the role of my grandmother in this period. I was not only to procure him an *entrée* to my grandmother and my father, but also to place my knowledge at his disposal. A prerequisite to my participating in the preparation, shooting and editing of the film was my passionate interest in disclosing the darkest epoch in the family history.

Having informed Syberberg that I was also working on a TV documentary on the subject – *The Festspiele Centenary* – for the BBC with Brian Large, Syberberg drew up a contract which took this other project into account and cleared important rights for me. I showed the contract to Father and he agreed to our beginning filming in April 1975. Beatrix and I used the time until then for further research which was later to come in useful for the book with Hans Mayer.

However it turned out to be the start of an obstacle race, as my father had no intention of handing over all the documents on "The Wagner family and National Socialism", that I found listed in the archive catalogue or that my grandmother had told me about. For example, there was the correspondence between Adolf Hitler and Winifred, Wieland and Wolfgang Wagner from 1923 to 1944, which my grandmother had secretly removed from a special steel-lined cupboard and handed over to me for a short time to look into. The letters were evidence of the great familiarity between my grandmother, my uncle, my father and Hitler and were full of declarations of belief in the Final Victory of the Third Reich. My father ignored inquiries about the letters between Hitler, himself and Wieland.

He was also irritated when I broached the subject of the presents from Hitler to my grandmother and the family, such as the gilt-edged copy of *Mein Kampf* with the dedication "From Wolf for Winnie" of 1925, and categorically refused to make such intimate family documents available for the Syberberg film. He watched over the preparations and the subsequent filming too with suspicion, not least in an attempt to prevent any of my grandmother's statements damaging the liberal-left image of the *Festspiele* at that time. I, on the other hand, wanted everything to come out into the open: it was only by exposing fully my family's involvement in National Socialism that it would be made to work through its guilt.

I showed Syberberg the films from the Nazi period that I had found in the BMW sidecar and I stupidly gave him some to take back to Munich. He ensured that he would look after them and would not use them without my permission. That Syberberg, as he claimed, had already devised an artistic direction and concept for the film when he was in Bayreuth was difficult to believe. Two basic factors were missing: knowledge of the material and any understanding of my grandmother's character.

She took over right from the beginning. What emerged from the Siegfried Wagner House was a film by Winifred Wagner, featuring Winifred Wagner, with assistance from Syberberg. The moment shooting began, he fell under my grandmother's control. She saw her moment of truth and seized the opportunity ruthlessly. Syberberg acted like a flirtatious six-former bowled over by the older woman. In so doing he was being absolutely true to his real intentions, which I was only later to learn. When he reported on the filming, he avoided the whole truth. For example, he kept silent on the fact that during filming my grandmother turned to me when she was singing the praises of her "Wolf". I did not agree at all with her statements on Hitler and it was difficult for me to suppress my anger while the cameras were rolling, especially as Syberberg requested that I should not make any comment. So during breaks in filming I discussed Grandmother's crazed statements about the Führer with her. Syberberg wanted to just let Winifred talk, so he didn't get involved and was evidently relying on her giving herself away. Woe betide me when I lost my temper through frustration with Grandmother's version of events! Each time Syberberg claimed he was being hindered in his art, and so Grandmother went down on record saying such things as, in connection with the "Jewish question": "We [Hitler and Winifred Wagner] never talked about these things...to be frank I didn't feel competent enough, I'm a totally nonpolitical person and I was extremely astonished that in the trial court [during denazification in 1947] I kept being accused of politics. I said politics didn't enter into it. Then they all laughed. They said of course you dealt in politics. I didn't deal in politics."[21]

The members of the trial court were right of course to laugh: Grandmother was in reality a very politically active woman. That also applies for allegedly private episodes:

"At Christmas in 1923 I made a collection among the National Socialists here, they all brought their Christmas presents here and I packed them all in boxes and sent them to the director of Landsberg [Fort Landsberg, where Hitler was imprisoned]...with the request to distribute them and so on. That was done. Well, and I had asked what he wanted and he said, well, writing paper was something he urgently needed and so I sent him masses of writing paper. Good God, now people are accusing me of having supplied the paper for *Mein Kampf*, aren't they? Sort of almost as though indirectly it's my fault *Mein Kampf* was written. Whatever you did you were constantly attacked for it."[22]

My relationship with Syberberg became increasingly strained. At first I had seen the potential in his film of publicly clearing up the family past. But during filming I began to mistrust Syberberg because of his undistanced and uncritical way of putting questions and his slavish attitude to my grandmother. He noticed my creeping mistrust and tried with my sister's help to keep me happy. I stayed in Bayreuth until the end of filming.

In the summer semester of 1975 I met my cousin Nike Wagner again in Vienna, the second daughter of Uncle Wieland. After this we met regularly in Vienna and an intensive dialogue developed between us, far from Bayreuth and family intrigues. Syberberg's film about our grandmother was a key talking point and through that we came to the role of our fathers in the Nazi period. The subject proved ticklish as, at that time, Nike didn't want to talk about her father's privileged role in the Nazi period, whereas I saw my father and Wieland in such a light and spoke openly about it. Only at the beginning of the nineties was she to talk about the subject of Wagner, Hitler, antisemitism and the Wagner family in Bayreuth from her point of view. We were agreed, though, that it was necessary to deal with Jewish artists as we did in our theses – she with Karl Kraus, I with Kurt Weill. Wummi probably felt something similar; it was no accident that he was living with the daughter of one of the people who had tried to assassinate Hitler, Nona von Haeften.

When I informed my father and Eva of my warm friendship with Nike this immediately caused consternation in Bayreuth. In father's and Eva's eyes we were unworldly crackpots, out of touch with reality.

I also told Nike about my mistrust of Syberberg, which continued to grow, as Syberberg kept me only vaguely informed about the progress of the film, and then over the phone. At the beginning of June Father, Syberberg and myself met up in Munich. Prior to this my father had had Winifred make out a power of attorney, according to which he could decide whether he accepted or rejected the film and how the material could be made further use of, for example in books.

At the meeting Syberberg showed us a version of the beginning of the film, which my father passed. Immediately afterwards, in an interview on 9 June, Syberberg summarised our meeting from his point of view. On the same day, my father issued a statement in response to Syberberg's account. As he was gradually recognising his own contradictory role, he had suggested "other solutions" for the legal position of the film, which his legal advisers had worked out for him, unbeknown to me. On 10 June Syberberg produced a five-page protocol which seemed to sum up everything that had been agreed between him, my father and his lawyers. For my part, I completely lost track of the legal situation. At the time I had no idea that the version Syberberg had shown father and me bore little resemblance to the finished thing and when I phoned him, he told me that Hans Mayer had seen excerpts from the film and was enthusiastic.

Then problems arose over my BBC project. Syberberg wanted to market my grandmother exclusively, which pleased the British TV team as little as it did me. I asked my father's lawyer to look over my contracts with Syberberg and with the BBC. Despite countless reminders, I never saw the contracts again. The following was decided on: the British were allowed to film Grandmother driving through Bayreuth to the *Festspielhügel* in her old Volkswagen and posing silently in front of the *Festspielhaus*. Brian Large got film records of the productions of *Meistersinger* of 1975, of *Parsifal* and of the centenary *Ring* of Chéreau and Boulez. My situation did not look very favourable: I was ousted from the BBC project. Large now had his own Bayreuth connections.

At the end of June 1975 I visited Syberberg in Munich, accompanied by Nike and Beatrix, and was shown some insignificant excerpts. When I asked him to show us certain scenes with Hitler and he explained that this was impossible, as those scenes were being edited, my suspicions grew. By chance I noticed in another room that he was projecting my father's films – the ones that I had found in the BMW sidecar – onto a screen that had a stills camera standing in front of it. It transpired that Syberberg was not only taking stills from these films, but had already had complete copies made. Furious, I demanded that he hand over originals and copies. These weren't returned until the autumn and I decided to store them with Beatrix's parents, where they remained until my father's lawyer demanded them back. Later they were moved to my sister

Eva's house, subsequently to mysteriously "vanish", which caused irreparable damage to our relationship. But I am jumping ahead.

When I demanded an explanation from Syberberg during our visit to Munich he promised not to make improper use of the material. In April 1976 I discovered in *Die Zeit* a series of articles on my grandmother, and the next year Syberberg published a book on his film. In both cases he had used pictures from my father's films under his own copyright. So much for his promise.

The situation had already become confrontational. In July 1975 the world premiere was due to take place in the Cinémathèque Française in Paris. Syberberg had neither informed me about it, nor invited me. Quite rightly he feared a row if I discovered how he had assembled his film. It was my French cousins who told me and Nike, Beatrix and I rushed to Paris. The premiere was a nightmare: I found myself in the large auditorium in the middle of a swarm of sensation-hungry onlookers and journalists all keen finally to learn everything about Winifred's "affair" with "Wolf".

While the film was running I realised with horror that it didn't have much to do at all with the version Syberberg had shown me in Munich. It was in fact a different film with new captions and cuts that through an altered sequence, conveyed quite a different content. My French relations understood at once what had happened. They remained the only ones in the family who did not attack me. I sat in agony in the Capitol restaurant after the premiere with Syberberg, Nike, Nikolaus Sombart and Wolf Donner from *Die Zeit*.

There Syberberg and I had our first serious dispute. I preferred talking to him alone, to avoid a public scandal. My anger was not because he had revealed my grandmother's Nazi mentality, but rather because he had broken our agreement and had not only disregarded my right of veto on the use of the films, but had also reneged on other agreements. Before a public showing of the film there should have been a private viewing, in front of experts like Hans Mayer. I particularly resented the fact that Syberberg had overlaid stills in the film – partly taken from Father's films – which included cynical remarks made by my grandmother which he had recorded during breaks in the filming without her knowledge. The director reacted with threats.

By his lack of objective filming, Syberberg had contributed to the monumental myth about the role of my grandmother during the Nazi period. His cuts and commentaries altered basically nothing in this, as they were governed by the visual presence of my grandmother in the film. As an "actress" she was both convincing and demagogic, as proven by the reaction of the audience. Instead of toning this down by artistic means, Syberberg reinforced the effect through his directing. And so the film was construed, by those who did not want to repress the Third Reich, as a piece of Nazi propaganda.

Today I admit that, at the time, the project was beyond me in every way. I realised too late that I had been walked all over both by my grandmother and by Syberberg. I should have known from the style of other Syberberg films that this project would ultimately be a mythologising of my grandmother as time's witness. When I got back to Bayreuth I was deluged with criticism from all sides, as people identified me with the film. I was sharply attacked by the psychoanalyst Eberhard Pöhner, whose father Konrad had played a considerable part in the reconstruction of the Bayreuth *Festspiele* after the war and whose Jewish wife had been persecuted by the Nazis. Unfortunately he did not give me a chance to defend myself and so an important friendship was destroyed. Jewish Wagnerians suspected me of being a Nazi sympathiser. Right-wing Wagnerians dubbed me a nest-fouler. And the liberal-left publicly disowned me, on the grounds that I had allegedly crossed over from Syberberg to Winifred. The Society Of Friends Of Bayreuth and the representatives of Bayreuth decided to distance themselves, as the film had allegedly damaged the image of the city. Doubts were even cast on the honesty of my intentions in writing my doctoral thesis on Weill.

Amidst all of this confusion I was particularly annoyed by the opportunism of the Bayreuth newspaper, the *Nordbayerischer Kurier* and its editor-in-chief, Erich Rappl. Rappl regularly gave the introductory talks for the *Festspiele* and at the same time worked as their critic – even as a teenager I had nicknamed this paper the *Festspielhügel Express*. The *Nordbayerischer Kurier* now carried as reaction to Syberberg's film a headline on my grandmother:

"Monument to personal courage." There was no better way to render innocuous the fascist past of Hitler's friend Winifred Wagner. Rappl's article was sublimely non-committal. His *Festspiele* introductory talks were not in danger.

In July 1975 an international press conference was held in the *Festspielhaus* restaurant. There could only be one subject: Winifred and Wolf, so my father asked me to stay away. He announced to the media that my grandmother had acknowledged that her remarks were made "without due consideration" and had consequently withdrawn them. He also said that he had for the time being, forbidden her to enter the *Festspielhaus*. Regarding his own role in the Syberberg affair, he remained silent and although he had been well aware of the conditions I had laid down prior to collaborating with Syberberg, and had initially approved them, he remarked that I had "collaborated in the film with youthful impetuosity" and was "horrified by the result". I later protested over such a public declaration of incompetence, but it did nothing to help my cause.

Afterwards, I went purposefully to my grandmother. Opening the door I saw with horror that on her desk, next to the picture of my father, was Hitler's photo with the dedication "From Wolf to his Winnie". When I asked her why she had put the photo out she retorted furiously: "Wolf[gang] is treating me the same way Wieland did with all his talk about me still believing in the Final Victory. He was there at all the negotiations with Syberberg after all. Now he's being celebrated as a left-wing resistance fighter." Of Hitler, Wieland and my father she said bitterly: "They understood one another perfectly, even though he is now pretending they never had anything to do with him. In 1945 I sacrificed myself for the two of them."

At the end of the 1975 *Festspiele* season I sent Hans Mayer, with whom I had been working for some time on the book *Richard Wagner In Bayreuth*, everything that I had collected on this subject in the last few years. It was a mountain of documents and pictures. Mayer had already been grappling with Wagner and the Bayreuth *Festspiele* for a long time and he knew what it was all about. For that reason there was no dissent in the compilation of the documents and photos. He also worked-in some text excerpts from the

Syberberg film. It hardly needs saying that Syberberg was foaming at the mouth when he got word of this, as he had wanted to market my grandmother exclusively, in book as well as other forms. In a telephone call to my father's lawyer, Syberberg announced that he no longer considered himself bound by agreements he had made in June and requested that I did not make it known that I had withdrawn from the film. Should I do so, he threatened to issue statements which would damage me.

The German premiere of the Syberberg film took place in November, 1975. My father asked Ewald Hilger, the chairman of the Society Of Friends Of Bayreuth, to be present and it was Hilger who later informed me in writing what happened. On 25 November he wrote among other things that he had no objections to Frau Winifred's remarks. The film was an honest and fascinating account of a life, and was also understood in this way by the public. If people hadn't wanted to hear about it, then they needn't have asked Frau Winifred about it. The excitement about the film he, Hilger, considered unfounded, yet he had reservations on the publication of the interview in book form, because this would create a completely different impression. There was a difference, between hearing Frau Winifred's "explosive statements" being spoken and reading them in printed form.

It was farcical. Hilger assumed an almost prototypical position for people of his turn of mind. He accepted without question that Grandmother was continuing to consider Hitler as a private individual, as though Auschwitz had never been, nor *Mein Kampf*, in which Hitler had already described his annihilation plans, long before he put them into effect. What could be honourable about Winifred Wagner, even thirty years after the war, doggedly refusing to see the mass murderer in her "Wolf"?

This by no means concluded the Syberberg affair, however. During our last Christmas holidays together in Arosa in 1975 my father read me a reply from Ernst Bloch, in which the Tübingen philosopher refused my father's request for a contribution to the "Jubilee" volume for the centenary celebrations of the *Festspiele*. Bloch wrote that as a Jew and antifascist he was incapable of doing this: through Syberberg and Winifred Wagner, the old association between Wagner's music and the Nazis had reemerged and any denazification by Wieland and Wolfgang Wagner had been disavowed.

I regretted Bloch's refusal. I was and still am of quite a different opinion with regard to the role of my father and Wieland. There can be no question that Bayreuth has been consistently denazified. Father tried to change Bloch's mind, visiting him secretly, as my mother informed me, but he did not succeed.

Incidentally, Syberberg later showed his true political colours and became a right-wing chauvinist, believing in the new great Germany after 1990, something I felt was always behind his left-wing pose in the 1970s.

CHAPTER NINE

THE FESTSPIELE CENTENARY

I worked only one stint as assistant director in Bayreuth while my father was intendant. It was during the centenary *Ring* in 1976, directed by Patrice Chéreau, with François Regnault as dramaturg. I ought to have been happy when I was told at the beginning of 1976 that I was to be part of the *Ring* team, since it had been one of my childhood dreams to work on the *Festspielhügel*, after gaining my professional spurs outside Bayreuth. But my parents' imminent divorce was weighing on my mind, especially the circumstances. I was soon to learn that Dietrich Mack's wife was the co-respondent, which solved the riddle of Dietrich's sudden departure from the *Festspielhügel* in 1974.

My relationship with my father reached a new low, especially as he, in view of the change in his private life, no longer wanted me in the *Ring* team – in other words, he wanted me out of the way. But I was not prepared to give up working with Chéreau and Boulez, quite apart from the fact that I didn't want to leave my mother in the lurch in this situation. Also, the book project with Hans Mayer could not go ahead without Father's support and consent, as he was the source of some additional material I wanted to provide for Mayer.

The meeting with the new *Ring* team on 21 February 1976 in the *Festspielhaus* left a great impression on me. Despite all the subsequent marketing statements issued to the contrary after the production had been judged a success by the media, my father had at the time by no means agreed with Chéreau and Regnault's concept of the *Ring*. The atmosphere at that meeting was extremely tense, and thanks to my father's patriarchal German attitude the project nearly came to grief. The tussles between Father and Regnault continued until June 1976. In a letter to Regnault of 11 June that year, Father wrote, among other things, of Regnault's major written concept of the 1976 *Ring*, entitled "Richard Wagner's theatrical mission", that the theses presented by the writer were so misleading, half-baked and false, that in the final analysis it was obvious he hadn't the faintest idea what the *Ring* was about.

I knew of this disparaging text, of course: François, very upset, had given it to me to read and asked for my opinion. The brilliant analysis of key scenes, for example the *Rheingold* prelude, and of the characters of the leading figures, especially Wotan, fascinated me, as did his profound knowledge of different cultures and mythologies. I also found his interpretation of German theatre traditions from the classical and Romantic periods convincing. In a letter dated 20 June 1976, François ended his reply to Father's destructive judgment with the remark that in Bayreuth it seemed one had to capitulate before the power of the "all-knowing genius".

This meant that the hour had come for a new house dramaturg, later head of press and close adviser to my father until 1986, Oswald Bauer. Bauer shared Father's opinion on Regnault's contribution in every detail. Where I was concerned, he watched my every step in the *Festspielhaus* and faithfully reported everything back to his esteemed boss. No detail was omitted, however ludicrous. For example, he reported "upstairs" that I had made some photocopies in preparation for an interview with the *Nürnberger Nachrichten*. From then on, Father forbade me to use the copying machine in the *Festspielhaus*, as he suspected evil intentions behind my interview. But another affair hit me much harder. I had collected material on the subject of "Richard Wagner in Bayreuth" to give Hans Mayer for inclusion in the book. At roughly the same time the music historian Michael Karbaum had been collecting similar documents on the same subject as part of his work under the aegis of the Thyssen Foundation. As my father, on the basis of family membership and his position as director of the *Festspiele*, already had copyright privileges, Karbaum had to submit his material to him before using it. However, my father passed on this material to me – to supplement the material I had collected myself –

with the remark that this was material he had made available to Karbaum from family documents, and assumed that I would pass it on to Mayer.

This led to Karbaum filing proceedings against Belser Verlag, who were planning to publish the Mayer book and in fact did publish it, because – and this was the charge – "his" material had formed part of the Mayer book. Karbaum lost the case, however, as traces of his material were only proved in five per cent of the quotations at issue: by and large, Karbaum's material contained little that I had not already collected myself.

What inspired my father's action was the fact that the academics working within the framework of the Thyssen research project were thought to be too left-wing, and in particular he considered Karbaum's manuscript to be "scientifically dubious". Hence Father preferred a treatment by Hans Mayer, considered at that time as mildly left-wing, but with an established name in Wagner literature.

Looking back on it today, I would like to believe that Father wanted to help me at that time. Nevertheless it would have been better if he had told me the whole truth on handing over the Karbaum material. The incident subsequently earned me a reputation of being untrustworthy among German academic circles: even as an "intellectual property thief". It even caused problems for me when I applied for a research grant for my Weill/Brecht studies from the DFG [German Society For The Advancement Of Scientific Research] in 1977, as my application was finally rejected after more than a year. I further experienced how opinion had been whipped up against me in February 1976, when Dietrich Mack stopped in the foyer of the Stuttgart Opera House to ask, cynically, whether the Karbaum affair wouldn't soon be blowing up in my face.

It was only now that I learned that his wife, Gudrun, was the reason for my parents' imminent divorce. The news had greatly affected me and I reacted against the allusion to the "Karbaum affair" in a letter to Dietrich at the end of March 1976, protesting against such an attack on my reputation. In June Mack wrote me a fawning letter in which he tried to make amends. I rebuffed it, in writing.

Later it emerged that Karbaum's historical interpretation differed considerably from Hans Mayer's, as he (Karbaum) emphasised the significance of National Socialism in the history of the Bayreuth *Festspiele*.

Of course, today I know that my father's misleading statements were intended to foil discussion on the subject of "Bayreuth, Hitler and the Wagner family", which Karbaum was so thoroughly investigating.

Back to April 1976 and Beatrix and I had moved to Martinsreuth near Bayreuth, in order to distance ourselves more from my father and the Siegfried Wagner House. The following month I started work as assistant director with Chéreau. I tried to support him wherever possible, as he faced a lot of resistance in the *Festspielhaus*. My father urged me frequently, in view of the tense family situation, to give up the assistant directorship. From that time on, he wanted as little as possible to do with his first wife and their children. He even locked my sister out of the office, which was tantamount to giving her notice after nine years of collaboration. As I had no intention of leaving the team, he started harassing me. In a whole series of unpleasant letters he made threats and even gave notice of legal proceedings against me, when I tried to help my mother in everyday matters. Consequently my time on the *Festspielhügel* turned into a nightmare. For instance, even when the official group photo of the *Ring* team was taken in front of the *Königsbau* of the *Festspielhaus*, my father insisted I leave, on the grounds that I did not belong to the team: the rest of the group maintained an embarrassed silence. The photographer, Siegfried Lauterwasser, a friend of my father's since youth, who had been very attached to me for decades, was horrified and pointedly photographed me separately with my musical mentor Maximilian Kojetinsky. In spite of all the strain, I carried on rehearsing the alternative cast for the Chéreau *Ring*. Like Boulez, Chéreau understood my situation and neither one intended to suddenly ignore me the way the majority did in the *Festspielhaus*.

Even today I look back with horror on the centenary celebrations which took place on 23 July 1976. "Richard Wagner and the Germans": so many lies about the composer and his heirs! The high point was a "people's party", after the third act of *Meistersinger* (Festival Meadow) had been performed in my father's staging and under the baton of Karl Böhm. These two events meant that the celebrations were suffocated by Upper Franconian provincialism. Oswald Bauer was the organiser of this sorry spectacle.

Arriving at my father's reception in the *Festspielhaus* after the ceremony, without an admission ticket and, like my colleagues, in casual dress, I suddenly found myself in the hands of the police again.

I shouted at the plain clothes officer: "I demand to speak to my lawyer. These are police state methods." One of the onlookers explained to the policeman that I was "the son of the boss of the *Festspiele*" and at the word "boss" a bell rang in his brain, and he let me go. Deferentially he said: "But why didn't you say who you were. Please go and get your invitation." As I hadn't received one, I couldn't very well do that and knowing every nook and cranny of the *Festspielhügel* since my childhood, I decided to try to get into the hall by one of my secret routes. I had almost reached my goal when I was caught by two security officers who started to lead me off. This scene was noticed by the publisher Klaus Piper, who was sitting at Martin Gregor-Dellin's table. He hurried to help me, took the policemen to task and invited me to his table. I looked around at the piqued faces of the guests from the cream of West German affluent society, especially those of the Friends Of Bayreuth, and discovered my father surrounded by his chorus of yes men. No, I could not stay here. I left the room as quickly as I could. I could easily have left Bayreuth altogether right then, but I had promised Chéreau and Boulez that I would continue rehearsing with the second *Ring* cast.

At the end of July I learned from the *Bild* newspaper that my father had married the former Frau Mack. Although I had had nothing to do with the matter, the tabloid press now descended on me too. My parents' divorce during the 1976 centenary celebrations, after thirty-three years of marriage, came as such a shock to my mother that she never fully recovered. In an attempt to find a new identity, she absorbed herself in writing an autobiography and worked through the copious entries in her diaries and her correspondence with my father since their engagement in 1942, complementing them with countless revealing comments which often placed the official Bayreuth historiography in question. The conflict with National Socialism and the role of the Wagner family in it became one of her central themes, one which she addressed with great intensity, occasionally overtaxing herself.

It wasn't until 1978, after she had moved from Bayreuth to her native city of Wiesbaden, that my mother actually began constructing a life for herself according to her own ideas and needs. This painful process made me not only look more closely at the consequences of the Wagners' Nazi past, but also at my relationship with her. Through her total identification with the Bayreuth *Festspiele* and Father, as had been expected of her, she had scarcely had the opportunity to do justice to her role as mother as well, which she often regretted. But since my father's first *Ring* production in Bayreuth in 1960 she had looked more and more to me for advice and comfort, as Father was totally bound up in his role as director in competition with his successful brother, Wieland. The consequent discord in the two families worsened the situation even more. After Wieland's death in 1966 and subsequent social duties which went with her position as wife of the sole head of the *Festspiele*, she increasingly found life on the *Festspielhügel* difficult, as Father, Grandmother and my sister Eva, being representatives of the new era, offered her no support.

Pursuit of the will to power in the years from 1966 to 1975 isolated my mother more and more from the outside world. Naturally she was aware of this and tried to do something about it, but unfortunately she was unsuccessful – she was no match for the other family members. Not surprisingly, it was during these years my mother began to wonder what would have happened if she had not given up her successful career as a ballerina at the Oper Unter Den Linden in Berlin in 1942. She even started questioning her career in the theatre and regretting that she had not become a nurse. After her divorce at the age of fifty-seven, however, she was forced to realise that it was now too late to embark on a new career and so she concentrated – almost by way of compensation – on looking into National Socialism and Jewish history.

Several sensation-hungry journalists, especially those from *Bild* abused Mother's lack of experience to concoct one of the usual Wagner scandal stories. In fact, they distorted her statements so outrageously, that I had to take legal action. With her gradual liberation from the Bayreuth past, helped by her brother and his family, Mother's interest grew in my Italian family, especially in her grandson Eugenio. I was happy about this: it corresponds with our belief in harmony and peace, and the search for a meaning to life. A picture of her as four-year-old, playing the part of the child "Sorrow" in Giacomo Puccini's *Madama Butterfly* in 1923 in a Wiesbaden performance, is on my desk. Her beautiful, delicate childlike smile still shines through her features today and reveals what was always the real aim of her life: the theatre and its world.

CHAPTER TEN

IN SEARCH OF MYSELF

At the end of July 1976, at an international press conference, my father presented the newly published Cosima Wagner diaries, edited by Martin Gregor-Dellin and Dietrich Mack. Shortly afterwards I packed my bags. The only thing that made my departure difficult was leaving Gunda, my foster aunt since my childhood. She broke down in tears.

First Beatrix and I went to the Chiemsee to her parents. There we decided to continue on to Ireland to recover from the Bayreuth lunacy. During a stopover we visited Charles and Germaine Spencer in London. They received us warmly and Charles encouraged me to lead a life free of Bayreuth. In Ireland we were overwhelmed by the beauty of the countryside, although I could not really enjoy it: I was still too deeply distressed by my experiences.

Fortunately there were at least some glimmers of hope, professionally. I was negotiating with the theatre in Bonn for a production of *Fidelio* in the spring of 1977. There was also a generous offer from Lys Symonette in New York to work in the Kurt Weill archives on the publication of Weill's written works.

Dieter Rexroth, head of the Hindemith Institute in Frankfurt am Main and notable for his brilliant conceptual ideas on Beethoven, had made discreet contact with the Bonn Theatre in 1975. I also requested that Roland Aeschlimann be involved in the production. Dieter Rexroth and I kept our negotiations secret as I feared that my father and his circle would obstruct any engagements for me. The influence of Bayreuth in the opera world should not be underestimated: the then intendant of the Bonn Opera House, Joachim Heyse, informed me of Bayreuth's attempts to manipulate opinion. On hearing that the contract had been signed, my father said to Heyse during a meeting of intendants: "You've landed yourself in a real mess there. *Fidelio* in Bonn in the Beethoven centenary year as his first production. Can he really pull that off?" Doubt about my ability, expressed by my own father, spread like wildfire among agents, theatre administrations and the media, many of whom were already closely connected with Bayreuth. For agents and intendants it was more important to keep in with the *Festspielhügel* than to find engagements for me. It was now known in opera circles that my father looked unfavourably on those who gave me work.

Since the autumn of 1976 I had been living in the same apartment on the Wartburgplatz in Munich that I had lived in before. For me there were primarily two concerns: firstly, securing my mother's livelihood; and secondly, preparing myself for the "Rigorosum", the final oral examination, in Vienna, after my doctoral thesis had been accepted in May 1976.

My father meanwhile had stopped my monthly payments. One of my guardian angels at the time, the hotel owner Peter Kremslehner, knew of my precarious situation and generously took me in as a guest in his Regina Hotel in Vienna.

In December 1976 I passed my oral examinations in musicology, German literature and philosophy. Only my mother, Beatrix and a few Viennese friends came to the graduation party. Wummi called up and told me that he had informed Father of my success. The latter's sole comment was: "He copied it all anyway!"

In April 1977 I started my work in Bonn. Dieter Rexroth had merged the first and third versions of *Fidelio* to form a revolutionary interpretation. Now his concept had to be translated onto the stage. This theoretical exercise was explained too in an extensive, provocative programme including texts by Ursula Krechel, August Stramm, Ernst Toller, Kurt Schwitters,

Peter-Paul Zahl, Rainer Kunze, Paul Celan, Marie Luise Kaschnitz and Norbert Friedrich. To coincide with the premiere in May, Amnesty International had organised demonstrations for the release of political prisoners in Iran, Chile and the USSR.

At the curtain call I experienced my first clash with a predominantly conservative public, although the young members of the audience applauded my updated production.

The press reaction was varied. The tone for the German media was set by Josef Herbort in *Die Zeit* on 3 June 1977 under the headline: "No competition from junior. Wagner great-grandson Gottfried makes his debut as director with *Fidelio*." His pertinent negative criticism was only mildly irritating, but I deeply resented his further assertions: "When Wolfgang Wagner was asked a year ago about whether he would soon hand over a *Festspiele* production or even the running of the Bayreuth *Festspiele* to a younger member of the family, the shrewd Franconian answered diplomatically that he still did not yet see a suitable contender among the next generation. Now that Wieland's son Wolf-Siegfried has dabbled with *Tristan* and the *Meistersinger* reducing Wagner to the one-dimensional, and Wolfgang's son Gottfried has staged his vision of Beethoven's opera as non-dramatic, the Bayreuth *Festspiele* boss can sleep peacefully again. In fact, he faces no competition from either of the Master's great-grandsons. And if the rumour going round the *Fidelio* premiere in Bonn is true, that Wolfgang Wagner warned his fellow intendants against his son, one may make of the family quarrel between the guardians of the Nibelung gold, what one will. Fundamentally though, the father is right."[23]

Herbort's piece had the desired effect: it was a long time before I found further employment in a German opera house, and even today reviews of my productions still contain Herbort's prejudice and insinuation.

The Bonn critic Hans G Schürmann was the only one who did not share the opinion of his German colleagues. The further away from Bayreuth, the fairer opinions became. For example the respected critic Roy Koch wrote in the *New York Times* at the end of May: "Bonn...here, in Beethoven's birthplace, where every note of the Master's scores is regarded as sacred, a starkly contemporary production of his only opera, *Fidelio*, is bound to raise controversy – all the more so when the producer is making his professional debut, and specially when that producer is the great-grandson of Richard Wagner.

"Though visibly shaken by the few loud boos mixed with the enthusiastic applause at the end of the premiere Thursday night, thirty-year-old Gottfried Wagner stuck out the unmistakable Wagner chin, and his blue eyes flashed defiance at his detractors as he left the stage after several curtain calls.

"'I hadn't realised I would be so affected by the violent reaction,' he said after the performance, 'but the booing as well as the applause convinced me that we have achieved a genuine dialogue with our audience – and that's what we set out to do.'

...Gottfried Wagner is regarded by many observers here as a force among the new generation of opera producer."[24]

Even then I could see that I would be better able to develop professionally outside Germany.

Meeting Bettina Fehr again in Bonn was comforting too, having been introduced to her for the first time only the year before in Bayreuth. She helped me through this and subsequent crises and soon became my second mother. Since then she has taken an interest in all the essential professional and private events in my life. Her selfless involvement in matters of public concern has been an example to me for decades. For example, for a long time she worked as honorary manager of the Bonn Society For Christian-Jewish Cooperation, of which she has been a member since 1954. This involvement also has a lot to do with our common interest in German-Jewish dialogue, which she supports for reasons of family solidarity with her Jewish maternal grandfather. Through him she is a distant relation of Heinrich Heine. Classified in the insane system of the Nuremberg race laws of 1935 as "half-caste, second grade" she, as daughter of the respectable middle-class Christian doctor Arthur Lankes, was not allowed to study and became a bookseller, a profession allowed to her by the Nazis. Through her marriage to Götz Fehr, the long-time director of Inter Nationes, she was able, after the war, to ally people all over the world to her cause. One of our topics of conversation, apart from the German-Jewish one, is "Bayreuth" and my relationship with my father, whom she knows. It should come as no surprise that Bettina, despite her daily exertions for people in need and her large family, has also been active since 1992 in the Olga Havel Foundation For The Handicapped. Advising her to take it easy is a waste of breath.

Fortunately in this difficult time Lotte Lenya and Lys Symonette renewed the offer of joining the Kurt Weill Foundation Of Music. But before I travelled to New York in the autumn I had a difficult errand to Bayreuth. My mother was determined to stay there and had moved in with my grandmother, of all people. Beatrix and I turned up at Grandmother's eightieth birthday, where we, and Mother, were shunned by the high society guests. I had never heard so many feigned compliments paid to my grandmother. The Syberberg film had, if anything, strengthened her position with her right-wing admirers. The old-guard members of the Wagner Societies and of the Society Of Friends Of Bayreuth toasted Hitler's "Winnie" while my grandmother gushed about the Führer's favourite sculptor, Arno Breker who had just finished a bust of her. While she and her cronies wallowed in the good old times, my efforts to liberate my mother from this Nazi nest came to nothing. In fact, the attempt was to have unpleasant consequences.

Before my journey to New York there was an episode as short as it was curious. In August Wummi, Nike and I were interviewed by Klaus Figge for a programme on the German television channel ZDF, called *Aspekte*. The media immediately reported that the fourth generation of Wagners was standing at Bayreuth's gates ready to seize power. This was in spite of the fact that I had clearly described how I wanted to make my way outside Bayreuth. My father wasn't at all happy with this. The interviewer had realised that my father had written off the whole of this fourth generation as incompetent, without being able to give any specific reasons. In order to give weight to his opinion, at the end of August 1977, in a letter to the then head of programming and now intendant of ZDF, Dieter Stolte, Father described the interviewer's research as inaccurate and warned against any repetition of such procedures, as this would ultimately also affect the interests of the ZDF. It did indeed have an effect on the interests of the ZDF: the channel was later frequently allowed to televise Bayreuth productions.

In September I returned to Bonn, to oversee rehearsals for further performances of my *Fidelio* production. The damning judgment of the German press had had a negative effect on the atmosphere in the team and in the theatre. But despite all the forebodings the revival was a success with that section of the public that I wanted to reach at that time: young people, who normally never went to the opera.

I frequently met the neurologist and psychiatrist Johannes Meyer-Lindenberg, who lived in Bonn and whom I had met through Bettina Fehr at the premiere party for *Fidelio*. She told him about my difficult family situation and he offered to stand by my mother, who was in a particularly bad state at the time. Eva and I gratefully accepted this. One of our central topics of conversation, however, was the conflict with Father. Johannes had, through his own experience, a great sensitivity for difficult family situations. His father came from a Jewish family and his aristocratic mother from a Christian background. Hence his parents were forced to flee the Nazis and go to Colombia, where Johannes was born in 1938. After the Second World War his father was West German ambassador in Rome and Madrid, and Johannes only came to Bonn as a student.

In Cologne he had founded a psycho-social centre for Italians and Spaniards in West Germany and in 1989 became President of the Germany Society For Psychiatry And Neurology. He immediately understood my rebellion because of the Nazi past of my family and that my ethical and politico-cultural positions were incompatible with those of my father. Seeing how much I was affected by the situation, he offered to mediate between my father and me. From the autumn of 1977 until his painfully early death in 1991 at the age of only fifty-three, Johannes did all he could, through meetings and numerous telephone calls, to convince Father of the need to talk with me. When we saw one another in

Bonn for the last time, shortly before his death, he wanted to know everything about my relationship with my son Eugenio and the latter's adoption – more about Eugenio later. Johannes was very happy that I was experiencing being a father, and said in earnest: "I regret very much that all our efforts with your father have been in vain. Concentrate on your son and make something beautiful out of that! That seems to me the only way of coming to terms with the shattered relationship with your father. Repression and denial of his own past unfortunately include you too. Look to the future!"

Bettina Fehr kindly looked after me again in Bonn. Once she even invited me to accompany her to a reception at the Israeli embassy where she not only introduced me to the ambassador but also to Heinrich Böll, who said: "So you're the Wagner who got up people's noses here in the sacred city of Bonn with your *Fidelio*." I answered rather despondently: "People have been annoyed at me for that, just look at what was in *Die Zeit* at the end of May." I told him what Herbort had written and Böll laughed and replied: "Gottfried Wagner, what you dared to do there was perfectly right; don't be upset by people like Herbort, who swim with the tide. You have to learn to free yourself internally from the opinion of opportunists, otherwise you'll go to the dogs in the German cultural jungle. Just stop believing that *Die Zeit* has a monopoly on truth and honesty." I told Böll about the first time I had read his book *Wanderer, Kommst Du Nach Spa* and how my father did not rate his work. Böll was hardly surprised: "Your father certainly won't change now, try as he might to give that impression to the press." He was right about that too.

I also used my time in Bonn to apply to the DFG (German Society For The Advancement Of Scientific Research) for a grant, just to see what my prospects would be. The official responsible for my case was in favour of my project; in fact he had already expressed surprise by letter that the decision was taking so long. At the end of September I sent off further extensive documentation, including new research results. Shortly before I left for New York the official rang me up and told me that three members of the decision-making board had raised objections to my application;

one of the three was Reinhold Brinkmann, a colleague and friend of Michael Karbaum, who for obvious reasons had little good to say about me. So Bayreuth had even caught up with me in the DFG and my application was finally rejected by a small majority. Fortunately, I had long given up hopes of a grant. Now, with no money, no enthusiasm and no energy for an endless and expensive lawsuit against the Bayreuth mire, it was time for me to leave Germany and try my luck in America.

CHAPTER ELEVEN

ON THE TRAIL OF KURT WEILL

I n November Beatrix and I finally flew to New York. The leaden fatigue soon lifted once we landed in the murky yellow poison of exhaust gases at John F Kennedy airport. The border officials had a style of their own. Coming from Germany, it was a refreshing change for me to be greeted by a friendly Afro-American official with: "What do you want here, Gottfried?" I didn't exactly know myself. Rather embarrassed I replied: "I'm here for fun!" The official grinned, slammed his stamp in my passport and said: "So have fun, Gottfried!" In a terribly hot, crowded and stinking bus we drove to Manhattan. We went first to Beatrix's Aunt Gabriele, whose house was in Riverdale on the Hudson River, opposite the Toscanini house. Subsequently Francis de Vegvar and his wife Kitty, other relations of Beatrix's, invited us to their beautiful penthouse; they were to be among my most faithful friends in difficult times in the USA.

The penthouse overlooked Central Park and the seemingly endless Fifth Avenue up- and downtown – a view which made me almost forget my bitter experiences in Germany. But stark contrast to Beatrix's relatives' luxury lifestyle was not slow in coming: only a few blocks further uptown I witnessed the indescribable squalor of black Harlem. It had an effect on me like *Mahagonny*, but without the romantic sociological babble of German academics. My first stay in New York in November and December 1977 proved by no means as smooth-running as I had hoped. The legal status of the Kurt Weill Foundation Of Music was at that time anything but cut and dried. Lys

Symonette was trying desperately to hold together the archive that her predecessor David Drew had left in a rather poor condition. In fact Drew, insisting that he was still the actual executor, had sat on Weill's estate like a Fafner for twenty-five years while allegedly or actually working on a biography of the composer. Furthermore, Lotte Lenya and Lys Symonette had found out that he still had some important original documents, letters or compositions, in his London home, and it almost became a joke when Lys and I heard in connection with Drew that "something else had come to light". Drew only passed on information that had long been known anyway, and only answered letters after long delays. An attempt to get information from him in London came to nothing and it wasn't until February 1979 that lawyer Alfred Rice, who also administered the Hemingway estate, gradually began to clear things up and Drew finally departed as executor.

During this time I presented Lotte Lenya (who only wanted to be called Lenya) with the book version of my doctoral thesis, for which she had written an introduction. When she accepted the book she said, with emotion: "Finally Weill's name is in first place, and then Brecht! It was always the other way round – you are the first one to recognise that Weill is the equal of Brecht." I answered, no less moved: "Weill's music makes the joint works with Brecht immortal, because what will remain of Brecht will certainly not be his ideology, but his accurate knowledge of human contradictions and his wonderfully clear, poetic language!" Lenya shared my opinion. With great enthusiasm she started talking of her work with Brecht in the years from 1927 to 1933. "Brecht," she said laughing, "always said to me, 'You are epic theatre!'"

Of course I wanted to know more about Weill. The Jewish seminarian of 1927, as her "serious little Kurt" was called in those days, was certainly not looking for the intellectual, emancipated woman in Lenya, but the seductive "Lulu", with whom he enjoyed all the attractions of the Venusberg. Eagerly I listened to Lenya's stories of the nights in Berlin until March 1933. Often the names of people and cities were thought up during a boozing spree, when Brecht would wildly spin a globe and Weill would stop it with his index finger. Once the finger landed on a place called Benares, hence 'The Benares Song'. "It's absurd what all these pseudo-intellectuals cobble together nowadays about the origins of works by Weill and Brecht and what ideological nonsense they pile on to Kurt," said Lenya heatedly.

She would alternate, from one moment to the next, between talking about her past to wanting "to know everything" about me. "There's not so much to tell, and you can imagine why I wrote my doctoral thesis on Weill and Brecht," I answered. She asked anxiously: "Did you run into a lot of difficulties?" "Certainly far fewer than Weill and you did!"

We fell silent and looked solemnly at one another. Then she burst out laughing and told one of her Wagner stories from the time she worked as a stage extra in Zurich: "In the third act of *Parsifal* as a servant of the Grail, I and three others had to carry the coffin with the dead Titurel a long way from the centre rear of the stage, right down to the footlights. We were marching very solemnly, and even more solemnly I had to unveil the wax head of the dead Titurel, that was covered by a velvet cloth. But unfortunately for me, I pulled the cloth too hard, Titurel's head flew off and rolled down into the orchestra pit. The audience roared with laughter, the curtain came down and I was sacked."

Lenya became more and more merry. She still had the charm of a girl and I saw clearly how easily one could have fallen in love with this woman forty years ago. The evening ended with our singing excerpts from *Lohengrin*: she sang Elsa's dream, in her rather smoky, brittle voice, but with clean intonation and exact rhythm. She knew every note and every word by heart, although she couldn't read music. I parodied the swan knight from the Grail Redemption Company Inc. We were helpless with laughter and completely forgot our surroundings.

In the coming weeks I was to learn to my horror how indiscriminate Lenya was in her choice of friends, many of whom exploited her shamelessly. Lys was no match for Lenya's false friends. On my second meeting with Lenya I didn't manage to clear up all the questions connected with my work so I started looking for another job.

During various meetings with theatre agents I was once again sharply reminded of my origins and of Bayreuth. The agents were well informed about my rebellions against family tradition – the long arm of the *Festspielhügel* had made sure of that.

My life was further complicated by living in Riverdale. Everything important happened in Manhattan, and to get there I had to take the bus, which went through Harlem. I shall never forget the faces of these neglected young black people, distorted by hatred. As soon as they saw the bus coming they would run towards it, swearing at the passengers, sometimes even banging on the sides. The polite, mostly black, drivers tried to get through Harlem without stopping; accused of being "whitie's friends" for simply doing their job. If a traffic light turned to red, the driver would open his window to try to repel the onslaughts of black kids with choice words, but they just answered with obscenities. "No melting pot," I thought at such times. Many of these mostly unemployed young people hated us just because we came from the rich Jewish Riverdale area, a social division which triggered off an evil explosion of class and race hatred. I increasingly doubted whether New York was really so wonderful, and the clean, beautiful Riverdale neighbourhood took on more the image of an ivory tower.

During this period I also met Gert von Gontard, one of the most influential sponsors of New York operas and the Bayreuth *Festspiele*, in the Metropolitan Club. He was an eager and knowledgeable friend of art, theatre and music and I was only ever to hear good things about him. A member of the Budweiser brewery dynasty, which offered him ample means to pursue his love of opera, he was by no means a mere snob, rather as the offspring of a bourgeois family he obeyed the aristocratic motto *noblesse oblige*. He had once supported Max Reinhardt, when the great director had had to flee to New York to escape the Nazis. I described to him my unpromising professional prospects and explained my opinion of the *Festspiele*, which he had no good opinion of either. Although he could be described more as a conservative, he supported my criticism of the German cultural establishment, especially of Bayreuth, with fatherly sympathy.

I was pleasantly surprised when my sister asked me to be a witness at her wedding in southern France. With fewer illusions about a professional future in New York, I flew to Munich in December 1977, and journeyed on from there. Despite my time in New York being short, and only partially successful, I now felt ill at ease in Germany.

The weeks there had had a salutary effect on me and I began to view things in Germany with greater detachment. Job or no, I determined to return to America as soon as possible. What Everding, who was becoming more and more powerful in the German theatre scene, or any other theatre bigwigs, might say, was immaterial to me now. Even the fact that the German media ignored my book on Weill and Brecht didn't bother me much. America became for me the big challenge. I wanted to seek my fortune there, build up a life of my own.

How I enjoyed the vastness and beauty of southern France after the confinement of Germany and the wildness of the New York jungle. Although it soon became clear to me that Eva was only being more affectionate because Father had rejected her, the friendly and open nature of my brother-in-law, Yves Pasquier, worked wonders. In the end Eva and I tried to talk honestly to one another, without the constant feeling of distrust or rivalry for the post of *Festspiele* chief. I said to her: "The brutal way our father has frozen us out of Bayreuth can still turn out to have its advantages. Let's use them!"

This proposal was ultimately to prove a great illusion, but in those days in southern France the divisive shadow of Bayreuth could not come between us. The wedding and the Christmas festivities that followed were of such a cheerfulness and warmth that I became painfully aware of what we had never had as children: the feeling of belonging to a family, of security. Out of politeness, my new relations did not ask about Bayreuth and so the atmosphere was scarcely clouded at all by bitter memories.

In January 1978 Beatrix and I flew back to New York, making a stopover in London at the Spencers'. I now began systematically occupying myself with Weill's works after his escape from Nazi Germany and worked out some initial suggestions on how they could be promoted in Germany. I also received a first lesson in "How to behave to get a job" from Betty Smith, a well-known New York media agent, who generously helped me. Betty presented me with twenty questions typically asked in job interviews with agents, theatre directors or publishers. I answered them all wrongly, because I spoke the truth. Betty was horrified. For example, asked how I viewed the Bayreuth family tradition, I answered: "Why do you think I'm here? Because I don't want to have anything to do with the whole Bayreuth business!" Laughing at first, then seriously, Betty said: "Do you wanna get a job or not? Your capital is also to be a Wagner. Use it in the right way!"

Of course she was right. I had to learn how to handle my past and to present the relationship with my family in Bayreuth without doing myself a disservice, or losing my identity. I began painlessly to de-Germanise myself and aimed at becoming a "liberal American". I began to frequent the doors of literary agents, which is how I met Eliot Ravetz, who worked for the influential Scott Meredith Literary Agency on Third Street. I soon enjoyed a warm friendship with Eliot, although it unfortunately ended as abruptly as it had begun. The agency wanted to make my revolt against the family heritage the focus of advertising for my book. I on the other hand had no intention of being acclaimed as the uncouth, hot-headed revolutionary. Eliot had to obey his boss, and we parted company without coming to words. I was sorry, as I could really talk to Eliot openly about Germans and Jews of our generation and he helped me overcome my superficial philosemitism. I shall never forget Eliot's simple words on one of our drives from Manhattan to Riverdale: "Here in New York, where there are more Jews than in Israel, you'll meet a lot of unpleasant Jews who'll make you feel really antisemitic. Stop thinking we Jews are better than other people, especially here in New York. We aren't."

Beatrix's uncle, Francis de Vegvar, and his wife Kitty invited us to see some shows on Broadway and in the Metropolitan Opera. I must confess that these performances didn't impress me very much. I thought the much-praised musical *Chorus Line*, with all its technical perfections, trashy and shallow and the directing and sets of Verdi's *Trovatore* at the Met seemed grotesquely old-fashioned.

On one visit to the Met I met Milcom and Yveta Graff, who were sponsors of the opera house. They had attached a condition to their terms of sponsorship: that the money be invested in Czech music since Yveta came from Prague. The Graffs lived in one of the luxurious apartments on Park Avenue. As had been predicted, the "entry ticket" to the Graffs' home and consequently to New York society was my name, however, people were extremely curious about everything concerning Wagner and Bayreuth. Talk was by no means confined to

Richard Wagner and his works; I was also questioned on my father's style of management and my relationship with him. Again and again came the question of whether I would follow him as head of the *Festspiele*. Despite my hosts' charm and generosity I found this kind of conversation unpleasant. Most of the very conservative questioners were interested more in the private world of the Wagner family than in my views on culture and art. But with Betty Smith's advice in mind – "Do you wanna get a job or not?" – I endeavoured to answer politely and noncommittally. But when I was asked why I had written my doctoral dissertation on Weill and Brecht of all people, I had had enough of evasions. I spoke bluntly about Hitler, Bayreuth and the Jews and, with passion, confessed that the book was the consequence of a disastrous marriage between politics and culture in Bayreuth. Mrs Graff, who as a child had gone through the horrors of the German occupation with her family, showed sympathy for my commitment. But she remained an exception. The majority of the art sponsors present, some of whom were members of the arch-conservative Wagner Circle and Bayreuth pilgrims, maintained a polite silence. This was their way of saying that they were more than sceptical regarding what I then, together with Alexander and Margarete Mitscherlich, described as "mourning work". Their motto was: "What you can't alter, is no longer a worthwhile topic of conversation." Nor was my impression improved when some of them assured me in private how courageous they found my attitude.

After a few moments of silence those present broached the subject of whether Wagner had been a Jew. If there were any truth in this assertion it would have been tantamount to a vindication, in view of my great-grandfather's well-known antisemitic attacks and the traditional family line culminating in Winifred Wagner. I was familiar with those speculations made by Ernest Newman in his biography of Richard Wagner. In Bayreuth, support for and denial of such theories changed as frequently as the weather, according to which seemed most appropriate at the time. I pointed out that it was by no means clear whether Ludwig Heinrich Christian Geyer had been a Jew or that he was Richard's biological father. All that was provable was that Geyer was Richard Wagner's adoptive father. I had no proof for my denial of the claim and could only promise to go in search of the answer.

I finally succeeded a few weeks later in New York. The Leo Baeck Institute had kindly looked out for me genealogical documents on Ludwig Heinrich Christian Geyer, which proved that he was not a Jew. Several weeks after that I met Milcom and Yveta Graff once again in the Met, at a performance of Debussy's *Pelléas et Mélisande*. I told them of the results of my research. Yveta was a little surprised and commented that for her only Wagner's music mattered anyway and not his ideology – an opinion I could not share in view of my knowledge of Bayreuth's history.

That evening will always remain in my memory although for quite another reason. After seeing the moth-eaten production, which I had dressed up for as an invited guest, I missed the last bus back to Riverdale. To make matters worse, there was a fierce snowstorm that day in New York. As a taxi would have been too expensive, I decided to go home by subway. I somehow took the wrong line and ended up in Harlem. I only noticed my mistake when I was standing in the middle of a snowstorm on 154th Street, with black faces peering at me from all sides. A black guy sitting next to me on the subway had warned me to avoid the area: "Hey, Mister, what are you doing here? Take care you get out of here! And take a yellow cab. The other taxis can be dangerous." Looking around, I saw silent people, clothed in dirty rags, warming themselves around fires they had made in oil drums. Seeing such an elegantly dressed white man their expressions combined scorn and suspicion. My heart stopped and I frantically looked for a yellow cab. It wasn't until over an hour later, and a number of dubious offers, that I finally found one. Before asking for any address, the somewhat surprised driver wanted to know if I had any money. When I then told him I came from Riverdale he said aggressively: "That's the rich Jews' district, and we've got a snowstorm. So you can pay double." I offered him twenty dollars but he demanded forty – "or you can walk there in the snow". The thought of walking twelve kilometres to Riverdale through this district and in this weather overcame all my resistance and I agreed.

Thus began a second adventure. The driver raced like a madman through short cuts and over enormous potholes. I was flung from one side of the cab to the other, and several times my head collided with the windows. I implored him to drive more slowly but that just made him even more daring and he started skidding his Buick over the snow-covered, uneven streets. The weather was so bad I couldn't recognise where we were and already had visions of myself as a corpse in the Hudson River. Suddenly the driver slammed on the brakes and demanded his forty dollars. White as a sheet, I had hardly handed them over when he got out and tore my door open. With a broad smile that stood out particularly in the snowstorm, he shouted: "Hey, man, you better learn something about Black Harlem!" I got out, he slammed his door and disappeared like a phantom. I took heed of this experience from March 1978 on all subsequent journeys into New York and elsewhere. It was certainly another illustration of the obscene gulf between rich and poor in that city. That night I doubted whether my life in elegant Riverdale as a private researcher into Weill's history and as frequent guest of New York society really had that much meaning.

But I had little time for social conscience. My financial situation was becoming critical and Lenya was further delaying the promised contract. She had a fear of being poor, which made it difficult for her to commit to paying wages, although she was otherwise very generous. This fear was probably also the reason that Lys and I, on our visits to the beautiful Weill House on the river in New City, New Jersey, had to take our own lunch, although it did not stop Lenya inviting us to a restaurant afterwards. None of this bothered me much: I was happy to be in the Weill House.

The composer had financed the house with the monies he had received for his work in Hollywood. I was particularly impressed by his attic work room with its spartan furnishings: simply a desk and a chair in it. Here he had written some of his major works, such as *Lost In The Stars*.

Lenya suggested that I write a biography of Weill, especially as it looked as though David Drew would never finish his book. Unfortunately she didn't tell me that the journalist Ronald Sander was already working on a similar project, and with her approval.

Another month passed before I explained to Lenya that I would have to return to Germany if she couldn't give me a contract. She realised I was serious. Lys had also told her that I was already busy with Weill's work in America and had developed ideas on how best to promote his work. Furthermore, an interview with me was about to appear in the *New York Times*, which would help publicise the Weill Foundation. This time it worked. By March I had a contract in my hand, which ensured a modest living. It at least meant that I wouldn't have to depend on the loan that Gert von Gontard had generously offered me.

It was through Gert that I met John White, an unusual witness of Austrian-Jewish history, at a splendid lunch in the New York Metropolitan Club. As a former Viennese Jew, he had fled the Nazis to the USA and after an adventurous life had become the successful managing director of the New York City Opera. With great empathy, he immediately grasped my situation: "The great-grandson of the antisemite Wagner is working on the left-wing Jew Weill. That won't make you very popular in Germany. And I won't even ask you about your family. You follow your Aunt Friedelind's anti-Nazi attitude!" He had got straight to the heart of the matter and I replied: "I do respect my aunt's attitude to National Socialism, but I don't share her uncritical attitude toward Richard Wagner's antisemitism. Unlike her, I can see an ideological line running directly from Wagner's article 'The Jews In Music' to Hitler." When he noticed how important a conversation with him about National Socialism was for me, he invited me to his office, where he made some interesting points relevant to my work on Weill and gave me the results from contemporary research into National Socialism. He also recommended some standard works, such as Eugen Kogon's *The SS State: The System Of The German Concentration Camps*. White had a lot of enemies as a businessman, but I myself owe a lot to him.

My meeting with Eric Werner a few days later went quite differently, a meeting which was important in the search for my own identity. After several telephone calls I finally met up with the distinguished music historian, whose important writings on Mendelssohn I was familiar with. Politely, but warily, he enquired why I was occupying myself so intensively with Weill. Although Werner thought him interesting, he did not consider him important. Scarcely had I revealed my interest in German-Jewish history than he started to deliver a lecture on Wagner's antisemitism that was as knowledgeable as it was filled with strong aversion. Nor did he just refer to Wagner's 'The Jews In Music', but also commented in detail on Cosima's numerous antisemitic remarks in her diaries, which had just been published in New York. I understood his horror at the antisemitic cult in Bayreuth and was not offended when he expressed loathing for Wagner and the Bayreuth "cretinism" (Nietzsche).

More difficult to accept was his condemnation of Germans in general, which included my generation and myself, of course. In fact he considered me part of the antisemitic tradition of my family, an opinion I was quick to refute. I described to him those decisive moments in my life as I confronted National Socialism and he finally understood why I had written my doctoral thesis on Weill. But his fundamental opinion remained unaltered. The meeting left me feeling like an ugly little German, a Nazi-Wagner, who could do no better than change his name as quickly as possible. Werner's bitterness and hatred strongly affected me, and I felt quite distraught when I left: dismayed by such a lack of interest in even talking to those who, like me, were suffering under the burden of their parents' Nazi past. I later discovered that he had suffered a particularly harrowing Jewish fate, although he never spoke of it in detail. That softened my judgment.

At the end of February 1978, I gave my first big interview in the United States. It took place thanks to Betty Smith, who had negotiated a discussion for me with Donald Henaham of the *New York Times*. As I had no experience at all of the American media, Betty prepared me for it with practised patience. We went through my life in a game of questions and answers. As usual I answered her twenty questions on Bayreuth critically and had nothing good to say of Wagner and the German cultural scene. She was horrified: "You haven't learned a thing since our last talk. Just realise how important a successful interview with the *New York Times* could be for you!" So we went through the questions again and worked out a more diplomatic, but still tenable version of the answers.

Betty's advice was spot-on. Donald Henaham asked the questions she had expected, and my answers aroused his rather reserved but objective interest. In May 1978 the paper published an accurate account of what I had said regarding my production of *Fidelio*, music theatre in the twentieth century and Kurt Weill. Finally, I was able to read an article on me and my work that contained scarcely one word on the Wagner family and Bayreuth. This interview was the first of several with other important American newspapers, although none of it helped to improve my precarious financial situation.

One day I went to visit Lys in her apartment on Seventy-Third Street, Westside. By chance I noticed downstairs on the list by the doorbells, a name written in English ornamental lettering which triggered a quite particular memory. It said: "Dr Wolf, Kapellmeister." "Kapellmeister Wolf" was the alias Hitler had jokingly given himself. Until 1935, whenever he travelled between Berlin and Munich, Hitler would always make a stopover at the Hotel Bube in Bad Berneck, just outside Bayreuth; from there he would ring up "his Winnie", announcing himself jovially as "Kapellmeister Wolf", whereupon Grandmother would dash by car to pick up her Führer and take him back to Villa Wahnfried.

So who was this Kapellmeister Wolf on Seventy-Third Street? I was cheeky enough simply to ring the bell. The door opened and a distinguished, friendly-looking gentleman appeared, who asked with a strong German accent: "What can I do for you?" I didn't dare present him with the Hitler story out of the blue, so instead asked in German, not very originally: "Are you Kapellmeister Wolf?" He smiled and said he was. He opened his door wide and I spied a beautiful old Steinway grand that almost filled the small room. When I looked more closely, I saw there were a lot of yellowing photos standing on it. I don't know why, but to Kapellmeister Wolf's amusement I started looking at the photos and discovered to my excitement a photo from 1927 showing some people on the steps of the Baden-Baden Kurkonzertsaal. I read: "18 July 1927, Baden-Baden" and couldn't believe my eyes.

I burst out excitedly: "That was the day of the premiere of *Songspiel Mahagonny*."

Wolf was amused: "Yes, just look closely."

I recognised Kurt Weill, Bertolt Brecht, Lotte Lenya, Otto Klemperer and Paul Hindemith.

"That's me on the left," said Wolf with modest pride.

"What, you were at the premiere?" I asked.

"Yes, but you seem very interested in Weill. Are you a descendant of his?"

In all the excitement I had forgotten to introduce myself. I laughed and said: "Excuse me. My name is Wagner."

"As in Richard?"

I nodded, and he started to study my profile. Then he beamed: "A Wagner in my home!" and we shook hands with mock solemnity.

With growing sympathy we continued our discussion, during which I learned that he had not only been the repetiteur on *Mahagonny*, but also on the musical *Eternal Road*, based on the novel by Franz Werfel, with music by Kurt Weill. It had had its unsuccessful premiere in New York, directed by Max Reinhardt. We talked about the many good conductors of the Weimar years, and I named my favourites: Otto Klemperer and Bruno Walter. "Walter was my uncle," said Wolf. We roared with laughter. But the light-hearted mood came to an end when he told me his life story, which included persecution by the Nazis, and emigration. Thanks to his lively and many-faceted stories, for a while I was able, as though in a time machine, to journey back to the Berlin of the twenties. We parted like old friends.

It was only during our second meeting in his apartment a short time later that I hesitantly told Kapellmeister Wolf the association with his nameplate. He found my story bizarre and said magnanimously: "There are two sides to everything. Hitler brought us together here." I shall never forget Kapellmeister Wolf: he helped me to see myself not as a lousy German and even worse, a lousy Wagner in New York – an attitude so many German Jews had adopted, who were not by any means prepared to talk to the children of Nazi delinquents.

Working with Lys Symonette was an altogether pleasant experience. She had a demanding job at the Curtis Institute in Philadelphia, one of the leading conservatories in the USA, and gave up a lot of time to help Lenya, who left her all of Weill's mail to sort through. On top of that she looked after her husband and son like a true "Jewish Mamma", as I teased her. In spite of all her commitments we met regularly in her one-room apartment, where there was always such a stimulating atmosphere among music scores and historical photographs from Germany and the USA. The room was transformed into a glittering music theatre when Lys started introducing me step by step to Weill's work in the period after his collaborations with Brecht. As soon as Lys started playing Weill, she was transformed, released from the cares of her taxing everyday life.

I could go through thick and thin with her and despite several crises, our friendship has held until today. Lys helped me and encouraged me, although she had only modest means available. We often despaired at the state of the Weill archive and were hindered in our work by the fact that Lenya could not decide whether to transform the bequest into a professional centre for Weill research. But such concerns disappeared when Lys started telling me about her time with Weill on Broadway, sat down at her Steinway grand for a swing session and introduced me to American syncopation, jazz and the wide variety of Weill's scores. I owe to her my basic knowledge on Weill in America.

It became clear to me how many prejudices there still were against Weill and his work, even in North America. During one of our Weill meetings – "with love for our Kurt" – I noticed a black and white photo of a conservatively dressed gentleman, with a fine face, his melancholy eyes framed by round spectacles. "He looks like your son Victor," I blurted out. Lys smiled and answered: "That's my father." And she started telling me about her dramatic flight from the Nazis via Italy to New York.

There was also a connection between a cousin of her father, Emil Holzinger, and the Wagner family. He was a well-known member of the Jewish community in Bayreuth. After the First World War, when the general financial crisis even reached the *Festspiele*, my grandfather asked Holzinger to urge the rich Jews of Bayreuth to support the *Festspiele* financially. He advised Holzinger not to take Richard Wagner's antisemitism too seriously, which in view of his antisemitic writings and their effects even within the Wagner family, was not very convincing. I maintained an embarrassed silence throughout the tale. Her parents, who came from a Jewish family in

Mainz, had left the Jewish community, and so Lys had not been brought up in the Jewish faith. All the members of the family managed to emigrate from Nazi Germany in time.

Lys is also a distant relation of the liberal German-Jewish playwright Carl Zuckmayer (1896-1977), a fact of which she is proud.

How paltry my problems seemed in comparison with the fate of so many others. And my father's lamentations: always bemoaning the "sacrifices" he had had to make in the difficult wartime years and after 1945. What did he know? And what did the one-time Hitler protégé want to know anyway, about the suffering of the Jewish victims? The same suffering that Lys never complained about. When she noticed in her fine, sensitive way that her life story was moving me, she smiled and said: "I must confess to you that when I heard that you, a Wagner from that Bayreuth family had written your doctoral thesis on Weill, I thought you must be *meshugge*. Other than your Aunt Friedelind all the other Wagner generations before you had probably been Nazis and antisemites."

Our friendship strengthened after this conversation. In the knowledge that we had become spiritually elective relations, we got a lot of fun when, as "freethinking atheists", while eating kosher chicken soup and garlic bagels we blended the 'September Song' and the 'Tristan Prelude' or parodied the 'Waltz Of The Flower Maidens' from *Parsifal*, and Lys attacked the keys with gusto to create the "Hollywood Wagner orchestra sound". She confessed to me with mock bashfulness, her lively eyes twinkling: "My family and I are Wagnerians! Can you forgive me? In spite of everything?" I blessed her solemnly and pronounced: "In the name of the Richard, the Kurt and the Holy Ghost may you and your family be forgiven for the mortal sin of being Wagnerians."

Lys is always there when I need her. Something I can say of many friends, when I think of all the traps I've fallen into in my life and how I only emerged thanks to people like Lys.

Finally, my itinerary was ready to follow the trail of Weill in North America. I flew to Los Angeles, where Paul Vambery's wife collected me from the airport. Vambery had written the musical political satire *Der Kuhhandel* with Kurt Weill in 1934. After a cold three months in the aggressive New York jungle, Beverly Hills seemed quite unreal, with its summery weather, its palm trees, the sterile cleanliness of its ostentatious mansions and its snobs with their permanent impersonal smiles. This American artificiality became more bearable when I was able to spend a few days with the widow of Ernst Josef Aufricht, in North Canyon Drive. Aufricht had been the distinguished director of the Theater am Schiffbauerdamm in Berlin under the Weimar period and until 1933 had staged the premieres of works by Bertolt Brecht and Kurt Weill, Ernst Toller, Robert Musil, Paul Kornfeld, Georg Kaiser, Ödön von Horvath, Jean Cocteau, Karl Kraus and Marieluise Fleisser. I had read Ernst Josef Aufricht's autobiography of 1966, *Erzähle, Damit du dein Recht Erweist* in New York in preparation for the meeting with Margot Aufricht and Paul Vambery, who had been Aufricht's dramaturg in Berlin. I found the book interesting, not only for its description of how Brecht and Weill collaborated on the *Dreigroschenoper*, but also for the shocking account of Aufricht's flight from the Nazis to North America.

My passionate interest in her husband's work pleased Margot Aufricht and she knew a lot about it. She spoke German to me, to show that she didn't think of all Germans in the same light, and certainly not my generation, and she answered my questions quickly, accurately and with great kindness. She described Brecht's family, their craving for money and power, in terms which reminded me of Bayreuth, which I pointed out to her, to her amusement. Her warm words made Weill, whose gentle and modest character I had already learned of through Lys and Lenya, more and more likable and easier for me to understand. I thought again and again during these talks how much generosity it must take for her to talk in an unprejudiced way with the grandson of Winifred Wagner, whose friend Adolf Hitler had driven the Aufricht family out of Germany. When we were talking of Nazi and New Bayreuth, she said kindly: "Your family with its view of German history has bequeathed a legacy to you which you will carry for the whole of your life."

During one of my visits I was surprised to find a beautifully decorated, candlelit table, with coffee and cake. It was 13 April – my thirty-first birthday. She gave me one of the last copies of her husband's book with an affectionate dedication; it is one of my most treasured possessions. I was so moved I couldn't hold back my tears: the gesture was made all the more meaningful as I hadn't had any kind of birthday greetings from my family. At such moments I identified strongly with the German Jews of my grandparents' and parents' generation and my anger against my family had grown to such a degree that after the four days in Margot Aufricht's house I toyed with the idea of becoming an American citizen and changing my name.

In mid April, I visited Ira Gershwin, the lyric writer and brother of George Gershwin. He had suffered a stroke only a few weeks before, but agreed to see me nevertheless in his luxury mansion in Beverly Hills. His staff, however, were obviously not enthusiastic about my visit. Ira sat immobile in a wheelchair and had great difficulty articulating. We spoke briefly of his screenplay for the Hollywood film *Lady In The Dark*, which looks critically at the psychoanalysis of a woman. The little he was able to tell me was revealing. On Kurt Weill he said: "You Europeans will never understand that the *Volksoper* was the model for the American musical, as George and I showed in *Porgy And Bess* and Kurt and I tried to do in the two works we did together. Kurt was a fine, soft-hearted gentleman. Lenya never understood his character, but she felt the greatness of his work." When I told Ira how much I liked *Porgy And Bess* he wheeled himself laboriously to his desk and pulled out an LP double album with all his well-known lyrics and gave it to me. At the end of my visit he said: "Richard Wagner was a bastard but a great composer!" Then he let one of his minders know that it was time for me to go.

A year before in Bonn, at Bettina Fehr's home, I had met the Germanist Cornelius Schnauber, the executor of Fritz Lang's estate and great expert on Jewish exile literature. On meeting him again now, he invited me to his home. Among the guests were Ronald Schoenberg and his wife and Martha Feuchtwanger, whose Bavarian origins were evident every time she opened her mouth, even when she was speaking English. In spite of her great age she had a very lively mind when she was talking about the work of her husband Lion and about her life with him. She said: "Your work on Weill is a pleasure for us emigrants. In this way we shan't be entirely forgotten either." What melancholy there was in her eyes when she said these words.

The discussion I had with the judge Ronald Schoenberg, Arnold Schoenberg's son from his second marriage, and his wife, the daughter of the Austrian composer and Schoenberg-pupil Eric Zelsi, went quite differently. I wanted to know everything about his father and his Jewishness, and the Wagnerian Ronald wanted to hear everything about Richard Wagner, but nothing about his antisemitism. We talked very pleasantly at cross purposes. He enthused about Bayreuth and was quite amazed that I had a different opinion. Although he is ten years older than me, I identified with the role of the parents' generation of Jewish emigrants, whose children, born in America, don't want to hear any more of the stories of their parents from the Nazi period and in defiant reaction sometimes act almost pro-German. All attempts at finding a common subject for discussion came to nothing. When we said goodbye we promised to try afresh should we ever meet again. I said: "But please not Wagner!", to which Ronald retorted: "And please not Schoenberg!"

During one of my meetings with Paul Vambery, who passed on fascinating impressions of his time with Weill and in the Theater am Schiffbauerdamm, I got to know a close childhood friend of Weill's: Joseph Joachim. Joachim has never got over his flight from Germany, – even assuming an English name, Jackson, in an attempt to sever any ties to Germany. He was completely unaware of how German his manners were, however. Outbursts of hatred against everything German were followed without pause by wild enthusiasm at the beauty of the German language. There we sat on Paul Vambery's veranda with a view over Los Angeles and still we couldn't get away from Germany. "Weill," said Vambery and Jackson, "was ruined by being kicked out by the Nazis."

The two asked me about my grandmother and the rest of the family. It was difficult for me to answer without opening old wounds, and I wanted to convey a discriminating picture of the generation of the children of the perpetrators. So I spoke reservedly about Bayreuth and the Germans. In so doing I gradually realised that I had become an outsider. I only liked being with Germans who had de-Germanised themselves abroad and tried to become cosmopolitan.

Hitler, again and again, occupied centre stage in my discussions. They were often interrupted by silence, to suppress tears.

How many uprooted people I met, with broken off lives. Not all emigrants were as successful as Weill. How much I learned through Paul and Jackson of Germany, and how good it is for me today to read Paul's letters!

On 20 April I flew via Chicago to Bloomington, Indiana, the last stage rather hazardously in a single-motor propeller plane. In Bloomington I hoped to meet another witness in time: Hans Busch, who has since died. He was the son of Fritz Busch, who conducted *Die Meistersinger* in Bayreuth in 1924 and had to leave Nazi Germany because of his liberal views. He was subsequently one of the founders of the Glyndebourne Festival, a sort of anti-Bayreuth. He had worked together with Weill in 1923 and conducted the premiere of Weill's *Der Protagonist* in Dresden. His son Hans had directed the premiere in 1948 of Weill's one-act opera *Down In The Valley*, to a libretto by Arnold Sundgaard, in Bloomington, in Weill's presence.

Hans Busch spoke openly about his loathing of the conductor Karl Böhm, describing him as a "Nazi minion", who in 1933 had ousted his father as conductor at the Dresden Opera House. My grandmother disgusted him too. A lot of hurt resonated in his tales of the brutal ejection of his family from Germany and I felt ashamed.

But scarcely had he started to talk of his time with Weill, when his face became radiant, and he spoke warmly of the great kindness and modesty of the composer. Hans invited me to the dress rehearsal of John Eaton's opera *Danton And Robespierre*, which after dedicated and thorough preparation, was premiered in Bloomington.

While the dress rehearsal was in progress that evening, I briefly left the darkened auditorium. Pushing open one of the two swing doors, I went through and was about to let the door go when I noticed a small figure who called to me with an unmistakable German accent: "Attention, please!" I held the swing door back, and a little lady, whom in the darkness I couldn't really recognise, thanked me. I answered: "My pleasure," and introduced myself.

The lady in the dark asked curiously: "Like Richard Wagner?"

I answered rather amused: "Yes, but with mixed feelings. May I know who I'm talking to here in the dark?"

A friendly, laughing voice said: "You may, my name is Busoni!"
Upon which I asked just as curiously: "Like Ferruccio?"

She said yes, and suggested we should continue our conversation in the light in the foyer. So began one of my most important friendships: with Hannah Busoni, who in the summer of 1978 took me into her apartment in her "Hansel and Gretel House" behind Carnegie Hall, which was to remain my New York base until 1994. Hannah helped me in her discreetly generous way, when I was up to my neck in trouble.

She told me a lot about Busoni, Weill, her husband, the painter Raffaele Busoni, Lotte Lenya, the premiere of the *Dreigroschenoper*, which she had attended as a girl in Berlin, and about her flight from Nazi Germany. Her maiden name was Apfel, and she was the daughter of a very respected Jewish lawyer in the Weimar Republic, who had fled to France in 1933. As Hannah's parents were divorced, she escaped with her mother to England.

Hannah had an extremely lively mind, a dry sense of humour and spoke such excellent German that she reminded me in her style of expression of my favourite German authors of the 1920s. She was gratefully affectionate towards New York, where she had survived by doing a whole variety of jobs, until the Federal Republic finally awarded her the pension of a German judge as "restitution", the Nazis having prevented her from finishing her law apprenticeship.

Committed and selfless, she was now assisting young musicians and musicologists interested in her father-in-law Ferruccio. It was through Hannah that I saw for the first time in America the other, better, intellectual legacy of my family: that of Liszt, whom Busoni had thought highly of.

Anyone staying with Hannah might have thought he was living in the Berlin of the Weimar Republic. Many of her friends had a similar German-Jewish history, and all of them welcomed me, the grandson of Winifred Wagner, like a grandson of their own.

It was also at Hannah's that I met Paul Falkenberg, among others. Until 1933 he had lived in Berlin as a prominent sound editor. He thought it exciting and plausible when I told him that Weill had also appropriated Jewish sacred music in his songs with Brecht. One day when I was asking Hannah about her identity, she answered: "It's good to be Jewish," by which she meant the fated community of the persecuted German Jews, and not the religious community. Hannah will always be with me, even though she never answered my letters – alas, none of her friends could induce her to do that. When I called her up she asked immediately: "When are you coming? You can sleep in the sitting room!"

Time stood still between us. Our goodbyes were always quick, as we assumed that I would soon once again come puffing and sweating up the steep stairs to the second floor. With my suitcases standing in front of her door, we would hug and she would set to cooking for her greedy guest. I put a stop to it in the end by taking her out for meals, but I will never forget Hannah's shining eyes when she opened her door. Hannah died in 1994. I miss her.

After my trip to Bloomington, I stayed in Chicago for a few days with Peter Jonas, at that time artistic administrator of the Chicago Symphony Orchestra and before that personal assistant to Sir Georg Solti. I met the famous conductor too. He had offered to help me in America with a letter of recommendation, and now fulfilled that promise.

At the end of April I returned to New York, where I moved into new lodgings in the Lincoln Tower in Westend Avenue, that Lys had fixed up for me. I started writing a synopsis for a biography of Weill and together with Lys, studied all his works that had been written in America. Although the rather sparsely furnished apartment was on the thirteenth floor, I felt as though I was living in the middle of the street: day and night cars and trucks thundered to and from uptown and downtown.

It was during this time that I first heard that Lenya had made materials for a Weill biography available to the journalist Ronald Sander as well. My agent at the time, Eliot Ravetz, wanted to sue her for this, as she had assured me exclusivity by contract. But I had no desire to take legal proceedings against Lenya: I was very fond of her despite all her weaknesses. Once Sander's biography of Weill was announced, my business relations with Eliot Ravetz and his agency deteriorated and contacts with publishers became more difficult too. I learned what it means to try to do business in the jungle of New York publishers and agents. As always, Lys Symonette and Hannah Busoni stood by me with advice and practical help.

In this situation I noticed that I was still far from becoming Americanised. I could not come to like an existence in which all my energies were devoted solely to a better chance of survival.

Amidst this crisis of identity and work, I met by chance in Greenwich Village one of my closest childhood friends, Eckart Grebner. Eckart's mother had worked for many years in the *Festspielhaus*, so he knew what had been happening to me, even after we had lost contact with one another. If we spoke of the past in Bayreuth, then we did so with the awareness of two Germans who wanted in no way to be typically German.

Eckart is a dentist in Munich. He does his job well, but does not regard it as the be all and end all of his life. In addition to various other crazy things he collects old cars. Above all though he possesses a strong if unfocused creativity which vents itself in pictures and poems. He lives intensely for the moment and always has time for important discussions.

When I talked with him then, I realised how much I still had in common with Germans such as this and I felt the facets of the German language and culture as a great enrichment in my homelessness. Eckart was, like me, fascinated at first by everything that was different from himself and loved every kind of cultural stimulus. He lived an alternative life in every respect, and with such charm that I loved listening to him, even though he couldn't always convince me of his "really new art or ecological trends". Unwittingly, he made me feel like an old man. Eckart never thought for a moment of his financial security or insurance for his old age. He never moaned, even when he fell flat on his face. He registered every essential change in my development with curious sympathy and never made me feel I had to justify myself for the drastic changes of direction in my life. On the contrary, in his eyes nothing should stay as it is. And so he started, without self-denial or false politeness, to live with me in my new world beyond traditional morals. Out of interest and out of aversion to prescribed Christianity he immersed himself in Eastern cultures and meditation. He also looked into Judaism. In Eckart – with his inner unrest in the search of new facets of one's own identity – I recognised something of myself too.

When Hannah Busoni went to a German health resort, as she did every summer, she invited Beatrix and me to move into her apartment near Carnegie Hall. We gratefully accepted the offer: it saved us paying expensive rent, and moreover the location was much better and quieter. We took every opportunity of going to concerts, operas and Broadway productions. I went mainly to the less well-known and much more lively venues which had arisen as alternatives to the New York establishment. The more avant-garde the production, the more curious I was.

At the end of June we saw the first signs of summer in New York. It resembles a visit to a sauna, but with clothes sticking to your body. The only salvation is offered by the omnipresent whirring air conditioning.

An invitation from Schuyler Chapin and his wife Betty came like a bolt out of the blue. I had known Schuyler since his time as Leonard Bernstein's permanent adviser. He had been chief administrator of the Metropolitan Opera for some years and at the same time dean of performing arts at Columbia University in New York. He is one of the least typical representatives of the New York establishment: always modest, discreetly helpful and unselfish in his advice. Of a warm-hearted spontaneity that ignores all social boundaries, he is a real liberal international gentleman. Betty came from the famous piano-manufacturing family Steinway and was just as modest as her husband. With them we celebrated Independence Day on Long Pond in their country house with its own lake and surrounded by beautiful forests. Such pleasure reconciled me to all the bad experiences with New York theatre and literary agents.

In Schuyler's beautiful apartment on the corner of Sixty-Sixth Street and Lexington Avenue I met Leonard Bernstein again after many years, and the memory of the bad years in Bayreuth came back. He enthused about Wieland and fulminated against my father, whom he held to be a closet Nazi in spite of all his liberal-left airs. When I enquired how he had reached this opinion he told me about a meeting with my father about a planned assignment conducting *Tristan* which eventually came to nothing. "As long as he is *Festspiele* boss in Bayreuth, I won't conduct on the *Festspielhügel*," he declared angrily.

On the other hand, like many Jewish artists Bernstein had a lot of sympathy for Aunt Friedelind. "You seem to be continuing the tradition of your aunt with your work on Weill," he said kindly.

I answered: "Friedelind still believes in Richard Wagner's innocence where antisemitism is concerned. I don't!"

It was obvious that this subject moved Bernstein. He became thoughtful and pondered aloud: "How is it that I as a Jew love the music of this repulsive antisemite, especially his *Tristan?*"

I replied: "I have no right, as a great-grandson of Wagner, to say anything to you. But in *Tristan*, with all my aversion to the man Wagner, I can't see any antisemitism. And you should record it one day."

He did record *Tristan*, later in Munich, and produced a video on his Wagner dilemma. In 1990 he gave me the still incomplete film and asked for my opinion. I didn't think it very well done and told him so at our last meeting in April. Amused by my answer, he asked me to work with him on it. He died shortly afterwards, having helped me with my lecture tour on Wagner in Israel, in opposition to the machinations of Bayreuth.

CHAPTER TWELVE

THE LONG ARM OF BAYREUTH

At the end of July 1978 Beatrix and I travelled back to Germany: my mother was moving house and I needed to make professional contacts. My flying visit was clouded by the bad state of my mother's health. Finally, she agreed to leave Bayreuth, so together with Eva, Beatrix and I planned to set up a home for her in Wiesbaden.

I was worried about my professional future and so tried to pick up some commissions in Germany, in theatres or in the media. My efforts were all in vain. I had one unpleasant meeting at the end of September in Mannheim, where I applied for the job of dramaturg with Friedrich Meyer-Oertel, who was head of opera production there at the time and later would be my boss for a short period in Wuppertal. He loved recounting episodes from his career, but with my friends in New York and Los Angeles and my conversations with them still fresh in my mind, the German opera gossip was unbearable.

After the initial meeting with Meyer-Oertel I had strong doubts as to whether I had a future in the German theatre scene with its uptight, intellectual proceedings. It was a curious situation. I wrote about Lotte Lenya's eightieth birthday for the *Neue Zürcher Zeitung* and the Viennese *Die Presse* and couldn't wait to pack my bags again and get out of Germany. This longing was increased even more when I collected my mother in Bayreuth, where she had been living with Grandmother Winifred.

"Grandma" was once again the politician of yore. Although she had initially made out that she would support her former daughter-in-law and her grandchildren, she had now swung completely the other way, to my father's side. When I asked her for an advance of 4,500 Marks against my inheritance, shortly before we left, she answered with a cold smile: "You can get money from your rich New York Jews or the Kurt Weill archive." She was all enthusiasm now for my father's second wife and secretary, Gudrun, although she hadn't had a good word to say about her in 1976. No wonder I felt less comfortable "at home" than ever before. By mid October 1978, with a cheap Pan Am ticket, I flew back to New York.

Immediately after my return I put the final details to plans I had made with Betty Smith for a Weill concert in honour of Lotte Lenya, to be held in the Avery Fisher Hall. I had started to plan the concert with David Gilbert months before my visit to Germany. I met David in 1976, in Bayreuth, when he was Boulez's assistant and he had meanwhile become the permanent conductor of the Greenwich Philharmonia Orchestra.

A trial run of the Weill concert was given on 12 November in the Avery Fisher Hall, Greenwich, New York State. Lenya attended – coiffured, made up and dressed like an ageing Hollywood star. Our timing was unfortunate as far as the media were concerned: on the day of the premiere the press in New York were on strike and in America, what doesn't happen in the media, hasn't happened in America. So there was no improvement in my job prospects.

I was now working with even greater intensity on the structure of my Weill biography, while my new literary agent Elsie Stern was looking for a publisher. Furthermore, the theatre agent Germinal Hilbert had promised me direction of a *Don Giovanni* in Marseille. I would have been able to live carefree for several months on the expected fee.

In this hectic period Beatrix and I moved twice, ending up as lodgers of Marion McLaughlin in two small rooms in a house on the corner of Seventy-First Street and Lexington Avenue. Our time there was oppressive: our landlady liked to discuss her personal problems with me, even at night, added to which some of the neighbours didn't like us being there. For example, I was frequently rung up after midnight and sworn at in German by a quavering male voice: "Dirty German swine, get out of our house. We don't want any Nazis here. Clear out, or we'll bump you off!" It literally took my breath away: I had never encountered such aggression before. I inhaled deeply and said: "We should get to know one another personally. I am German, yes, but I'm not a Nazi and anyway I was born in 1947." On that I heard a furious snorting, and the anonymous caller with the nervous male voice slammed down the receiver. This malicious game was to be repeated several times. It wore me down, not least because I couldn't get a good night's rest any more. I later noticed that silence fell whenever I got into the lift from which, only moments before, I had heard German being spoken. Now I suspected the kind of circle the caller came from. Obviously people with a German-Jewish history were living here. As I find any form of hatred offensive, I tried to dismiss these incidents quickly. But unsuccessfully.

In mid June, 1978, in Hampshire House, I had already met the man who wielded influence over the world opera market: the big boss, Ronald Wilford. As an agent he commanded the highest fees for himself and his artists, although such exorbitant demands were jeopardising the whole opera market and in particular the opera repertoire. Anyone wanting to make a career in opera took care not to criticise his business methods: no one wanted to land up on Wilford's black list. He seemed interested during our hour-long discussion and was distantly polite, like many of the powerful people in the opera business. Most of all he wanted to know how things stood between Father and me and whether, in spite of all the tensions, of which apparently Eva had informed him, I would be the successor. I understood: he was already "networking" for future business. When I answered him evasively he cut short our conversation. But I hadn't come to exchange civilities with him. So I presented him with my CV, showed him interviews I had given and supplemented it with other things which might be useful to an agent. He concentrated on the interview in the *New York Times* and declared he would give it to his best agent, Matthew Epstein, and ask him to see me. He then asked me to pass on his regards to my father. The upshot: after one hour I was as wise as before.

After nine months of many humiliating attempts, I finally got an appointment with Epstein, in mid February 1979. The words of a highly dramatic American singer, who shortly before had not been exactly encouraging, still rang in my ears: "Don't expect anything! You're neither gay nor Jewish, and people know your father is against you!" I heard many similarly memorable comments about Matthew Epstein.

We met in his New York office and I quickly realised that he was making it hard for me to find any kind of basis for discussion with him. The man was hysterical and, from the first moment to the last of our hour-long conversation – constantly interrupted by telephone calls – made it quite clear that he was the boss and I was a little nobody who should be honoured to be received by him and whose career now lay in his hands.

He didn't question, but rather *interrogated* me on my views on opera. When I spoke of Bertolt Brecht, Konstantin Stanislavsky, Vsevolod Meyerhold, Erwin Piscator and other writers and directors, he said at once: "Unmarketable! You are only marketable as a Wagner, who produces Wagner and who is the future director of the *Festspiele*. If you want to get into the business here in the USA, and that applies for Europe too, then you'll have to give up your left-wing ideas, because you won't get anywhere with them. Drop Weill too! You're entering an area there that doesn't belong to you."

I interrupted his monologue and asked: "Why shouldn't I work on Weill? I've written a book on him, after all, that earned me my doctorate at the University of Vienna and the job with the Weill Foundation."

Epstein answered with a disparaging smile: "For a grandson of Winifred Wagner there's no place here for anything to do with Weill."

I had to stop myself telling Epstein that this was racism under a different name and answered guardedly: "I am a convinced liberal, even in the American sense of the word. Out of all the Jewish intellectuals I have met here in the USA, I have never heard anyone say I am unwelcome because of my work on Weill and because of my origins."

Epstein became rather embarrassed, bit his nails even more and said irritably: "I know. Things have changed. We're also doing business with Bayreuth, although we know everything about Wagner and Hitler. But that doesn't mean we have forgotten that you come from the Nazi Wagner family."

I became more self-confident and retorted with some energy: "I find any form of discrimination and ideological fanaticism repulsive! A wide variety of opinions in art and life is part of my identity, and that has nothing to do with the character of my family in Bayreuth!"

Epstein was cool and condescending. "You'll never make a career for yourself like that!" he said. "Your only chance is: Wagner makes Wagner, and in line with Bayreuth, and with your father."

I remained silent and wanted to leave. Epstein noticed my aversion and said: "I'll write you a recommendation, as no one knows you here in the USA, and introduce you as a Wagner who does Wagner and is right in line with his father and Bayreuth."

Now I said something I shouldn't have said: "No thanks! I'll try to make my way in life without making false statements against my convictions."

Epstein was thunderstruck. "You'll never find a job here or anywhere else if you don't follow my advice. I only want to help you."

Disgusted, I left the office and hoped I would never be dependent on people like him. Sadly, that was to prove one of the many illusions I had with regard to agents.

Germinal Hilbert, meanwhile, who had offices in Paris and Munich and collaborated closely with my father, was now talking not only about Marseille, but also about Buenos Aires, where he held out the prospect of a *Lohengrin* for me. He said preliminary contracts already existed. I worked out detailed plans for both productions and asked Hilbert to conclude the contracts. But it now transpired that Hilbert could not even produce negotiation documentation. He had totally misled me. When I told the conductor Karl Böhm about this and considered bringing an action against him, Böhm said: "If you cross swords with Hilbert, you'll never set foot in any of the bigger opera houses in Europe again. Come to terms with Hilbert and your father and there'll be no lack of work."

But I had no intention of coming to terms with them, although

I did not want to risk legal proceedings either, given my desperate financial situation. With the help of a lawyer, a compromise was reached, after much to-ing and fro-ing: I was eventually fobbed off with a job directing in the theatre in Trier. But more of that later.

CHAPTER THIRTEEN

RETURN TO GERMANY

Unable to earn enough money in the USA, I flew back to Germany in February 1979, where I started looking for work without an agent, writing to every theatre in Germany and generally rushing from pillar to post. In mid March an offer from the Kammeroper in Vienna seemed to be firm and I began working with my friend Johannes Dreher on Johann Nepomuk Nestroy's *Tannhäuser* parody. In the sixties Johannes had been projection painter and artistic collaborator for my uncle and father, but he remained a fatherly friend, one of the few from my Bayreuth past who did not swim with the tide.

Johannes had had a colourful life. As a pupil of the painter Otto Dix he had been on the Nazis' black list. They had persecuted him and the torture to which he was subjected had left him with a permanent limp, but he had remained a nonconformist. He was a painter, and his set paintings were in demand in all the important opera houses of the world. He was always up to the latest developments in stage and lighting techniques and the Bayreuth and Salzburg *Festspiele* owe him a lot. His modesty made him endearing, but didn't do him much good in the hostile opera jungle which exploited him, much to my anger. With him I could talk about everything and he followed, with amused approval, my ideas for ridding the theatre, opera business, in fact the world in general, of corruption.

When we worked together he was sometimes as enthusiastic as a young man. Both sanguine types, we raged and screamed at one another if things didn't go as we had planned, afterwards hugging one another with the greatest affection. We were equally glad when things on the stage finally worked out as we had imagined.

I owe thanks to Johannes not only for essential knowledge on how one employs theatrical means, but also for the warning, never to forget for whom one makes theatre.

For Nestroy's *Tannhäuser* parody I wrote a new prologue and read it aloud to the writer Hilde Spiel. She liked it, and so in April we started rehearsing. But after only two days Hans Gabor, director of the Kammeroper, had rehearsals stopped, without giving reasons and refusing to discuss his surprising action. I was upset and confused – more so when the Kammeroper gave guest performances of the parody in mid August 1980 in the Bayreuth Margravian Opera House. Someone in Bayreuth had evidently once again been pulling strings.

At the beginning of May 1979, my mother and sister's lawyer notified me that I could collect my furniture and other items from Bayreuth. I wanted to get the disagreeable business over quickly, so I hired a small van and drove there at the end of the month with Beatrix's brother for moral support. As my father refused to see me, I turned to the caretaker, successor to the kindly Grandpa Lodes, who had always been a faithful servant of my father. Despite having known me for many years, he treated me like a stranger and in great haste unlocked a shed that had been named *"Rüdelsheim"* (after one of the Bayreuth chorus masters). It was cold and dirty inside. The caretaker pointed into the corner where my things were stored, then stayed close by me to check every single piece I loaded into the van. I lost my temper and shouted at him to kindly clear off. That was precisely the language the caretaker understood. Deferentially he apologised and said he was only following Father's orders and had "nothing at all against me personally". Angry, I recalled: "Father has always surrounded himself with such people."

The caretaker finally got off my back and moved to stand between the door and the spot where my things were piled, and I set to sorting through everything. When I looked more closely I found that the furniture which I had lived with for many years, was missing and that in its place Father had put a few shabby old wardrobes. I didn't want them, and gave the caretaker the job of telling my father so. Amongst the dirty pile I discovered my puppet theatre and the sets I had made as an eight-year-old, with the help of the set painter Otto Wiesner.

Everything was falling to pieces and useless. But the puppets for the theatre were in an old Bavarian chest and by some miracle had survived storage. Not so my diaries, which I had been keeping since the beginning of the sixties. Unfortunately, they were mouldy and dirty, the pages stuck together and unreadable. I only had one thought: get out of here, where they let memories of one's past disintegrate. One day I shall build my son his own puppet theatre!

All I took as I left the shed were the puppets and a chair by the famous Viennese furniture-makers Thonet. The chair had been used in Wieland's production of *Parsifal*, to carry Amfortas into the temple of the Grail. When I recognised the *"Parsifal* chair" I decided to take my own compensation and save it from the pile of junk.

How many memories came flooding back at the sight of that stage prop from Wieland's time: thoughts of George London and Thomas Stewart, singers of the Amfortas role, and of the guest appearances of the Bayreuth *Festspiele* in Franco's Barcelona. Before I drove off, I told the caretaker that he was welcome to tell my father about the "theft". Then, in the almost empty van, we tore along the Siegfried-Wagner-Allee, past Breker's heroic Wagner bust in the *Festspielpark*, and then past Wahnfried on the Richard-Wagner-Strasse, without visiting my grandmother. I wanted only one thing: to get away as quickly as possible. Later I gave up my claim to all the furniture. It would have been too constant a reminder of Bayreuth.

The *"Parsifal* chair" didn't bring me much luck and it is now standing in the Bödiger Gallery in Bonn. When I see my son Eugenio playing with the puppets today, I'm glad; his games remind me of the few lighter moments of my childhood.

Although I didn't want to give up America as the big alternative, I nevertheless still clung to the illusion of being able to build an existence for myself in the German theatre and opera world, especially as my finances were at a very low ebb. And so in summer 1979 I accepted a job as assistant director at the Salzburg *Festspiele*, working on Dieter Dorn's production of the Richard Strauss opera *Ariadne auf Naxos*. Dieter is, in his personal relations outside the theatre, a witty, sensitive man with brilliant ideas, and I greatly admire his directorial work. But as soon as he entered the Salzburg *Festspieltheater*, he changed into one of the most stereotypical of theatrocrats.

The Salzburg *Festspiele*, like that in Bayreuth, is a collection of prominent or allegedly prominent figures, who regard nothing as being more important than themselves – the acme of high society. These people were only interested in me in so far as I was part of Bayreuth gossip. They asked about the family quarrel and whether I would follow my father as boss of the *Festspiele*. It was made clear to me that a Wagner without Bayreuth connections would not get a footing in Salzburg either.

In Salzburg there was also the bombastic celebration of Karl Böhm's eighty-fifth birthday. Leonard Bernstein had his Jewish melody performed by Christa Ludwig as 'Piccola Serenata' and the great Herbert von Karajan congratulated his friend Karl, greatly moved. Everybody was moved in fact: the public no less than the fine gentlemen of the classical music industries. The biographical grey areas of the music heroes of the Nazi period were not mentioned: that had all been long forgotten.

In September 1979, after weeks in Salzburg, I flew to Ankara, to direct Carl Orff's *Carmina Burana*. When Johannes Dreher, who had negotiated this contract for me, and I arrived at our quarters, in what was at the time a rather unattractive Ankara, after a tiring flight and a wild drive, we felt quite ill. The sanitary installations were not functioning and when we went out for a walk we saw that the city resembled a besieged fort. The ruling military junta feared an armed resistance.

During the first night we heard shots and then a bloodcurdling scream. I dashed to the window and saw two soldiers in the twilight beating a man to death with their rifle butts, after they had shot and wounded him. It was the first time I had witnessed someone being murdered. Angry, but paralysed by fear, my instinct was to fly back to Munich immediately. When I told the directors of the opera house the next morning of my traumatic experience they retreated into aloof silence. That made me even more uneasy and strengthened my urge to get out.

What determined my decision to stay on until the dress rehearsal, however, was my first meeting with the opera house chorus and with the ballet master Attila and his group. The majority of the chorus were young, open-minded conservatoire graduates who were eager to learn. They agreed with my concept and wanted to play *Carmina*

Burana, out of political conviction, in the Ankara of 1979. I threw overboard Orff's mythological *kitsch*, which was incomprehensible to them. They amused me in particular with their embarrassed giggles as we worked on the many erotic scenes. But prudery and embarrassment soon disappeared and together we discovered the political statements contained in *Carmina Burana*, which similarly to the *Ring des Nibelungen*, portrays a struggle between love and power.

However, for some friends of the military junta the concept caused bad blood: for "inexplicable" reasons the stage equipment wouldn't work and rehearsals were boycotted for days.

After the dress rehearsal, as I said goodbye to all those who had gone through the last weeks with Johannes and me, we were overwhelmed with presents and invitations.

What was particularly important for me in those days in Ankara, though, was the beginning of my friendship with Pulat Tacar and his wife Selda. Pulat came from one of the few families who had a lot of influence in Turkey. He had been general consul in Munich and had enjoyed great esteem among the Turkish population there, earning the honorary name "Workers' consul" because of his efforts on behalf of their interests. When we met in Ankara at the beginning of my rehearsals, he had our quarters transformed into a place fit for human habitation within a few hours, before disappearing off on diplomatic affairs. Both then and later, when he turned up at the end of rehearsals, he opened my eyes to his country, its culture and its people, whom he felt bound to in critical sympathy. He is extraordinarily cultured, speaks eight languages and is passionate about art, philosophy and world religions, in particular the Chinese philosopher Lao-tse. It came as no surprise that he knew Richard Wagner's works well too.

His wife Selda was just as unusual, and as an Austrian had not found it easy integrating into the Turkish diplomatic corps: a sensitive artist receptive to Chinese culture, she had no interest in small talk.

Both were superb hosts. In October 1979 Johannes and I left before the premiere in protest against the obstructing of our work. It was difficult to say goodbye to Pulat and Selda and we felt sad on the plane to Munich. Later, I proudly told my son the story of the Turkish carpet which is now lying at the side of his bed. Pulat had got it for me at an incredibly cheap price at a bazaar in Ankara. It represents my director's fee for *Carmina Burana*.

After giving some lectures in Washington, New York and Toronto in the second half of October 1979, mainly to do with Weill and the theatre of the Weimar Republic, I began work on 1 November at the Frankfurt Opera House as evening director – the journalist Wolf Rosenberg had got me the job. At that time the conductor and composer Michael Gielen was director of the opera house. I only saw him once, for a brief, impersonal conversation when he asked me whether I really needed the job so urgently, as it wouldn't bring anything other than the salary. I was surprised by this comment. I thought highly of Gielen as conductor, and it was because of him that I had accepted the job in Frankfurt. The deputy director Christof Bitter told me which parts of the repertoire needed freshening up in addition to managing the evening performance and gave me *Carmen* in an old production by Jean-Pierre Ponnelle and an old warhorse: a production of Johann Strauss's *Die Fledermaus* from the sixties.

The preconditions for the job were pathetic. There was no piano score of *Carmen*, just a rather useless video recording. The opera house officials were totally indifferent to this miserable state of affairs and it was made clear to me yet again that a Wagner who has crossed swords with Bayreuth finds no allies on the administration floor of German opera houses. Even in Frankfurt, people acted left-wing and progressive – the vocabulary of 1968 – but were authoritarian in their management of people who didn't find it all so wonderful.

As lowest of the low in the opera house, my colleagues and I had a bad deal in the day to day tussle. Many depended on the job, although they found what they did pointless. To use the words of one of the intellectual super-cynics on the administration floor of the Frankfurt Opera House: we were "alienated wage-earners". People revelled in unworldly ideas for saving the workers and indeed all the oppressed of the earth, and understood theatre as an instrument for overcoming social contradictions or as a platform for doctrines of salvation. This masturbatory theatre comprised incompatible elements: absurdly luxuriant programme books dripping with pseudo-left jargon, keeping one eye on the media and sponsors, deferent towards political power and contemptuous of the public. And the whole time their gaze was directed at the next free chair in Everding's intendants' merry-go-round.

And so when, on top of everything, I saw Dorothea Glatt, now with the married name of Behr, creeping round in the ugly underground shafts of the opera house, with its linoleum flooring and washable bright green walls, as ambassador from Bayreuth, I resolved yet again to have nothing to do with these theatre managers, who confuse their little stage universe with reality.

Gielen had been right. The job was only the means to earn money. But it did help me to understand more clearly what was happening in the West German opera scene. By the end of January 1980 the Frankfurt nightmare was over and a new one could begin, in March in Trier.

The intendant of the Trier municipal theatre, Manfred Mützel, proudly called himself a "faithful follower" of August Everding. On the administration floor, gossip, elitist behaviour and tactical manoeuvring were the norm. Such people must have considered me and Johannes Dreher, whom I had brought again as set designer, crazy eccentrics. There were other colleagues in the theatre, on the other hand, whom we got on with well, as they based their work on craftsmanlike professionalism.

I had chosen Busoni's *Turandot* as a parody of opera and his *Arlecchino* as a caustic settling of accounts with moralising ideologies of every kind. As the performances were taking place in right-wing Trier, I had incorporated harsh anticlerical allusions which were taken up by the chorus, the ensemble and the excellent extras with great enthusiasm. Our popularity among our colleagues grew, to the great annoyance of the administration, when I started reacting to the despotism of the administration in the interests of chorus and soloists. The intendant tolerated the chorus master not even turning up for the dress rehearsal. So I brought in the media to draw attention to the unbelievable working conditions in the Trier theatre. Despite all the obstacles, the premiere was a success and the intendant endured our practices. Later Mützel blackened my name at a meeting of German intendants.

After my experiences in Trier I accepted an offer of working as dramaturg and director at the opera house in Wuppertal. It only later transpired that opera director Friedrich Meyer-Oertel and general intendant Hellmuth Matiasek were only interested in working with me because my name was Wagner and I therefore may, albeit in the distant future, play a role in Bayreuth. Moreover, when Richard Wagner's first opera, *Die Feen*, was performed in Wuppertal in February 1981, they thought it appropriate to pass me round the media like a museum piece. Meyer-Oertel also approved when I collected 60,000 Marks for the Wuppertal Opera House from Wagner Societies and a private sponsor.

But the mood changed when the media showed greater interest in my dramaturgical work on *Die Feen* than in the conventional staging of the opera director. In fact it triggered off some melodramatic scenes, and petty jealousies. In a crowded canteen Meyer-Oertel made it clear to me, in a loud voice, that he was the opera director and I was only his employee. The intendant regarded Wuppertal merely as a stopover point in his career, and his then assistant played the boss in Matiasek's absence. So, tensions were almost inevitable.

The only bright spots were new friendships. First I got to know and value the set designer Hanna Jordan. Our conversation revolved around matters which we believed important: German-Jewish history, National Socialism, and its effects on the cultural and political climate in Germany. Hanna and her family had been victims of the Nuremberg race laws, and she reacted violently to any form of intolerance or discrimination. She is a trusty left-winger, a person who has suffered a lot and by no means always feels at ease in Germany, with its undigested past. Such feelings bind us in a special way. The fact that I am a Wagner amuses her, in particular as at the time she was living in the Wotanstrasse, of all places, in Wuppertal-Elberfeld. "Hanna of the Wotanstrasse": we still make jokes about it as we do about Wagner, whom she considers important as a "theatre animal", as I do. When we met again years later in Wuppertal, in 1992, at my lecture on the "The Case Of Wagner In Israel And Germany", it was as though we had seen one another only yesterday.

On 5 March 1980 my grandmother died in the hospital in Überlingen. I had seen her for the last time three weeks earlier, a visit which will always remain in my memory because of the way she spoke with such disconcerting clarity about her approaching death. It was only Aunt Friedelind whose grief was genuine. The solemn burial on 10 March in Bayreuth was an embarrassment from beginning to end. My father had worked out a seating plan separating the family into the pro-

Festspielhügel and anti-*Festspielhügel* contingents. A string quartet provided the only relief from interminable speeches in which my grandmother was acknowledged as the saviour of Bayreuth. Not a word was said about the intimate friendship between Winnie and Wolf, and even Mayor Hans Walter Wild distinguished himself by maintaining total silence on her National Socialist past.

And then there was a media circus adroitly handled by the Bayreuth PR professionals. Among the onlookers were delegates of the NPD and old friends of my grandmother's from the Nazi period. I avoided their attempts at condolence. Free of his mother's presence, my father now exuded omnipresence as *Festspiele* boss and did not consider it necessary to receive his own family or the guests. Whilst the family feigned mourning to the outside world, they privately rejoiced that the domineering shadow had finally lifted and got down to business: dividing up the inheritance.

Far more traumatic than the death of my grandmother was the break-up of my marriage to Beatrix. At Christmas 1980 Beatrix and I faced up to the fact that our weekend marriage between Munich and Wuppertal was ultimately unsustainable: among other things we disagreed about having children and on the paths our careers should take – especially mine, since I had no intention of returning to Bayreuth. She didn't want to move to Wuppertal, as the prospects for her career as a lawyer were better in Munich and though I hoped to dissuade her from separation by offering to give up my job in Wuppertal, she wouldn't agree to that either. As divorce proceedings began, so did one of the most difficult periods of my life. I took refuge in my work and it soon became a drug for me.

After four years of trying, Johannes Meyer-Lindenberg finally succeeded in persuading Father to meet me face to face. So it was that in February 1981 we drove through a snowstorm to Bayreuth. The only place we could find to stay was the Hotel Goldener Anker, on the first floor, right next to room number twenty-three, where Hitler had stayed in 1923 when he met my grandmother for the first time. To me this boded ill, but Johannes quickly talked me out of such superstition.

Father received us in the *Festspielhaus* out of consideration for his wife and my half-sister Katherina, who I didn't meet. The conversation began superficially, with commentary on the weather. It was obvious that Father found the meeting awkward: he kept repeating that he had very little time and had a lot of other important things to do. But neither of us let ourselves get irritated. Johannes' tactical skills left me amazed. He told Father to stop his public attacks and derogatory remarks and to meet me regularly to air our views. However, when Johannes tried to arrange the next meeting, Father was reluctant to commit himself. Annoyed, Johannes, insisted we meet in Wuppertal.

What we had achieved though was an agreement in principle to have regular conversations and for Father to no longer make negative remarks about me in public. Satisfied, Johannes left my father's office on the second floor of the *Festspielhaus*. As we parted, I tried to look my father in the eyes, but he avoided it and something told me he would not hold to the agreement.

In March 1981 my father and his second wife Gudrun attended a production of mine for the first and last time: Mozart's *Bastien und Bastienne*. For the administrative staff of the Wuppertal Opera House, Wolfgang Wagner turning up was a great event. The performance took place in a school in Wuppertal-Ronsdorf under extremely modest conditions. There had been no publicity and the hall was half empty, on which my father's wife commented: "In Bayreuth we are swamped with audiences. You seem to have quite the opposite problem." An embarrassed silence followed and the atmosphere was ruined.

In April 1981 I met Johannes Meyer-Lindenberg again and asked him to help me cope with my divorce. With some reluctance I took the sedatives he prescribed and then the treatment began. I started talking. After I had talked on for half an hour, Johannes declared with a kind smile: "You don't need psychoanalysis, you need your own family and the right professional environment, which you certainly don't have in Wuppertal with career-conscious types like Meyer-Oertel and Matiasek." The very next day I stopped taking the tablets and, to the amazement of my boss, stopped living for the theatre. After the premiere of my production of Berlioz's *Béatrice et Bénédict*, which to my great joy Aunt Friedelind attended, I flew to Paris, to attend a Jewish wedding. I had a brief, refreshing flirtation with an enchanting Parisienne and slowly began to recover. In this new, positive frame of mind, I became aware of the pointlessness of my former existence. Things had to change.

CHAPTER FOURTEEN

TERESINA

My new appetite for life was not impaired by the appearance of my father plus his new wife. Things could only get better. I started freeing myself from my self-imposed isolation and enjoying the generous society of my landlady, Dodo Koch, who accepted me into her household like a son and spoiled me. Dodo took a warmhearted interest in both my professional experiences and private escapades. I lived in a small annexe situated, like the main house, at the beginning of a forest path leading to the Gelpe valley amid beautiful countryside – compensation for the depressing ugliness of Barmen and the opera house!

In the first week of July Dodo started preparations for her seventieth birthday with the skill and attention to detail typical of such a perfect hostess. Belonging to Wuppertal high society, she enjoys great popularity and so had invited a large number of guests, meticulously planning the seating arrangements. As she knew about my divorce from Beatrix she asked me in her pleasantly direct way: "And who should I invite as your lady partner at the table?"

I said defensively: "Better not have anybody!"

Dodo wouldn't give up and said jokingly: "Teresina Rossetti would be a charming partner!"

The comment slightly annoyed me: "Her of all people. I had such an awful row with her a year ago over the Pope and his reactionary views. You can't do that to me."

Irritated, Dodo replied: "How silly you are not to see Teresina's human qualities just because of your excessive views on the Pope!"

She had much affection and respect for Teresina, who had been a regular visitor since 1973, first as *au pair* girl, then as friend. A few days before the birthday party Dodo and I were sitting in her drawing room talking about the party arrangements when the telephone rang. Dodo picked it up, listened, and answered: "Teresinchen, how nice that you've arrived! Get straight into a taxi and come here. No, wait. Dr Wagner will pick you up at the station." I could hear Teresina's comments quite clearly as I was sitting next to Dodo. She said firmly: "I'd rather take a taxi." But Dodo was firmly against it and insisted. On the drive to the station I weighed up whether I should direct the conversation immediately to the Pope or to the emancipation of women. Then when I saw her waiting in front of the station with her suitcase, tired from the long train journey from Milan, I refrained from all the little digs and greeted her in a friendly way: "*Ciao, come stai?*"

Surprised at my unusual friendliness, she answered with an irresistible smile: "*Bene, grazie per essere venuto a prendermi.*" [Thank you for coming to collect me.]

From that moment on I preferred talking Italian with her. When we were sitting smiling in the car I couldn't resist asking her why she had insisted on the telephone on not being picked up by me. "I didn't want to start straight away fighting with you about the Pope, as I can hardly imagine you have altered your opinions since our argument a year ago," she said with disarming hilarity.

"A lot has happened in my life since then," I said. "I have altered a lot and I am more capable now of listening to you."

From that moment on until the time she left we met up whenever we could, telling one another the story of our lives with an openness that only old friends are capable of – or people who have just fallen in love. We made it clear to one another from the first moment, based on our own bad experiences, what we thought meaningful and what was not. And yet the hurdles before us were anything but insignificant: my divorce proceedings, my difficult professional situation, the incurable illness of Teresina's father, the geographical distance and our very different families. Amidst all the plans we had for our future together, we completely forgot the Wuppertal world around us. With some satisfaction, Dodo immediately sensed that we had fallen in love. My change didn't escape the other guests either, and people whispered behind our backs: "How happy and open Gottfried Wagner has become, and how well this charming Italian woman suits him."

Teresina and I were amused by the sugar-sweet interest of Dodo's guests, who were already starting to hear wedding bells. When, on the evening of 12 July 1981, I watched the train on which Teresina travelled back to Italy leave Cologne station, I knew that with her I had a chance of a meaningful and fulfilled life. Lots of things that had seemed insoluble to me lost their importance. I began to understand who I was. I became myself through Teresina's love.

After her departure I made preparations for a discussion with my old teacher Maximilian Kojetinsky in Bayreuth on the various versions of *Tannhäuser* for a planned production by Meyer-Oertel for the coming season. Beforehand I had met the set designer Arno Adar from Israel, a friend of Hanna Jordan's, who was working with Meyer-Oertel on a production of Volker David Kirchner's opera *Die Trauung*. At that very first meeting we had a frank, intensive discussion on the role of the artist in society and on whether and how far art could be politically effective. Arno was not against politically committed art, but he doubted that it could influence politics. At once we were thrown into discussion on the dependency of art in totalitarian states like Nazi Germany and the Soviet Union. Only after that did Arno start talking about his experiences as an Austrian-Jewish emigrant. I had finally found a new discussion partner in the Wuppertal period, which was otherwise not very stimulating.

I was impressed by Arno's scepticism towards my often too idealistic arguments, as well as by his reliability as a human being. He brought me closer to Erich Fromm, Hannah Arendt and Viktor Frankl, authors I only knew superficially. He also broadened my horizons and motivated me to investigate the subject of art and politics more profoundly. I asked Arno if he would like to go with me to Bayreuth. "With you, yes," he said curtly.

On the way there Arno told me of his flight from Nazi Austria, speaking exhaustively and fascinatingly about Israel and it aroused my own curiosity about that country. We stayed with my mother who, against my advice, had moved back to Bayreuth.

One afternoon we wanted to attend the dress rehearsal of *Tristan*, with Ponnelle's conventional set and directing. When I went to pick up the tickets for the dress rehearsal from my father's office, I wasn't allowed in. The porter, whom I had known for thirty years, clearly found the situation painful and apologised: "The boss's wife said you're not allowed into the *Festspielhaus* any more. Frau Pitz will bring you the tickets." Arno was surprised and asked: "But this is the son of the *Festspiele* boss. Can't he go in?" At that moment Frau Pitz arrived. She wanted to avoid any lengthy and painful discussion and invited us into her office, which was crammed with flowers and presents – small tokens from those fortunate enough to attend dress rehearsals or performances. For the first time in my life I had to sign a receipt for the tickets for myself and my guest. When I introduced Arno as a friend from Israel, my father's colleague reacted with exaggerated friendliness. "Herr Barenboim is an Israeli too," she declared, enthusiastically. Evidently a new chapter in Bayreuth's tactical philosemitism had opened. When I asked whether we could see my father, she answered that she would first have to discuss that with his wife Gudrun. "Then I'll tell you at the beginning of the first interval."

Without asking for permission I showed Arno the *Festspielhaus*. People either returned my greetings unenthusiastically or not at all. My presence was obviously undesirable. Arno quickly picked up on it and I told him about my father. The story clearly moved him. After the first act interval we went back into the auditorium: I was peered at as if I were a half-wit. Behind my back I heard, "He's back, he's made it up with his father" and similar stupid whisperings.

Finally the curtain went up on Act Two and in spite of myself I was enthralled yet again by Wagner's *Tristan* music. I completely forgot the coldness of my reception. Arno was thrilled by the acoustics and the stage and said during the second interval: "Let's just go up and say hello to your father!" Without announcing ourselves, I led Arno to my father's office. In front of his door his secretary intercepted us and requested in some excitement that first a time be agreed on. I answered drily: "I'm sure my father would receive Mr Adar from Israel." At this magic word the secretary threw herself into a perfect paroxysm of obsequiousness, and after a few minutes we were allowed to see my father. Arno said in greeting, almost provocatively: "I would never have dreamt it: me sitting in the Bayreuth *Festspielhaus*." My father misunderstood the remark, felt flattered and answered: "We have a great tradition of Jewish conductors, and now Barenboim too." I restrained my comments. After two minutes the secretary burst in and reminded my father of an appointment, a familiar trick Father used when he wanted to get rid of troublesome guests. Generously, he allowed us to visit Barenboim in the interval.

I didn't particularly want to join the queue of fans waiting in front of Barenboim's room, but did so, more for Arno's sake. He spoke to Barenboim in modern Hebrew – quite new and unexpected sounds in the Grail temple. Arno introduced me to Barenboim as the son of the *Festspiele* boss. I spoke of Aunt Friedelind, who had known him since he was eleven. The conductor remained diplomatically silent; he knew my aunt was *persona non grata* for my father.

The following day I met Meyer-Oertel and Maximilian Kojetinsky in the Siegfried Wagner House, in order, as agreed, to discuss the Dresden and Paris *Tannhäuser* versions. Afterwards I showed Meyer-Oertel round the house. I noticed that several valuable family objects had already disappeared, although the final division of the inheritance had still not taken place. After visiting the "Führer's room", we came to my grandmother's bedroom, where we saw photos of my Uncle Wieland in a Nazi helmet and my father as the Führer's soldier, standing on the bedside table just as they had years ago. Meyer-Oertel understood my horror and my wish to leave the house immediately.

It was then on the *Festspielhügel* that I understood why he had engaged me as his colleague: he had totally succumbed to Bayreuth-connection fever. Thank God Arno was nearby, who had closely observed what had happened. We understood one another without saying a word.

After the dress rehearsal of my father's *Meistersinger* I set off for Italy. There the first meeting with Teresina's family awaited me. The first separation from Teresina had seemed like an eternity to me, although it had only lasted eleven days. Smirking, Arno hoped I'd have a good time. "Italian families, like Jewish families, are run by women," were his parting words.

The 24 July 1981 will always remain in my memory. On that day a new chapter in my life began: my integration into Teresina's family in Cerro Maggiore near Milan. It was not without friction. Being from such a broken home it was not easy for me to fit into the Rossettis'. Also, knowing Italy only as a tourist, I had to overcome a few prejudices. It made me realise just how questionable my social and cultural conditioning by Bayreuth had been. Added to this was the fact that my divorce had not yet gone through and I didn't know how a Catholic family would react to this case history. And last but not least, my professional prospects were pretty thin.

Teresina assured me that the fact that I was German didn't bother her family. But nevertheless the SS had had a base in Legnano, very near Cerro Maggiore, and had terrorised the population. With my heart pounding, we drove into Via Saffi, where Mamma Antonietta, Papa Antonio, Uncle Luigi and his wife Maria, and Teresina's sister Francesca and her husband Enzo and their little daughter Silvia were waiting for us. I was scrutinised by curious, expectant eyes and they all concentrated totally on me. I was received as Teresina's fiancé. Teresina had advised me not to blurt out everything at once and mention my still pending divorce, as I had originally planned. I restrained myself: partly out of concern for her father's serious illness.

The *fidanzato* (fiancé) Goffredo was automatically assigned a place in the home – the idea of having the future son-in-law put up in a hotel would have seemed absurd to Teresina's family. In the living room the evening meal was waiting on a beautifully decorated, long marble table. Mamma Antonietta gave one of the unforgettable proofs of her cooking skills, which immediately won me over to her. I earned a few "merits" in her eyes too, when much to the amusement of the whole table I helped myself liberally to every dish. To my joy I was soon to learn that food was a valuable item in the culture of my new environment. There was a relaxed, jolly atmosphere at the table, such as I had never known before. But I was equally amazed by the intensity of discussions which the family members were able to have. I also relished the fact that Richard Wagner was not the key topic of conversation: Uncle Luigi, Mamma Antonietta's brother and onetime musician in the local band, turned after a few well-considered remarks on Wagner's orchestration to his favourite composers, Verdi and Puccini. Wagner was, to my relief, only one of the many music subjects.

The family were at the liveliest on the subject of "mother and child".

In Italy children are the centre of attention for female members of the family. And so the then nine-month-old Silvia soon became the main subject of discussion. It almost made me a little jealous, when Mamma Antonietta, Francesca or Teresina said to Silvia: "*Fai un bel sorriso!*" [Give us a nice smile.]

How unkindly in contrast my sister and I had been treated. Again and again, often with inner reluctance, I compared experiences from my past with the gift of my new family to live with a unique intensity in the "here and now". Confused and happy, I started acclimatising myself in Cerro Maggiore. The introductions to relations and the festivities each introduction entailed were endless. There was no question of any intimate time alone with Teresina. But when she looked at me with an understanding smile, I felt the warmth of the reception and gladly gave in to it.

Then at a stroke everything changed. At the beginning of August Teresina's father was admitted to the Legnano hospital. There we learned that the bone cancer from which he was suffering would not give him much more time. From that moment on I witnessed what it can mean when a family is united through grief. There was no longer a moment when Papa Antonio was not being cared for by Mamma Antonietta, Teresina, Francesca, his still living four brothers Ernesto, Franco, Angelo and Luigi and his sister Giannina with their respective spouses, children and grandchildren. It was the first time I had been present when someone died. The silence was only interrupted by prayers in Papa Antonio's sickroom, by the shouts of the children in the corridor or the nurses dashing to and fro. Seldom, but then with great convulsions, one of the relations burst into tears. Teresina's constant suffering moved me in a way I had never known before. Mamma Antonietta, who sought comfort in prayer in the hours in the hospital room, when her husband was sleeping, held the family together. As always, she forgot herself and lived with superhuman strength for us. She remained silent and showed us with great, calm dignity, how to overcome this sense of paralysing helplessness, pain, sadness and vain hope.

When Papa Antonio had moments free of pain, I could talk to him. His concern was only for Teresina, who was suffering too much pain to talk to him, and needed all her energies not to break down constantly in tears. One night, when I was alone with Papa Antonio, we spoke frankly about my coming marriage to his daughter. In view of his imminent death I now felt responsible for Mamma Antonietta and Teresina and told him: "Don't worry, Papa, I'll be there for Teresina and Mamma."

At that moment I felt such a loss at my own fatherlessness: my father had never been there for me, while Papa Antonio, who had accepted me as a son, now lay dying. In my despair I rang my father, intending to ask him to come. But his secretary informed me: "Herr Wagner can't be contacted, he is in a meeting." I left my number with the secretary, along with a request for my father to ring back. He never did.

That night something strange happened. A notary from Legnano who was on the same floor in the hospital as Papa Antonio, regularly wandered around the corridor of the intensive care ward. I don't know how, but he had learned that I was a great-grandson of Richard Wagner. As he was a passionate Wagnerian, he wanted at all costs to get into conversation with me. So softly, but quite audibly for me in the sickroom, he sang in the corridor with pure intonation the story of the Grail out of *Lohengrin*, in Italian. That even amused Papa Antonio, who faintly smiling said: "*È matto, ma simpatico, il notaio!*" [He's mad, but nice, the notary.] Papa Antonio knew some of Wagner's most popular pieces; we had listened to Toscanini's 1954 recording before he went to the hospital. "Tell him he's got to stop singing Wagner in the middle of the night, or the others will get annoyed," he said.

I hurried out into the corridor and saw a scene Fellini couldn't have improved on. The notary and Heldentenor *manqué* stood there in operatic pose, with transfigured gaze, waiting for an imaginary Grail miracle. "Bravo, bravo!" I said and shook his hand with melodramatic gratitude. The self-styled "Lohengrin" replied: "How does one as great-grandson of the great composer experience mankind?" I answered: "I'll tell you if you promise me to let people sleep now at three in the morning." He sighed and said ecstatically: "*Che bello. A domani, maestro!*" But I didn't have the time then and even less the inner calm to talk about Wagner. The notary understood and showed a delicate sympathy for our difficult time.

Only three nights later Papa Antonio died. I shall never forget Teresina's horror and shock, when the coffin was sealed. His death touched me, too: for the first time I became painfully aware that our life must one day end. I began to respect just being alive.

Despair had triggered off in Teresina a crisis in faith. Who was this God who had let her father die in terrible pain from bone cancer at the age of fifty-nine? In this mood we went to a place that was to become a refuge for us: to Cannero, to the Order of Augustinian Fathers of the Assumption, who lived over Lago Maggiore on a rock with a splendid view of the lake. Over these difficult days one of the priests, Giuliano, became an important helper and friend. No subject was excluded: Teresina's religious crisis, my indiscriminate aversion to Christianity, in particular to the Catholic Church, my divorce. I had to acknowledge with some shame, what stupid prejudices I had against priests too.

Giuliano was not only a warmhearted, modest discussion partner with a lively vision of the Bible and Christianity, who possessed wide-ranging culture. I realised that the Catholic Church does not merely consist of a repressive hierarchy, but lives in worldwide spiritual dialogue with the other monotheistic religions and with atheists. Teresina's crisis of faith and the discussions with Giuliano strengthened in me the need to look into religious questions again. I saw that I had made it too easy for myself when I criticised from outside, instead of helping to bring about a little of the Sermon on the Mount in my own world.

Once back in Wuppertal, I made contact with the Franciscan monk Ising, who was anything but conventional. In a district of 128 different communities of faith and sects, he had turned his Catholic community into one of the liveliest and best-attended spiritual centres. He raged against the Pope, the ecclesiastical hierarchy and corrupt priests and considered his brother, Leonardo Boff, the Brazilian liberation theologian, Hans Küng and other rebels in the Catholic Church to be true Christians. He spoke with such sensuality about men and women, marriage and bringing up children, that I couldn't believe my ears.

On 31 October, Reformation Day of all days, I decided to enter the Catholic Church.

For the event Mamma Antonietta went on her first flight, and Bettina Fehr also came as witness. Father Ising, who later converted to Protestantism, got married and became a father, said to me after the ceremony: "The Christian church is a heterogeneous universe. You will never subject yourself unconditionally to the Church and its hierarchical ideology. But the Church needs heretics like you, otherwise it would die as it did in the Nazi period! Just don't give up your dialogue with the Jews. That is part of your life." He was to be proved right.

CHAPTER FIFTEEN

THE MONASTERY AND THE BANK

In the weeks immediately after my return from Italy, and conversations with Father Ising, my preoccupation with my life as dramaturg and director in the Wuppertal Opera House seemed pointless. By the time Meyer-Oertel scrapped a *Mahagonny* production that I had planned with Arno Adar, and which had been announced as my production for the coming season, I had already mentally served notice. I was simply waiting for the right moment to leave Wuppertal. I needed another job and one came up quite by chance.

I had met the former director of the Deutsche Bank, Hans H Asmus, at a premiere party in Wuppertal. Asmus is a keen friend of the arts and thinks highly of my theatre work. Despite any objection on my part, he saw me as the future boss of Bayreuth and opined: "What you need is training and ordeal by fire in the Deutsche Bank! The German intendants have no idea about balancing the books. If you can read balance sheets and music scores, the world is your oyster!"

He had no sooner made the suggestion than the deed was done and on 16 December 1981 I stood, dressed as a junior banker, in front of Adolf Sievers, one of the three personnel directors of the Deutsche Bank in Frankfurt am Main. The meeting had nothing to do with banking. Mr Sievers was of a cheerful amiability and sensitive refinement and steered our one-hour talk in a direction that made me almost forget why I had made the appointment with him. Like me, he loved Mozart and understood interpretation to a degree which surprised even a professional of the classical music scene like myself. For him Otto

Klemperer or Bruno Walter was a question of conscience. When I finally reminded him of the reason why I had come, he asked laughing: "What do you understand of the banking business?"

"Nothing," I answered, "and I never want to be a banker, only to learn how to handle money. And I need a job because, for various reasons, the Wuppertal theatre doesn't interest me any more."

Sievers retorted: "Seeing that you, as an exotic bird, will first have to prove yourself in our cage, I'll give you a half-year trial period. Where do you want to go?" With my imminent divorce in mind and a desire to live as close to Cerro Maggiore as possible, I suggested Munich.

The Christmas of 1981 was the first with my new family. It was also the first Christmas without Papa Antonio, and a pall of melancholy hung in the air relieved only by my then one-year-old niece Silvia. As every year, the family went to midnight mass on Christmas Eve in the overcrowded main church of Cerro Maggiore and during the following two Christmas days everyone met in Enzo and Francesca's house. Despite the sadness over the loss of their father, people danced and sang, determined to give little Silvia a merry Christmas. This merriment, out of love and respect for the children, made me wistful, reminding me of the quarrelsome Christmases in my family, in which children were assigned the role of decorative extras.

It occurred to me that this was perhaps the fundamental difference between the Italian Catholic and the German Protestant family: the former being matriarchal and the latter patriarchal. In my Italian family, mother and child form an inviolable unit – the cult of Maria. Mamma Antonietta explained to me that respect for the child is a fundamental value that she had passed on to her daughters.

It was clear that, after the death of my father-in-law, I was expected to support the family with all my strength. It was taken for granted that, as Teresina's future husband, I would be completely integrated into the family. What objection could anyone have to joining a family such as this, which stuck together in good times and bad and which accepted me as I was? Until that moment it was something I had never experienced.

Before long I had the opportunity of proving my loyalty to my new family when I learned that Teresina and her mother would soon have to leave their home. It was the last thing we needed after the death of

Papa Antonio: I was not yet divorced, a probationary trainee of the Deutsche Bank and still not yet officially finished at Wuppertal. But no matter, we went looking for an apartment. With the courage of a lover I finally signed a purchase contract on an apartment, despite my lack of assets. I was relying on the fact that Father would pay me my inheritance which, for the moment, was only putting money into the lawyers' pockets.

The year 1982 began dramatically in every way. With the help of Father Ising I had found a room in the Franciscan monastery in the Annagasse, Munich. My furniture wouldn't fit into the room in there, so I had to store it in Dodo Koch's garage in Wuppertal; it later ended up in a furniture warehouse in Bonn. In mid January I ended my contract with the Wuppertal theatre, to the horror of Aunt Friedelind and many friends. My last task in Wuppertal was to organise a matinée. With great inner detachment I saw what Meyer-Oertel had thought up for himself as director of *Tannhäuser*.

Relieved rather than feeling any regret at leaving the German stage, I travelled to Munich at the end of January. After I had unloaded my car, Prelate Guardian invited me into his room, looked at me somewhat sceptically and declared: "Brother Ising has told me you were working in Wuppertal as director and dramaturg. Now you want to work in the Deutsche Bank and live with us. Theatre, church, bank: that sounds like a novel. But it is a monastery here. Please respect that!"

In return for a nominal rent, I was given a relatively large room on the first floor of the monastery, which looked down into the garden. It wasn't easy for me to share a bath and telephone with high school children and students – they looked on me as a rather strange old man. But I knew that the coming months would only be a transitionary phase in my life.

First I had to visit the personnel office of the Deutsche Bank Bayern, in the Ungererstrasse. One of the personnel heads explained to me that I was now number 42,411 of the Deutsche Bank and as such had to give up my former identity. When I mentioned my Munich address, it caused roars of laughter. Bank and monastery – that was almost provocation to a member of the great Deutsche Bank family. I got the impression there was more to come.

On 1 February 1982 I began working as trainee of the branch in the

Schwanthaler Strasse. The director welcomed me warmly and made no attempt to hide his amazement at my former life. He assigned me a narrow place between the many desks behind the counter, and I was immediately let loose on humankind. As I hadn't even the slightest idea what I was supposed to be doing, I copied my new colleagues and played the part of the experienced banker to the customers. When I didn't know what to do – as was frequently the case at first – I would say, with a friendly smile: "Excuse me, my colleague is more experienced in this matter," and turn for help to one of my colleagues, who with a certain amusement helped me out of often embarrassing situations.

At noon, walking from the branch to the main Deutsche Bank canteen on the Promenadenplatz, I was struck by three things along Schwanthaler Strasse: banks, brothels and dubious export and import shops. The owners and employees of the latter enterprises formed the core of the clients I had to deal with in the first stage of my rather awkward training. They had no sympathy for my lack of knowledge and reminded me of it with a brutality I have never before experienced. I put up with it, thinking of Brecht's *Dreigroschenoper*, but found that the reality had nothing to do with the world of theatre. After working their night shift on the streets, the ladies of the horizontal trade would come into the bank and sullenly tip their earnings out of their cleavages, growling at me when I didn't know immediately what I was supposed to do. It took some effort not to pay them back in the same coin.

When it finally got too much for me I complained to my superior. In reply, the deputy branch manager gave me a lecture: "The fact that your name is Wagner, that you've studied musicology and philosophy and worked in the theatre, is totally irrelevant. Here only one thing counts: that you stop costing us money and finally close some deals. With whom, why and how, doesn't interest us. And if you don't like it, there's the door! There's a long line of people outside it who would do your work without complaining."

I said nothing, simply giving him a withering look, for which he paid me back whenever he got the opportunity. He was a classic "crawler": kowtowing to his superiors and trampling those beneath. As such, he was no different to most little bosses I've met. I soon worked out how I could avoid being affected by them though: I pretended I knew the big bosses and anyway my academic title impressed them. Ultimately they even believed I was on the threshold of a long career and held back.

The branch manager was, in his Bavarian stolidity, rather predictable. He taught me how to arrange credit loans and then expected immediate results. Every morning before the bank opened he asked his employees for the "racing lists" – their signed agreements. I did not fulfil expectations and saw with some horror how my colleagues targeted foreigners in particular, talking them into risky overdrafts and shamelessly exploiting their language difficulties.

I started working against these methods and became immune to the daily reproaches for not having concluded any deals. As scarcely any of my colleagues spoke foreign languages, I was often called in as interpreter for Turks, Italians, Yugoslavs, French or Americans. I warned poor clients against signing long-term policies with the branch, especially if it were clear that they would be incapable of repaying the respective debt. Word of this got around among Turkish, Yugoslav and Italian workers and to the annoyance of my boss they came to me in droves. I had to see to them in a side room – foreigners without fat wallets were not welcome.

It happened that these groups brought me presents out of gratitude and invited me for meals after work. When this reached the ears of the deputy branch manager, he bellowed through the bank, to the amusement of clients and employees alike: "We are not a charity, Wagner!" and shunted me off to the cellar to sort savings leaflets. My protests were to no avail. The only comfort was that my time in the Schwanthaler Strasse would soon be over.

In an attempt to stop the situation getting me down, I started looking around for colleagues who thought as I did. And so I got to know my friends Florian Lauermann, an excellent organist and lawyer, Günther Maier and Axel Ohse. With them I could discuss my experiences in the Schwanthaler Strasse and they helped me fit into the banking business. At that time nothing was further beyond my ability than understanding balances. But I realised that economic knowledge and experience would help me to understand social power structures better. I began reading and understanding the financial section of the newspapers and this newly acquired knowledge was soon to prove helpful in winding up my divorce and later in the tough negotiations with my father's lawyers, on the payment of my small inheritance.

When I left the Schwanthaler Strasse branch at the end of April 1982, I felt I had been living on a different planet. From May, working in the Ungererstrasse in the heart of bank administration, I was initiated into the secrets and techniques of banking. As I was only tolerated as an observer, mostly reluctantly, people preferred it if I didn't disturb them with questions, which meant that I could finally pursue my own interests. To the amazement of my banking colleagues, I spent my time under the desk, reading the Jerusalem Bible Old Testament with growing enthusiasm, and the works of Shalom Ben Chorin, whose *Brother Jesus: The Nazarene From The Jewish Viewpoint* impressed me in particular, as did Pinchas Lapides' books on Bible translations. Back in the monastery, after my boring day at work, I would continue my reading of the Jewish Bible in the German translations of Moses Mendelssohn and Martin Buber and compare them with the New Testament. It made my isolation in Germany bearable and later my integration in Italy easier. It became clearer and clearer to me how inconceivable Christianity was without Judaism and I grew more remote from Bayreuth, with its Wagnerian pseudo-religion.

In May I visited my sister, who was living with her husband in the elegant Schönbergstrasse in Munich. Both were working for Leo Kirch, the future media tycoon, who was already powerful. Eva didn't understand my professional and private direction, but unfortunately it never came to a frank discussion. The gulf between my spiritual development and my new family on the one hand, and Eva's opera/film world on the other, was unbridgeable.

After my bogus activity in the administration department I finally moved to the Bavarian headquarters of the Deutsche Bank on the Promenadenplatz. For two months I worked my way through the foreign department. There was no question of the much-quoted trainee principle "learning on the job". I was allowed to observe what the others did and only showed interest because I hoped to get a place in the branch of the Deutsche Bank in Milan or in an Italian bank.

The monotony at work, squabbles with lawyers over the divorce settlement and the struggle for my inheritance were all left far behind, however, when I drove at weekends to Teresina in Cerro Maggiore or met friends in Munich. Unlike my colleagues at the bank, I had no desire to join the trendy set with their CSU party and BMW cars. I felt removed from the opera world too. It was more important to improve my Italian for my future with Teresina and attend marketing courses that might perhaps one day help me.

To the outside world I continued to feign great interest in the banking business, determined to prove that, contrary to all the predictions of friends and relations, I would stick it out in the Deutsche Bank. The first positive evaluations of my banking activities amused me. Adolf Sievers was the only one I did not need to pretend to and he constantly encouraged me to keep going.

At the beginning of June I happened to be passing my sister's home and dropped in to find out how she was, as in May she had given birth to her son, Antoine, in the USA. My brother-in-law proudly showed me the baby's American passport with the name Antoine Wagner-Pasquier.

In August and September 1982 I was initiated into the deeper mysteries of capitalism in the property department of the Deutsche Bank. I also visited the Munich stock exchange. The stockbrokers, screaming hysterically and rushing around like hungry wolves, brought Brecht once more to mind: he saw no moral difference between bank robbery and bank business. But to be fair, in the Deutsche Bank in Munich there were superiors and colleagues like Günther Maier and Axel Ohse who with great commitment provided me with essential insights into the banking business. I am still in contact with them today. They understood that my professional life would not end in a bank, and found me – the exotic – a welcome change in their professional life day to day.

I was bored to death in the property administration department too. My only comfort was the monthly cheque. In my free time I again went into Wagner's idea of religion in *Parsifal* – it now seemed dishonest to me.

I wanted at all costs to work in the theatre again, so I went to see Alberto Zedda, who was influential in Pesaro and in the left-wing cultural scene in Italy. I also consulted the conductor Claudio Abbado. Both assured me they were convinced of my professional competence, but did not help me in my search for a job.

Meanwhile the dispute over my inheritance entered a new phase.

First of all my father demanded that I hand back the rolls of film from the Nazi period. They were still being stored with Beatrix's parents, but in January 1983 he had his lawyer's chauffeur collect the originals from me. I sent the copies to my sister, making it clear to her how potentially explosive the material was that she was now guarding. I had further use for it. Without a projector I inspected the films once again by holding them up to the light: Hitler with the Wagner family in the Wahnfried garden and in the *Festspielhaus*, Father as a sturdy member of the Hitler Youth on the Bayreuth Sternplatz, his arm upraised. What unfortunate intimacy and foolish merriment! Then pictures from Nuremberg of the Nazi rallies with my grandmother and other family members, being cheered by fanatical masses.

The divorce hearing took place before a Munich court and was remarkably unpleasant. Beatrix and I left the court building like two strangers – after a relationship of almost eleven years.

But now there was no turning back for Teresina and me. As I hadn't been married in church the first time round, there was nothing to prevent us having a classic Italian wedding. In the months up to the big day, 3 July 1983, I became aware of just how important the marriage ceremony was to my new family. After an atheist upbringing and the spiritual and ethical neglect in Bayreuth, the Catholic rites seemed very strange to me, as did the various other important feastdays and holidays. I envied Teresina and her family, especially Mamma Antonietta, their deeply rooted piety, that had and has nothing to do with bigotry or dependence on the Catholic Church. In time I learned to understand that what my new family possessed was a much more realistic philosophy of life than that of my pseudo-Protestant, idealistic, German worldview, in which the idea has nothing to do with human nature in all its inconsistencies. Irrespective of all the dogma and the omnipresence of the Catholic Church, I realised that in my new family a strongly pronounced individualism prevailed, which made any form of state and ecclesiastical tutelage impossible. Fascinated, I discovered the capacity of my new family environment for living life here and now with all the sensuality of Mediterranean culture, that reflects by no means just Christianity, but also pre-Christian rites and myths. Much of what I had believed began to waver. I started one of my many, often painful self-re-evaluations, that still go on today.

In February 1983, even before the wedding, I had agreed in Munich to a disadvantageous settlement of my inheritance, mainly because I had to make a downpayment on our future home together in Cerro Maggiore. Bad though the settlement was for me, it nonetheless meant a further step in the direction of Italy.

It was also in February that the celebrations began for the centenary of Richard Wagner's death. Although I lay low in the bank, my Bayreuth past still came back to haunt me. I received idiotic offers from the media to appear as a great-grandson, all of which I rejected. An enquiry from the Munich *Abendzeitung* seemed to be of somewhat higher calibre: I was asked my opinion on Wagner's work and influence and I thought I could answer that with a clear conscience. But, yet again it was only the gossip about who would succeed my father as head of the *Festspiele* that was printed.

The bookshop windows were crammed with Wagner literature, although the only significant title was the new edition of Hartmut Zelinsky's *Richard Wagner: Ein Deutsches Thema*. On the other hand, I found the commentaries superficial in the ten-volume Wagner edition by Dieter Borchmeyer, who tried in particular to gain status in Bayreuth with his remarks about 'The Jews In Music'. Yet again there was a Wagner boom in the book market. But I wanted to have nothing to do with it.

Meanwhile I had advanced in the bank from the lowest of the low to potential management material, and pressure to perform increased. In February I was allowed to speak in the Bayerischer Hof Hotel in Munich before Dr Siegfried Gropper, known as "God the Father", director of the Deutsche Bank in Munich, and his humble retinue from affiliated Bavarian branches. My topic was "Strike Insurance" from a liberal-left viewpoint. A few days before I had assisted Peter Glotz of the Bavarian SPD as electoral assistant in Munich's working-class district of Haselberg. Contrary to expectation, my talk was calmly received.

Afterwards there was a dinner to which the trainees had been invited. Many of them wanted to seize the opportunity to play up to the big boss – all jolly and deferential. It brought to mind Heinrich Mann's novel, *Man Of Straw*. I was under no pressure to gain status and so conversed in a relaxed way with Gropper, even daring to contradict him when he entered the – for him – uncertain territory of "art and music" and started giving me some private coaching on Wagner. My friends among the trainees enjoyed the spectacle, while the others just stood agog at such lack of respect.

The meeting had one distinct advantage. I could present myself as a specialist on Italy, although I didn't even hint at the true reason for my interest. Lo and behold, after I had finished my basic training in the Munich credit department, my request for transfer was granted. The Munich bankers were glad to see me go and found me a new job at the Deutsche Bank in Milan. I could now plan my move to Cerro Maggiore.

CHAPTER SIXTEEN

MY ITALIAN WEDDING

Most of my friends from Germany had already arrived for the *Polterabend*, the pre-wedding party, on 2 July 1983, the evening before my marriage. My new family weren't familiar with this tradition. In Antonio Lazzati's little summerhouse with its huge garden, we celebrated in glorious weather until far into the wedding day. In the morning, at the church ceremony, it was mainly the Italian friends and relations who came into Mamma Antonietta's home. I was only allowed to talk to Teresina through a locked door, as the groom could only see the bride again in the church in front of the altar. However strange such rituals seemed at the time, I kept to them and throughout the day, Uncle Luigi discreetly whispered instructions. The wedding guests gathered on the piazza in front of the Borretta church.

My extended Italian family created a merry atmosphere that prevented me feeling any regret that my father had declined his invitation for reasons which were quite transparent.

My mother, however, did come and she accompanied me to the altar, with Teresina following shortly after with her father's eldest brother. She and Mamma Antonietta were visibly upset that Papa Antonio could not be there, but as she came towards me to the wedding march from *Lohengrin*, which the Cerro Maggiore choir had studied for us in Italian, the church resplendent with roses, the months since July 1981 flashed again through my mind. Curious and happy, to my right in front of the altar sat my witnesses, Eva and my friend Louis Landuyt, a singer and music teacher from Luxembourg. The choice of my sister as witness represented my hope that we could start our relationship afresh. Behind us, in the nave, sat my mother and my cousin Christa as representative of my mother's relations and behind them Bettina Fehr and the friends who had helped me in the difficult transition period from theatre to bank: Eckard, Rosi, Dieter, Ulf, Dodo, Walter, Maureen, Florian and their partners. On the left side sat my brother-in-law Enzo and my sister-in-law Francesca, behind them Teresina's relations on the paternal and maternal side, including Mamma Antonietta and her brother Luigi, and Ernesto, Papa Antonio's third brother, all of whom are still particularly close to me. They knew from the beginning that it would be difficult for me, as a foreigner, to be fully integrated into Italy society.

The marriage ceremony was performed in German and Italian by our friend Father Giuliano. Teresina and I had chosen the text from I Corinthians 13.XIII on the love that overcomes all obstacles. I was caught totally unprepared by the request to read out a text from the Bible for our German guests. The words were printed so small that I could barely decipher them. Added to this was my profound emotion, and so I improvised, much to the amusement of guests better acquainted with the Bible. When Francesca, quite unexpectedly, sang the Gounod 'Ave Maria' with wonderful tenderness and pure intonation, accompanied on the organ by Franco Pasquali, the leader of the *Ars Nova* choir, there were few in the church who were not moved.

In those moments, full of hope, a new chapter began in my life. Behind me lay crises. I had even toyed with the idea of taking on Teresina's family name in order to make a visible break with my Bayreuth past, but she convinced me that this would be a pointless denial of my identity and that I should soon continue my path in my actual professional milieu. When I came out of the church with my new wife to Mendelssohn's wedding march, which I had selected in preference to my great-grandfather's wedding music, I felt a completely different Wagner.

The exalted mood was abruptly broken by loud cries from the Italian wedding guests and curious on-lookers: "*Evviva gli sposi!*" [here's to the newly-weds] and a relentless hail of rice showered down on us, and

Back view of
Villa Wahnfried

Winifred Wagner saying goodbye to the
children as they leave Bayreuth station for
their holidays in the early 1930s. L-r:
Wolfgang, Verena, Friedelind, Wieland and
their nanny Emma (in the background)
who devoted fifty years to the family

Siegfried (left) with Arturo Toscanini in
June 1930 during the *Festspiele*

Siegfried and his wife Winifred in the grounds of Villa Wahnfried, 1924, the year the *Festspiele*
reopened after World War I, with their children. L-r: Wolfgang, Siegfried, Verena, Winifred,
Friedelind and Wieland

The racist writer, Joseph Arthur Graf Gobineau (1816-1882), in 1880: one of the many forbidden topics of conversation after 1945

Parsifal by Fidus, 1890. Despite being brilliantly innovative even Richard Wagner's early works were antisemitic including the *Ring*, *Parsifal* and *Meistersingers von Nürnberg*

Houston Stewart Chamberlain (1855-1927): the English racial theoretician and one of Adolph Hitler's mentors. He married Richard and Cosima Wagner's daughter, Eva

Alexander von Spring and Heinz Tietjen (standing) with Wilhelm Furtwängler, Winifred and Arturo Toscanini. Taken in the garden of the *Festspielhaus* in 1930

Festspiele artwork, 1908-1927

Winifred, Hitler and Wieland
ahead of Wolfgang and Hitler's
guards in the villa grounds.
Adopting the role of father
figure to Wieland and Wolfgang
after Siegfried's death in 1930,
Hitler felt very much at ease at
Villa Wahnfried whether
attending official functions or
relaxing in a family atmosphere

Winifred greeting Hitler at the front entrance of
the *Festspielhaus*

Hitler, Winifred and some of her guests in the
Siegfried Wagner House. It was extended
especially for the Führer

Bust of Richard Wagner by Hitler's favourite sculptor, Arno Breker. A similar bust was shown in the Nazi-occupied Paris in 1942, then put in the festival's park in 1955. A third copy in the *Festspielpark* in 1955 created some understandable protest

Winifred, Goebbels and Hitler, 3 August 1938

Crowd gathering outside the *Festspielhügel* to see the Führer at the window of the Wagner family box

Verena, Hitler and Friedelind

Lebrecht Collection

Wieland, Uncle Wolf and
Wolfgang, 1935, at Villa
Wahnfried

Lehrecht Collection

Wieland at the piano with Wolfgang

Below: Wolfgang in Nazi uniform, proud of his
active role for the fatherland. Hitler even
overcame a phobia to visit him in hospital when
he was injured and despatched his private
ambulance to bring Wolfgang back to Berlin.
Wolfgang has always held dear the memory of his
times with Uncle Wolf

1938: in the
uniform of
Arbeitsdienst

Taken in
September 1939,
the week the
Nazis invaded
Poland

Wieland and Wolfgang in Wahnfried Park,
1945

L-r: Wieland, Verena, Winifred, Heinz Tietjen (artistic director of the festival from 1930 until 1944. Wolfgang became his assistant in Berlin in the 1940s), Wolfgang and Friedelind

Margarethe Matzenauer (1881-1963): famous international Wagner singer who took a role in *Twilight Of The Gods* in Bayreuth, 1911

Hermann Weil (1876-1949): sang leading Wagner roles in Bayreuth from 1911-1925 as well as internationally

Henriette Gottlieb (1884-1943?), murdered in Auschwitz. Gottlieb also sang a role in *Twilight Of The Gods* in Bayreuth

Ottilie Metzger-Lattermann (1878-1943): famous Wagner singer of the twenties, also died in Auschwitz

Gottfried's mother Ellen (left) and her brother Gustav (right) at their confirmation in 1934 with their parents, Adolf and Thora Drexel. Gustav is now Gottfried's only surviving uncle

Ellen Drexel. She gave up a career in dance when she married Wolfgang, something she regretted after their divorce. This picture summed up for Gottfried her eternal innocence, something which made her a victim of Winifred's powerful personality

Wolfgang and Ellen in Wahnfried Park, April 1945

all of a sudden wild merriment erupted. Before driving off to the wedding feast, we laid roses from the church decorations on Papa Antonio's grave and on the graves of other deceased relations – such contrast to my family's indifference toward the dead, who were only remembered on official occasions, with an eye to the media.

Our honeymoon took us to a magical place on Crete, the cradle of European and Mediterranean culture. Surrounded by sweet-smelling, lush, flowering woodland and the chirping of crickets, in the following days we forgot the rest of the world and our worries. In August 1983, however, we went to Bayreuth together with Mamma Antonietta and Italian friends. As Father did not want to receive us in his house, Aunt Friedelind invited us to dinner in the chic Schloss Tiergarten Hotel. On hearing that we had no tickets for a *Festspiele* performance, she rang Father up against our will and demanded three tickets for *Tristan und Isolde*.

I took Teresina and Mamma Antonietta on a guided tour of Bayreuth, through Wahnfried Park, Villa Wahnfried and the *Festspielpark* where there was whispering behind my back. The *Festspiele* court lackeys, once they were sure no-one was watching them, greeted us with insincere friendliness.

In the *Festspielhaus* we encountered my father's army of yes men. When I asked to see him, to introduce Teresina and Mamma Antonietta, I was told that he could see only Teresina and me briefly. In outrage I threw the *Festspiele* tickets on the desk and left the room, shouting: "Either my father receives my wife, my mother-in-law and me or I leave the *Festspielhügel* immediately. Who does he think he is? My mother-in-law is not going to be discriminated against here!" The guests waiting in the corridors pointedly turned their backs on us. When I asked Mamma Antonietta indignantly to leave the *Festspielhaus* immediately with us, she pulled me back with a strong grip and said: "Calm down. You're going with Teresina to your father: she certainly won't have the the opportunity again to meet her father-in-law. Don't think of me now." Gunda, my loving foster aunt, who thank God was on duty that afternoon, pulled Mamma Antonietta down beside her next to her desk in the telephone exchange and pushed Teresina and me onto the stairs leading to the first floor, in the direction of my father's office. When

Teresina and I arrived there, Gudrun greeted us with a gracious smile and offered me her hand to kiss. I shook it. Shortly after we met Father. Without looking at us, he shook our hands. Then he started talking without pause and in a strong Upper Franconian accent, which Teresina could not understand, tactlessly comparing his second marriage with mine. I replied calmly, but firmly: "Everyone has to make his own decisions." He didn't go into this. I remained silent for Teresina's sake, but tried to persuade Father by meaningful looks to change the subject. Instead he continued praising the second marriage as a source of renewal for a man. This torrent of words was only interrupted by one of his secretaries, who flung open the door to indicate to us that we should now go. Turning to my father she said in a thick local accent: "Herr Wagner, you're wanted on the stage!" Father bowed deeply and hastily on saying goodbye, so that he didn't have to look us in the eye, and tore out of the room. As we left the room I recognised the secretary: she was the daughter of one of my nannies. We had met many times previously, but she didn't seem to know me now.

Teresina and I collected Mamma Antonietta from Gunda's office and, as the performance was soon to begin, we hurried to our seats. Briefly I explained to Mamma Antonietta the story of the first act of *Tristan und Isolde*, while we were heading for the stuffy family box where Gudrun had rather tactfully seated me next to the lawyer who had drawn up the inheritance settlement.

During the intervals we went to the *Festspiele* restaurant, where most of those present pointedly ignored us, apart from Philip Wults, who was writing a history of the Wagner family and appreciated with great sensitivity what was happening. I waited impatiently for the end of the performance; the brief visit to my Father and his lackeys had put me in a bad mood. I wanted to prevent Mamma Antonietta and Teresina taking home an even worse impression of Bayreuth.

Mamma Antonietta was pleased with the music and Ponnelle's production. However, when I asked her after the performance how she found her stay in Bayreuth, she answered concerned: "The opera performance was beautiful. But I don't think you could be happy in Bayreuth." On what she had had to put up with in Bayreuth as my mother-in-law she remained silent. This first trip was her last.

At the end of August 1983 I organised my transfer to Italy, paid for by the Deutsche Bank. They also enabled me to enroll at the expensive Bocconi School of Economics in Milan, but more importantly they gave me an advantageous contract for a position in the credit department of the Deutsche Bank. Four weeks later I began my new life with Teresina.

I started work immediately and attended the Bocconi School every evening, pursuing both activities purely to earn money. The most valuable possession for anyone involved in the theatre scene at that time was a membership card of Bettino Craxi's Socialist Party. I didn't have one. This type of corruption disgusted me. Besides, being a banker precluded me joining the opera and academic circles and my attempts to deny the image failed.

My superiors in the credit department made a varied impression on me right from the start. With one, Eleonore Finsterbusch-Horn, I was to develop a warm friendship over the course of time. The other superior, a man we only called "Semmel" [bread roll], made an awkward and stiff impression and I soon suspected we would not see eye to eye. In fact it was through Semmel that I experienced first hand what it means to be a subordinate in a bank hierarchy in which deviations from the prescribed norms are not tolerated. This system, which was only for the profit of the bank, stifled any individuality below the leading positions. There were two options: submit or get out.

As I fully intended handing in my notice once my course at the Bocconi School had finished, I could afford to stand up to Semmel. I analysed the hierarchical mechanisms to avoid seeming an ignorant fool, and gave some thought to his psyche, his servile mentality and his unbounded career drive. He was the prototype of the German *petit bourgeois*. After I had caught him repeatedly talking disparagingly about "the Italians", I requested he stop such discrimination: my family was Italian and I too felt insulted.

That was the prelude to a series of spiteful gestures, for which I was fortunately well prepared. News of our feud spread like wildfire. Eleonore took my part and our Italian colleagues started trusting us. Pleased to be able to offer them help, I advised them to join a union, but most were frightened of losing their jobs and scarcely dared demand changes. Semmel took the coward's way out and complained to the director, a former Luftwaffe officer, who now tried to intimidate me. But I soon brought his efforts to a halt by casually mentioning that as a sideline I worked as a journalist. Semmel and he then started preparing a report on me for the Frankfurt headquarters.

Shortly afterwards, I noticed that Semmel no longer greeted me and seemed relieved if I closed my door, which was directly opposite his. Any contact was via the internal mailing system and minutes of meetings filled whole files. I collected these documents and in spring 1985, when I had enough valid material in my possession, I asked for a meeting at the headquarters in Frankfurt am Main. The ever-kindly Adolf Sievers saw only one way out in the short term: my transfer to Berlin. I asked for time to think it over. Besides, I wanted to see Semmel's report and hear his justification. White as a sheet he tried to present his outrageous criticism, but I constantly interrupted him and he never got to the end.

CHAPTER SEVENTEEN

BACK TO THE CULTURE JUNGLE

Amidst guerrilla warfare at the bank, Götz Friedrich, intendant of the Deutsche Oper in Berlin and the Theater des Westens, made me an enticing offer. I was to write a programme feature for a production in the Theater des Westens of the opera *Aufstieg und Fall der Stadt Mahagonny* by Weill and Brecht in April 1985. I accepted the offer gratefully. I had unlimited resources to draw on: in fact, I had only to think of my experiences in the Deutsche Bank and in Bayreuth. I called the article "I Remember, The TV Memoirs Of Leokadja Von Begbick". My story of *Mahagonny*, with its strong autobiographical allusions, was based on the idea that there is scarcely any difference between methods of procedure in the banking and in the opera world, where ultimately everybody is trying to out-do everyone else. I played off the decadent, bourgeois world of Wagner against the progressive forces in the opera scene of the Weimar Republic, hinting too that there was not much difference between the past and our own times.

Götz Friedrich understood my allusions immediately, and he commissioned another feature, this time for the programme for the premiere of his new production of *Götterdämmerung* in autumn 1985.

Re-entering the cultural scene at this time, I brought newly-gained and valuable experience. My work in the bank had taught me more about economic and political forces, including those in opera.

Shortly after the publication of the article my sister sent me an interview that my cousin Wummi had given to Karsten Peters, editor of the German edition of *Harper's Bazaar*. I had heard nothing from Wummi since my move to Italy. Entitled "I Always Have The Feeling Everything's Going To Happen Today", the interview contained statements I couldn't possibly endorse. Unfortunately Wummi didn't just restrict himself to his work as an opera director, and his comments on my situation and attitude, although he didn't know my opinion on many things, made me angry. It proved once again that even Wummi and I had not learned to talk, not really talk, to one another – a consequence of the distrustful and hate-filled atmosphere in which we had grown up. The interview certainly portrayed a reaction to long-endured humiliation.

I did, however, endorse his criticism of my father's work as director. When Peters asked him about the succession of *Festspiele* head in Bayreuth, Wummi answered: "Wolfgang Wagner wants to be the longest [sic] and last *Festspiele* head of our family. And actually I don't find that a very responsible attitude." So far, so good. Not so good, however, was his response to the question of whether Wummi wanted to be my father's successor: "Yes, I would really like that. That's not just wishful thinking on my part, but a definite ambition."

Peters: "Who other than Wolfgang Wagner could hinder you there?"

Wummi: "Oh, Wolfgang can't hinder me there either, I think. It's just a matter of under what circumstances it happens."

Peters: "Is there a practical possibility, then, of taking over the *Festspiele* before your uncle's decease?"

Wummi: "He ought to bring me on board now, instead of waiting for the moment when catastrophe strikes or something else unexpected happens."

Peters: "And he expressly rejects that?"

Wummi: "He rejects it."

Peters: "And does he give any reasons for that?"

Wummi: "Yes, he says I should have worked my way up from the bottom after my father's death. But he forgets that he made that impossible for me. I also find that it is more beneficial to make one's way outside a firm one belongs to, than inside."

Peters: "Among the other 'Young Bayreuthers', who aren't actually that young any more, are there no other candidates?"

Wummi: "Oh yes, there's my cousin Eva, who is already heavily involved in arts administration, and there is my cousin Gottfried, who is not concentrating on administration any more for the moment, though."

Peters: "How is your relationship with them?"

Wummi: "I have – amazingly for our family – very good contact and we get on very well. And there's no reason at all why two or three people couldn't take it on together."

Peters: "Wagner directs Wagner – one generation after the other. Isn't that a sort of artistic incest?"

Wummi: "Of course it's incest. But I'm of the opinion that amazing things can come out of incest as well. And in my case that is so: I get most of my ideas while listening to this music."

The following passages of the interview made me particularly thoughtful:

Peters: "What characteristics would particularly apply to you?"

Wummi: "Fury and vindictiveness."

Peters: "And whom do you hate at the moment?"

Wummi: "Myself most of all."

And then Peters came back to his favourite subject again: "Do you want to be the heir of Bayreuth...here and now, today?"

Wummi: "Yes, rather the day before yesterday than yesterday. Wolfgang Wagner should stop dismissing the rest of the family as incapable...And if he were to look back on what he has done in the past, then I would say my qualifications are certainly worth more than his were then."

Peters: "What makes your uncle act like that?"

Wummi: "He must still be reacting to a distorted relationship which – and I can only guess at this – goes back to that battle he had to fight as younger brother. I can't understand that, especially as my father has been dead a long time now. Wolfgang established himself a long time ago, and he's recognised. He doesn't have to fight for his reputation for ever."

Peters: "Was the enmity between big brother Wieland and little brother Wolfgang so great?"

Wummi: "Yes, they were at daggers drawn."

Peters: "Isn't it a bit the envy of the less gifted too?"

Wummi: "It must be, I suppose, otherwise he wouldn't react the way he does."

Peters: "What's his relationship with his own children, Eva and Gottfried?"

Wummi: "That's the real tragedy of the whole story: he regards his own children exactly as he does his brother's children – they mean nothing to him. That is pretty alarming."[25]

The historical basis for doubts over my generation's claim to succession are for me further illustrated by an event which took place during the *Festspiele* of summer 1984. Friends told me of the exhibition *Wagner And The Jews* in Villa Wahnfried and I received details a year later by way of an exhibition catalogue. For the following reasons I still consider the exhibition and its catalogue a falsification of history:

First, the antisemitic inflammatory essay 'The Jews In Music' by Richard Wagner is presented totally without comment and without a critical comparison of the three versions.

Second, this essay is only the beginning of Wagner's antisemitic writings up to 1881.

Third, the historical development of antisemitism from Richard Wagner to Cosima Wagner, and then on via Houston Stewart Chamberlain to Hitler, Winifred, Wieland and Wolfgang Wagner, was only partially demonstrated in text and pictures.

Fourth, the biographies of the so-called Jewish friends of Richard Wagner – Hermann Levi, Samuel Lehr, Carl Tausig, Heinrich Porge, Angelo Neumann, Joseph Rubinstein and Joseph Joachim and Wagner's Jewish artistic paragons, Felix Mendelssohn and Giacomo Meyerbeer – were presented falsely.

These four points constitute an attempt to relativise Wagner's antisemitism and to falsify them to the point of philosemitism.

Fifth, an indispensable element of the exhibition should have been the inclusion of specialists on the historical connection between Wagner's antisemitism and the Holocaust.

Sixth, in the exhibition nothing is said about the connection between Wagner's antisemitic writings and the antisemitic content of his stage works.

In presenting Wagner's antisemitism I found the contempt for critical Wagner scholars such as Hartmut Zelinsky particularly unpleasant. Bayreuth was going in a direction that I now combated. In a subsequent telephone call to Father I asked him whether he was behind this shoddy attempt. "It's high time to draw a line under this," he said and hung up.

But before I could continue my attacks against the *Festspielhügel*, I still had my inner struggle to overcome, in which Teresina selflessly stood by me. After serving notice at the Deutsche Bank and receiving a surprisingly positive reference, I tried to keep my head above water financially in whatever way I could. For a time I worked as an insurance agent in Milan. After that I sold shoes with some success at the Milan Shoe Fair for a friend in Cerro Maggiore, who was a designer shoe maker. That gave me a bit of leeway for work on Liszt and Wagner. All attempts at finding a job in the cultural scene via Everding came to nothing, which didn't surprise me. I heard nothing from him except for a few pious phrases with a lot of compliments. His interest was solely in Bayreuth family gossip and I soon tired of asking him for favours. The only person in the opera scene who didn't abandon me was Götz Friedrich.

Because of the official historiography in Bayreuth and my desire to continue my German-Jewish studies, I concentrated intensively on the nineteenth and twentieth centuries. I also continued working on Liszt, fascinated by his contradictory personality: he was Mephisto and saint, social lion and Christian socialist. He considered himself cosmopolitan, and had occasionally shown courage when he had to publicly stand by his convictions, but he was incapable of building up lasting family and intimate relations.

As I studied, a new, exciting world opened up to me, a cultural concept that I felt more and more to be a counter-position to Wagner. The contrasts thrown up by Liszt's confrontation with the outside world seemed extreme. He experienced reality as a contradiction to his artistic idea of the world. In vain, Liszt sought a solution to the conflict by retreating into artistic isolation. Through his work as avant-garde composer, pianist, music theoretician, opera director, conductor, teacher and coordinator of all the essential musical trends of the nineteenth century, his effect on the music of his and our century is enormous.

I found myself confronting yet another giant out of my own family. But this one is far more likable than the one whose name I shall always bear like a millstone. I also realised while working on Liszt that I still had to find my own identity. It is not enough to read literature and music scores.

In the course of my research I drove to Eisenstadt in Austria, to the European Liszt Centre, which turned out to be an insignificant little archive. In nearby Raiding, the composer's birthplace, I discovered that Bayreuth had already stretched out its hand in that direction and had reached the Liszt museum there. To me, though, it was important not to leave Liszt to sanctimonious Lisztians and all-powerful Wagnerians, but to interpret his work independently.

After the disappointing trip to Austria I contacted my Parisian cousin Blandine Jeanson, a direct descendant of Liszt. Her mother Daniela Jeanson had looked after the artist's legacy and she tried to continue her mother's work. In accordance with family tradition, she had the Christian name Blandine and still owned a few valuable heirlooms. When I informed her of my Liszt studies, she gave me advice and told me of the coming international Liszt Congress at the Paris Sorbonne in the autumn of 1986.

This was to be Teresina's first trip to Paris, and I enjoyed the great museums, especially the Impressionists and the Louvre. I was particularly looking forward to the meeting with my cousin Blandine, whom I had not seen for years. Her sympathy and concern for my professional career and our conversations about our families' destinies helped me to find a non-Wagnerian family role.

In addition to my studies on Liszt's ethics as an antidote to Wagner, I was working on an article for Götz Friedrich on the final bars of the *Götterdämmerung*. At that time I still didn't recognise the antisemitic overtones, especially in Wagner's drama outline *Jesus Of Nazareth* of 1849, which had preceded the *Ring*. But I felt the end of the *Götterdämmerung*, compared with the whole *Ring des Nibelungen*, to be a sort of artificially imposed music theatre epilogue, with an operatic happy ending.

I then received an offer from the head of the Richard Strauss Institute, Stephan Kohler, whom I had met in 1978 during rehearsals of *Ariadne auf Naxos* in Salzburg. Kohler is an open European with wide-ranging knowledge, not just on Strauss, and is personally courageous when it comes to awkward subjects. He wanted me to give a lecture on Strauss and Liszt. As I had just been working on Wagner's vague final message of "love as redemptive salvation of mankind" in the *Ring*, I was interested in the transcendence and immanence in the *Bergsymphonie* of the unorthodox Christian Liszt and in the *Alpine Symphony* of the bourgeois and one-time Nietzschean Richard Strauss. The point of departure of my theme, "Christ – antichrist or the artist between transcendence and immanence", was Kant's definition in his 'Critique Of Pure Reason' of 1781: "We want to name the principles, the application of which is held completely within the limits of possible – not merely actual – experience, immanent, but those which should go beyond these limits, transcendent principles."[26]

In preparing for the lecture I read the correspondence between Liszt and Nietzsche of January and February 1872. Nietzsche, who at the time was still strongly influenced by Wagner, misinterpreted Liszt as an Dionysian: that is, as a man who follows his own daemon and gives his passions full rein because he is strong enough to master them. Liszt's answer was full of respect, but he wrote that he was a Christian. I then read in Nietzsche's essay 'The Case Of Wagner' (1888) the way Nietzsche's judgment of Liszt developed. In the epilogue I found the following lines, which became important for my exposition of Liszt: "If Wagner was a Christian, then Liszt was perhaps a church father! The need for redemption, the quintessence of all Christian needs, has nothing to do with such buffoons: it is the most honest expression of decadence, it is the most convinced, most painful affirmation of decadence in the form of sublime symbols and practices. The Christian wants to be rid of himself. *Le moi est toujours haïssable* [the ego is always hateful]."[27]

I started to better understand a few things in Liszt's thinking, when I read that the *Wunderkind* had had a nervous breakdown at sixteen and wanted to be a priest. His desire to escape from the world reemerged two years later, after his first love affair ended tragically. The composer's subsequent relationships ended tragically too and Liszt was disastrous as a father, which accounts for the character of his daughter, Cosima.

Liszt fought against the rigid musical forms of his time, but like Wagner, he allowed discussion about music to peter out in vague interpretations. At that time I saw Liszt as the complete opposite to Wagner, which was very important for my further understanding. In October 1985, in a lecture to the choir of Cerro Maggiore, I declared myself totally in agreement with Liszt's ideas, against a dogmatic, intolerant exercise of religion and music. My audience was not enthusiastic. In fact, my new views were the start of my growing distance from the intellectual life of Cerro Maggiore.

In mid December the conservative cultured classes of Munich heard my thoughts on Strauss and Liszt, in the presence of the Strauss sons, who were devoted to Bayreuth. Not only had I carried out my assignment, but I also had some money in my chronically low bank account.

It was only in the following year that I really discovered Liszt though. In lectures and radio broadcasts in Switzerland, Italy, Belgium, France and the USA I was to be offered many opportunities to exchange views, and I gradually came to understand Liszt's attitude to the Jews. His book *The Gypsies And Their Music In Hungary* of 1859 with the crucial chapter 'The Israelites' had certainly been prompted by Wagner's inflammatory and racist 'The Jews In Music' of 1850. Liszt ends his book, not like Wagner with the "decline" and "suicide" of the Jews, whom he understood as a nation, but with the advice to reconquer Palestine through their "own efforts".

At the end of October 1986, after attending the not very satisfying Liszt Congress in Paris, Teresina and I went on to Luxembourg, where Louis Landuyt and his wife Cathérine had invited us to a Liszt evening. With the assistance of the Luxembourg Ministry of Culture, the German Embassy and – of all things – the Deutsche Bank, Louis had put together a well-balanced programme of piano pieces, played by Cathérine, and songs, which Louis performed, accompanied by his wife in the Théâtre des Capucins.

I had given a lecture at the start of the evening, reading out mainly provocative quotations from Liszt's writings on all essential aspects in the life and creativity of the artist. An aggressive silence spread through the audience, which was composed primarily of bankers, when I read out the following passages from Liszt's book *Chopin* of 1852: "Among the kings and princes of the financial world on the other hand…everything is paid for in cash, even the visit of a potentate like Charles V, to whom, should he condescend to be accommodated by his banker, is offered his own bill to light his fire. Hence poets and artists need not wait in vain for a fee, which protects their old age from care…The enriched bourgeoisie lets artists and poets founder in the voracity of materialism. Here women and men know of nothing better to do than to fatten them up, as a King Charles spaniel on the boudoir sofa is fattened, until, at the sight of their Japanese porcelain dish, they die of obesity…The *parvenus*, who do not hesitate to pay for their gratified vanity, as they only feel great through the sums of money they have lavished, may hear and see with wide open ears and eyes, but they understand nothing of true poetry and art."[28]

Then, when I read out in Catholic Luxembourg Liszt's opinion of the Roman Church and his letter to the excommunicated social revolutionary, the Abbé de Lamennais, a slight coughing became audible in the hall. But they remained polite and refrained from heckling, which I had been hoping for. In the interval afterwards I stood alone with Teresina as a punishment. Louis and Cathérine were amused by the audience's embarrassed silence. But then like a *deus ex machina* a representative of the Hungarian Ministry of Culture came up to me to inform me that on the basis of my work on Liszt I was to be distinguished with the Liszt Medal for 1986, the only German to receive it. Louis announced this news before the second half of the evening, the concert. Suddenly I was "in" and Teresina and I were paid court to after the successful concert. People were amused by Liszt's "jokes" in precisely the way Liszt had intended, "with wide open ears and eyes". A director of the Deutsche Bank said: "Those are just the opinions of an artist who understands little of the banking world. For you, as for your great-grandfather, our world would certainly be quite alien."

I answered: "The banking world is alien to me, it's true, but I know it. I worked for three years in the Deutsche Bank." There was general amusement. No one quite believed me.

The year 1987 seemed promising. I got a contract from the Bonn theatre to act as dramaturg for a production of *Meistersinger von Nürnberg* in the 1987-8 season. The project required me to be in Germany, initially to research in the Richard Wagner Museum in Bayreuth, but it was some time before I was permitted to visit. The archive administration knew its master's voice and looked on my work with suspicion. A few violent scenes preceded my being able to read my own family's letters, without submitting detailed reasons every time. My resentment of bureaucratic obstacles led me to look around a little more thoroughly in the archive and I started again probing into areas taboo in Bayreuth: antisemitism, Gobineau, Cosima Wagner, Houston Stewart Chamberlain, Winifred Wagner and Hitler.

That was also useful for my introductory lecture at a Toscanini symposium at the beginning of November 1987 in Parma. Harvey Sachs, the internationally acclaimed Toscanini biographer, let me choose my own subject, and I decided to talk on "Toscanini's Bayreuth Conducting Style". Going through the *Bayreuther Blätter* and the *Festspiele* guides from 1878 to 1943, I felt so nauseated by this pre-Nazi and Nazi reading matter I had to break off several times and go for a walk in Wahnfried Park. So that was the cultural soil of my own family! I had all the material I needed copied, knowing that there were (and still are) a lot of sources in Bayreuth that are supposed to be withheld from public view or which my father and his team of history distorters would like to keep under lock and key for ever.

Every visit to the Richard Wagner Museum and Bayreuth was like a nightmare for me: the repression, the concealment and the distortions of German cultural history had reached a stage that ensured evil spirits of the past remained long in the archive cupboards. Even my route from the archive in the Chamberlain House towards the city centre took me along the Richard Wagner Strasse. And I was reminded yet again.

Before I left Germany I met Father in the *Festspielhaus*. I wanted to offer him an article on the centenary of Nietzsche's 'The Case of Wagner' the following year. He answered shortly: "Send in your concept. Dr Bauer will look through it." I was surprised that Bauer, in spite of his new job as general secretary of the Bavarian Academy Of Fine Arts, which my father had strongly advocated, still had influence on Father. His answer was equivalent to a rejection. Remembering how much Father despised Nietzsche, I asked: "Is Dr Bauer the specialist for Nietzsche too now? When he was still working in the *Festspielhaus*, he already had his problems with Wagner." Father walked off angrily. I knew that Bauer was now looking forward to rejecting my proposal, but I wanted his opinion and Father's in writing. I got them in April 1987: Father's comment was that the subject was still too charged with emotion and he consequently did not consider such topics desirable in the Bayreuth programme at the moment, especially from a descendant of Wagner.

In Munich, August 1987, through my mother, I got to know the Jewish Wagnerian Alfred Frankenstein from Tel Aviv. Mother had been in contact with him for years and had often mentioned him. His love of Wagner's music blinded him to my criticism of Wagner's antisemitic writings and the role of the Bayreuth *Festspiele* in German culture and politics. He did not want to acknowledge that Wagner with his racist writings and his Bayreuth *Festspiele* had contributed his ideological part to the Holocaust. Unfortunately, he didn't realise how shamelessly the *Festspiele* were exploiting him in marketing the new philosemitic Bayreuth. As part of this calculated attention, he was overwhelmed with *Festspiele* tickets.

Like many of my Jewish friends, who took Wagner like a drug, Frankenstein could never completely understand why I did not identify with my great-grandfather. Like many other Jewish Wagnerians, he wanted to repress all this. I didn't. But in spite of all the contradictions we liked each other, a feeling which he expressed when he found out that I was investigating German-Jewish history. We spoke about Kurt Weill, and then the question came up of whether I would give some lectures in Israel. Alluding to Uri Toeplitz, however, he pointed out that this idea would be difficult to put into practice. Toeplitz had written in a programme for subscription concerts in 1966 in Israel: "We speak of music to emphasise that we can only accept Wagner as a composer, not the ideologist of the 'total work of art', even less so the theoretician, the writer of inflammatory works on cultural or political subjects, the unprincipled, egoistic, ambiguous revolutionary, friend and exploiter of kings, friend of Jews and arch Jew-hater – in short, the man who acted out of all the contradictions of his complex personality. We do not want people to forget what the Nazis made of him, namely one of their spiritual ancestors, but we should also bear in mind that we can never know what Wagner himself would have said about it, because he had been long dead when National Socialism emerged."[29]

That attitude was typical of the majority of liberal German Jews in Israel, opposed at the time by the Israeli population's radical rejection: they equated Wagner with Hitler. None of this discouraged me, as I had gone my own way where my family and their past were concerned and I owe Frankenstein and his wife Esther my first contact with Israel. It was later to bear fruit.

In July 1987 I sat in on some dress rehearsals in the *Festspielhaus*. Although Barenboim was conducting, I enjoyed hearing *Tristan* there again. Among others I also sat in on the dress rehearsal of my father's production of *Tannhäuser*. I had tried beforehand to correspond with him on it, but he hadn't even answered my letters. I realised yet again during the dress rehearsal that we were worlds apart, illustrated by our ideas of the "Venusberg".

My interest now turned to an offer from France, from Orange. At the open air Roman theatre there, parallel to a *Ring* production, I was to help, as dramaturg, to produce a video, organise an exhibition and put together the programme for summer 1988. After an initial meeting with the director Raymond Duffaut I noticed that there were scarcely any differences between marketing methods in

Bayreuth and in Orange, where the administration wanted above all to market my name. As I was not exactly inundated at that time with offers, the idea of the video attracted me, so I thought of the fee and said yes.

Back in Cerro Maggiore, meanwhile, I was told on the telephone that I had become one of the short-listed candidates for directorship of the opera house in the northern Swedish town of Umea. Lennart Rabes, the pianist and well-known interpreter of Liszt, who was working in Umea as repetiteur, had proposed me as candidate and with no great hopes I had sent my details to Umea. I flew to Stockholm for the first time at the end of August and found it enchanting with its lakes and its architecture, untouched for centuries. I was received very warmly by Bertil Hagman, then dramaturg of the Royal Opera, the liberal politician Jan Eric Wikström and by Marietta Kardos, a prominent physician. Marietta and I soon developed a warm friendship – I later learned that as a child she had survived the concentration camp with her mother.

My new friends instructed me on what would be expected of me and, once prepared, I flew on to Umea. I was impressed by the sight of the wild landscape of lakes and forests and scarcely had I landed, when I was met by the whole of the opera personnel. I was completely frank and emphasised that it was a privilege to work in the culture and opera scene, and that any form of cultural work was based on individual initiatives and responsibility.

The cadre of Party Socialists in the opera house didn't approve of my views: they thought art should be fully organised from the cradle to the grave. Despite my opposition to such political nannying I was elected by an overwhelming majority as the new opera director. There was great disappointment when I decided, after discussions with Teresina, that I would prefer to continue my life in Italy rather than to do battle with Party functionaries in beautiful Umea. Many of my friends and acquaintances were horrified that I had not seized such a unique opportunity in the opera world. But there was no question of my pursuing an uncertain future in a field that had become strange to me, at the expense of my private life. As a friend in Bayreuth told me, the *Festspielhügel* sighed with relief.

I now started preparing some radio broadcasts on Goethe's *Faust* in musical versions by Liszt, Hector Berlioz and Wagner, and also on Liszt's youthful opera *Don Sanche*. I also soon had a lecture to prepare on "The Cases Of Nietzsche And Wagner" for the Bayreuth young people's *Festspiele* meeting.

CHAPTER EIGHTEEN

BONN AND ORANGE

Preparations for the *Meistersinger* in Bonn and the *Ring* in Orange seemed good opportunities to establish new contacts in the opera business, after an absence of six years. This new beginning did have its dark sides though: the then general intendant in Bonn, Jean Claude Riber, had brought me in solely because of my name and in the course of our preliminary discussions on the *Meistersinger*, I noticed that we had nothing in common on the intellectual front. He revelled in the absurdly large budget of his federal capital opera house, staked everything on the star circus, and anyone who didn't go along with it was frozen out. During one such discussion I saw the set model by Günther Schneider-Siemssen, whom André Heller had rightly called "Karajan's *Basteltante* [handicraft auntie]". The design was appalling: it reminded me of Bayreuth's *Meistersinger* productions of the thirties and forties. Schneider-Siemssen sensed my disapproval and retaliated by criticising Wieland's *Meistersinger* of 1956. As this was one of my favourite productions, I could hold back no longer and said: "Where content and aesthetics are concerned we don't seem to have anything in common. Wieland's *Meistersinger* of 1956 will make theatre history. This *Meistersinger* won't." With that, all further contact with the set designer came to an end. I realised that next year in Bonn I would have to concentrate on finishing the programme. Difficult times lay ahead.

Before that was the Toscanini congress in Parma and my lecture on "Toscanini's Bayreuth Conducting Style". The period of the great Italian conductor of the *Festspielhügel* was in the run-up to National Socialism and I was interested in the political environment, in particular the role of my grandmother, who from 1923 had made Hitler presentable to the German bourgeoisie. In preparation, I reread Aunt Friedelind's autobiography, *The Royal Family Of Bayreuth*, in which she describes in 1948 the unbridgeable gulf that lay between her and my father.

Shortly before my departure for Bonn, at the beginning of March 1988, I met the poet Karl Lubomirski and his wife, the painter Enrica Lubomirski, at a reception given by the Austrian consul Rudolf Novak in Milan. What a humane contrast they made to the seedy opera world awaiting me in Bonn and Orange! From the outset our talk ranged over many levels, including taking an interest in the fate of others. I soon became familiar with Karl's colourful narrative style with all its nuances of subtly caustic humour and deep melancholy alternating with explosive *joie de vivre*. I knew after our first hours together that our paths would often cross. I read for him a poem from his German-Italian volume *La Zolla Di Luce* [The Clod Of Light] which Enrica had translated with great sensitivity into Italian. Poems such as 'The Tree', with the line "The tree of my life bears doubts" won me over immediately to his work. He too had been induced by the *italianità* of his wife to leave the narrow confines of his native Austria.

Although Karl had left Innsbruck irrevocably behind him as I had left Bayreuth, we remained – whether we liked it or not, and Karl as a poet even more than I – marked by and dependent on German culture and language. Between us a quiet solidarity arose in opposition to the friendly, but ultimately impersonal, attitude of Italian Catholicism. Although it is clearly better for us to live in Italy than anywhere else in Europe, nevertheless we feel like cosmopolitan outsiders and nomads. How close we are in decisive questions became clear to me too when I read Karl's poem of 1990, 'Auschwitz', in which he manages to say the unsayable as follows:

Here fell a great leaf
from the tree of death
greater still than Babylon
Jerusalem and elsewhere too
a leaf
that follows no winds
that lies and lies and lies
and when history itself is blown away
then only will perish
with its place.[30]

For me there is no doubt of his importance as a poet. He also became a trusty fellow fighter for German-Jewish dialogue in the controversy over the Wagner cult in Bayreuth after my trip to Israel in 1990. What will always bind me to Karl is his incorruptibility in humanitarian questions. He was discriminated against by self-styled popes in a pseudo left-wing international cultural lobbying scene. Something else we have in common.

The beginning of our friendship in March 1988 already had a good effect: I went to Bonn without fear of Riber and co. At first I stayed with my "second mother" Bettina Fehr and as always we talked at length about Father, Mother and Bayreuth. Bettina always tried to work towards mediation and conciliation, but over time she had realised that there was little I could do about what seemed an impasse.

Inspired by our conversations, Bettina gave me something to read in bed on 14 March which was to have lasting repercussions: Ralph Giordano's *Die zweite Schuld oder von der Last, Deutsche zu Sein* [The Second Guilt or On The Burden Of Being German]. She said, knowing me all too well: "This book will have a big effect on you!" She was right. I didn't read the 363 pages, I devoured them, for what I read in Giordano's book touched my very soul. The clarity of the content, its linguistic beauty, his nuanced historical, political and cultural analyses and his humanity overwhelmed me. Here, finally, was a German-speaking author who had something to say to me. His life of suffering had made him unusually sympathetic as a human being, one who stands up with the courage of his convictions against the German society of repression. He seemed to put into words everything that was important to me.

On 15 March I got up at seven, wide awake, despite having had hardly any sleep at all. I couldn't resist waking up Bettina, who is not an early riser, by making a lot of noise during my morning ablutions. Still somewhat sleepy, she made coffee for me in the kitchen while I told her enthusiastically about my reading experience, asking impatiently: "Can't you ring Ralph Giordano?" Bettina laughed and said: "Now, at half past seven in the morning? Let's wait till nine."

At nine she rang him up and introduced me in her charming, irresistible way, not only as the "Weill Wagner", but as someone very much hoping for a discussion of German-Jewish history with him. Three days later, at Giordano's invitation, Bettina and I went to Cologne. Having rung the doorbell, we waited outside until the door opened and inside we saw a beautifully laid coffee table, among several other pieces of tasteful period furniture. Instead of a greeting by the host came the 'Prelude' to Act One of *Tristan und Isolde*. Then Ralph Giordano came towards us. Pensively he said to me: "This music is one of my favourite Wagner compositions." I answered: "It's impossible not to be fascinated by Wagner's *Tristan und Isolde*, but unfortunately we have to live with the 'other Wagner' as well." He agreed and shook my hand.

I had intended asking Ralph Giordano about his life and work, but I didn't get round to it during the next three hours. He had a lot of questions about my life. And as we sat on the sofa in a relaxed mood, I noticed how his fine and melancholy features began brightening up while I was answering him. I found it so easy to open up to him, and talked as though to an old friend. When I told him about "Winnie and Wolf", he gripped my arm and interrupted my flow with a question that annoyed me: "Are you really Wolfgang Wagner's son?" I hardly reacted as I thought I had misheard, and carried on telling him about the correspondence between Hitler and my grandmother. With friendly obstinacy he repeated the question: "Are you really Wolfgang Wagner's son?"

He was evidently asking about my father, so I countered laughingly with the question: "Why do you want to know that?"

He answered seriously: "I once interviewed your father in Bayreuth. I'm sorry to have to tell you that I didn't believe a word he said. There's no humanity in that man."

I answered: "You don't have to apologise – you're only saying what I've known and felt since my childhood."

Giordano reached for a copy of his novel *The Bertinis* and wrote in it: "For Gottfried Wagner – who I liked on sight." And then he said emphatically: "Whether you want to or not, you must write the story of your life. You owe that to your own generation and those to follow."

I didn't like this idea at all and said: "At the age of forty-one to write a sort of autobiography against the degenerate conditions in Bayreuth? Why? Who would be interested? To make myself even more isolated than I am now?"

Giordano replied: "You have nothing to do with the false Bayreuth of the Wagners, but you are a Wagner aware of his human and historical responsibility. Write your life story. Going over it will help you personally and one day may help you be reintegrated in Germany. I'll support you."

I was moved when Bettina and I left Ralph Giordano. I knew the meeting would have consequences for my life.

The day to day life in the opera house caught up with me again. My initial fears that Riber would misuse *Die Meistersinger* in Bonn to promote his own image were proved an understatement. In mid March I sat in on one of the rehearsals taking place on the small main stage. The set, which was already partly assembled, was even more tasteless than the model. According to the maxim "anything expensive must be good", Riber had bought in all the stars of the international Wagner market – René Kollo and Bernd Weikl among them. These "stars" stood around bored in the rehearsals and feigned interest in Riber's arrangements, which they then supplemented with ideas and experiences from other productions at other opera market places. At first Riber even made video recordings of these embarrassing scenes, to preserve it all for posterity. When I tried to point out to him grotesque mistakes in the way he was directing movement, he was insulted. He was so used to everyone paying him compliments and lauding him as an artist.

My work on the large *Meistersinger* programme booklet was going ahead well and, so as to remove my critical eye from his rehearsals as quickly as possible, he immediately agreed to all my suggestions for the programme, and then intrigued behind my back. He regarded me as a rival and did everything he could to trip me up. Every step I took – every telephone call I made – was watched over by his lackeys. The dramaturg, Monika Rottmaier, who like me didn't take these repressive measures lying down, was given notice – certainly not because of a lack of expert knowledge. Riber and co destroyed a respected opera repertoire house through a soulless, interchangeable star programme. And what was I to think of singers who ridiculed Riber in the canteen, while feigning admiration for his direction during rehearsals. Underpinning all this hypocrisy, however, was the box office. I hoped that this system, which was inimical to art, and which was prevalent not just in Bonn, would soon end. In fact, such inflated mediocrity was to explode in the 1990s.

One of the last of Riber and co's attempted coups against me, was when they tried to delete my name from my *Meistersinger* programme booklet. A visit to the lawyer clarified the situation. That wasn't enough for Riber and now he did everything to squeeze me out of the *Ring* production in Orange, in which he was also involved as director. He asserted that I had not made any contribution to his "brilliant" *Meistersinger*, although the public and the media had reacted positively to the programme booklet. Later Riber had to retract his calumnies in court.

The premiere, on 17 April 1988, was just as one would have expected from the rehearsals. The media and the public were taken in by the glamour and big name sensation, and not only in Bonn. The 1980s were obviously the culmination of a politico-cultural dictatorship of mediocrity, based on political and economic lobbies who only allowed what they wanted to succeed.

I only had one opportunity in Bonn to protest against this state of affairs, and that was through the content and shape of my programme booklet. I quoted from Wagner's writings and the *Meistersinger* and wrote articles which, if read carefully, opposed what was happening on the stage. I unmasked Riber and co via the revolutionary Richard Wagner and his avant-garde ideas on music theatre, while Riber tried to present the composer in the federal capital as a *petit bourgeois* garden gnome. Not even the contrary Wagner and his ambiguous works deserved that accusation!

So I quoted Wagner's letter of 14 October 1868 to Ludwig II, in which he complained about the production of his *Meistersinger*: "The utter wretchedness and deep decline into which the German theatre has sunk is something I shall discover to an even fuller extent by what happens to this very work of mine."[31] This was precisely how I felt about the Bonn production. The import of my subversive programme booklet was not appreciated in the federal capital, however.

I added fuel to the fire during a conversation with the Bonn music critic Hans G Schürmann. The resulting interview appeared on the weekend of the premiere in the Bonn *General-Anzeiger* under the title "The Other Wagner: Against The Flow Towards His Own Goal". In it, I criticised the opera jungle and advocated "achieving opera as a constructive group experience on the basis of individual responsibility, motivation, initiative and permanent evolution of professional competence and creativity".

Instead of prompting open discussion, my attack was followed by effusive compliments which, by being generally non-committal reminded me where I was: in Germany, the paradise of repression, in which silence, especially in the case of Wagner and his *Meistersinger*, has well-known, well-founded reasons.

Riber's intrigue against me in Orange was successful. The festival director, Duffaut, suddenly wanted me off the production and offered to settle with me for half my fee. It ended a quarrel that could be heard over half the town. I demanded that I be allowed to fulfil my contract as dramaturg, and Duffaut realised that legally speaking I held some good cards. I had delivered the large manuscript of the programme booklet, reasserted that any alteration must be discussed with me beforehand, and then left.

My next task was preparing the *Ring* video, for which I collected copious amounts of material. Inspired by events in Bonn, I chose the subtitle "The Consequences Of The Misuse Of Power" for the project. In my *Ring* story, Wotan and Alberich appear as two crooks in a struggle for world domination. My method of narration was to consciously address a public that understands opera and Wagner as it is presented: as a stage for the self-presentation of alleged high society. I owe considerable visual inspiration to the pictures of the famous photographer August Sander. In a crazy mixture of pictures from Botticelli via Roy Lichtenstein to Coca-Cola I show the decline of an apocalyptic society from Red Square to Wall Street, ending up with the launch of an atom bomb. Thierry Bénizeau saw to the technical assembly of my meticulously worked out material.

The next battle took place at the end of July 1988. Duffaut and Riber had altered the programme booklet without asking me – contravening the contract. My lawyer advised me to leave Orange and informed the media of this decision. It caused quite a stir – a few days earlier the *Ring* had won first prize at the video festival in Biarritz. The subsequent legal action against the administration in Orange dragged on for four years and ended in a settlement, as I did not have the financial means to continue the proceedings.

I now began to prepare a multimedia lecture for Bayreuth. In it I wanted to continue what I had begun in Bonn and Orange: an open attack on the Wagner money making machine.

At that time I was living in Bad Kissingen and was in poor health. I was being treated by my friend, the distinguished cardiologist Peter Deeg, who I had known since 1960 – the year in which my father had directed his first *Ring* on the *Festspielhügel*. He, like myself, had a strong father to contend with, one who had written a book in the Nazi period on the "court Jews" and had made a second brilliant career as a lawyer in Germany's economic miracle. Peter had been brought up by his father to be a conservative, but I knew that behind this apparently impenetrable conservative façade there were other qualities. They emerged when he married Jadwiga from Gdansk. Jadwiga, with her radiant *joie de vivre* and openness, altered Peter so much that, to my amusement, the effect of his years-long bachelorhood was completely undone. Their four lively children grew up in a stimulating German-Polish cultural environment. Jadwiga's cosmopolitan father, Stefan Angielski, had gone through Poland's Nazi occupation and been detained in a Stalinist labour camp in Siberia.

Throughout the first years of our friendship, Peter and I avoided talking about the Nazi past of our fathers as a point of principle.

It was also about this time, in July 1988, that I got into conversation with his father. Initially he had helped my father to draw up the "Foundation statutes of the Bayreuth *Festspiele*", until he discovered that they did not lead to a settlement of the succession within the family. That went against the grain with him as a strongly family-orientated man, as did the shoddy treatment of my mother in the divorce, whom he and his wife continued to help from 1976 on. I was surprised when, during our conversation, he also began to talk about National Socialism and the Jews. With some emotion he fully acknowledged the horrors of the Holocaust as a terrible crime in German history. I had never heard this kind of admission from my father. His admission also had an effect on my friendship with Peter. Gradually, we began to talk about our fathers' past and openly discussed antisemitism in the Third Reich and our responsibility for coming generations.

In the middle of August 1988, within the framework of the International Young People's *Festspiele* Meeting in Bayreuth, I gave my talk on "The Cases Of Nietzsche And Wagner". My politico-cultural collection of quotations from Nietzsche's 'The Case Of Wagner' and 'Nietzsche Versus Wagner' created an icy atmosphere which I found difficult to cope with. Nietzsche's marvellous analysis of Wagnerians was received with silent fury. I then described the reasons for the break-up of the friendship between Wagner and Nietzsche in 1878: because Nietzsche could no longer stand Wagner's woolly, late-Romantic conception of life with all its ideological dynamite.

I then turned to Nietzsche's description of the "Wagner

Neurosis", with its antisemitism, which he recognised early on as a danger. In summing up Nietzsche's convincing criticism of Wagner, his passionate attack on the opera public of his time and of the future, plus his gloomy diagnosis of "Bayreuth cretinism", which was already showing totalitarian aspects, I was clearly understood in the auditorium: namely that I was getting even with the *Festspiele* public of the dishonest New Bayreuth era. I garnished all this with provocative collages of Wagner's music and caricatures by Marc Sautet and Patrick Boussignac.

As I brought the lecture to a close with Nietzsche's eulogy of Bizet's *Carmen* and a resounding play-in of the end of that opera, the atmosphere in the auditorium was as I had expected: edgy and aggressive. Some of the *Festspielhügel* faithful managed to twist the facts in such a way, that no serious discussion with the audience came about. The Society Of Friends Of Bayreuth, whom I had kindly invited, preferred not to expose their world view to any upset. After the lecture, Teresina and I stood with a few friends and acquaintances in the empty auditorium.

It was impossible to discuss Wagner, Nietzsche and the Jews openly in Bayreuth. As we left the auditorium, a man came up to me with a friendly smile and said: "My name is Janos Solyom. Don't let yourself get discouraged by the reaction of this audience. I'm right behind your talk, which has to be unpopular here: you are not only questioning everything, but you are not allowing any repression of the past. Any form of truth hurts. You are unwelcome here, where nothing has changed." He shook my hand warmly and we arranged to meet in one of the intervals of *Meistersinger*, which was about to begin.

When we met, Janos told us of his international career as a pianist and of his wife Camilla Lundberg's work as a journalist. The friendship between the four of us developed in defensive reaction to the copper-bottomed dishonesty of the Bayreuth environment. We talked about Liszt and the misuse of his life and works by Bayreuth, and together made plans for the future. One of the joint projects was our much-admired Theresienstadt evening in Stockholm in 1994, in which Janos played piano works by Pavel Haas, Gideon Klein and Viktor Ullmann in a uniquely intense way.

His artistic and cultural richness and his tolerance made the hours with him irreplaceable. It was only in Stockholm that I learned that Janos is related to Kurt Weill and that the Nazis had murdered his father in Russia.

One day, after meeting Janos, my *Ring* video was being played during the Bayreuth Young People's *Festspiele* Meeting. The negative mood following my lectures had not abated, but because I was the son of the *Festspiele* boss, it didn't come to a head. As I played my video several times over, a large section of the audience indignantly left the hall. Such conservatism among these young people did not surprise me. It was a reflection of the *Zeitgeist* in which there was no vision, no protest, simply career plans. Discussions with younger participants of the Young People's *Festspiele* revolved mainly around aesthetic details instead of the politico-cultural phenomenon of Wagner in Bayreuth. Older members of the audience were just as shocked by the video, but to my amusement hoped that through it, I had disqualified myself as my father's successor.

The only positive outcome of my two events in Bayreuth was the offer from the *Neue Zürcher Zeitung* to publish my thoughts on Nietzsche. To my surprise, Josef Lienhart, president of the West German Richard Wagner Societies, invited me to show the *Ring* video to his Freiburg Society in the autumn of 1988. Shortly beforehand, both my video equipment and the only copy of the video were stolen from the luggage locker at Hamburg Railway Station. So I had to talk about the *Ring* video without showing it, which was awkward as, in addition to some inveterate Wagnerians there were also open-minded people in the audience. Before and after the talk, Lienhart enthused about Wieland's Bayreuth times. That surprised me, as my father and his lackeys had done everything to banish his great shadow. Lienhart also seemed to appreciate my critical examination of the Nazi past, in particular my intention to accept the invitation to Israel, and promised to do what he could after the trip to promote discussion in the Wagner Societies, as he too seemed to consider it necessary that the case of Wagner be placed under discussion in Germany and Israel.

But I soon discerned that, despite all my criticism of the

Bayreuth *Festspiele*, he believed I would go to Israel as a pro-Wagner propagandist. I made it clear that that was not my intention and on my return from Israel, I heard nothing more from Lienhart. In fact, he spoke indirectly against my opinion of Wagner and Wagner's antisemitism.

CHAPTER NINETEEN

ON THE ROAD WITH NIETZSCHE, WAGNER AND LISZT

A t the end of October 1988, after thorough preparation, I set off on a lecture tour that was to take me first to North America and then to Japan. My first stop was Washington, where I was to speak at the George Washington University. Before that the historian Stephen Gallup gave an impromptu party attended by stimulating academics from all over the world. From the first moment I felt at ease in this environment with its great expertise and kindly tolerance. What a contrast to the German academic circles.

During the party, passionate discussions had already broken out for and against Wagner, always conducted with mutual respect for the opinion of others. Just as stimulating were the hours I spent as a guest in the home of the Guenthers: Roy was the head of the music department at the George Washington University and an excellent trombonist, and his wife Eileen, a music teacher and distinguished organist. Roy is a happy mixture of scientific passion, which he easily conveys to his students, and pragmatism, having the capacity to carry through projects efficiently, a mixture which I had seldom if ever encountered in Europe but which I consider important for effective teaching. Roy helped me with the preparation of my talk on "The Cases Of Nietzsche And Wagner" and in the discussion afterwards.

The lecture was received with lively interest. Among the audience were several people who had had to flee Nazi Germany. Discussion was of quality and gave me some ideas for the coming talks.

My next appearance took me to Chicago where I was a guest of the Goethe Institute and the opera house. The conservative opera public reacted quite negatively to the recovered *Ring* video and Nietzsche's criticism of Wagner. Their number comprised a powerful German contingent, which had expected a eulogy to Wagner and the Wagnerians in particular were disappointed. The discussion with some liberal intellectuals, who were particularly interested in the subject "Wagner and the Jews", was more constructive.

Over the next stages of the tour (Bloomington, Atlanta, Victoria, Vancouver, San Francisco and Los Angeles) the arguments against my critical contributions to the subject of Wagner were repeated.

My last stop in the USA was of particular interest: in mid November I landed in Los Angeles and was the guest of Michael and Miriam Meyer in their beautiful home in Pacific Palisades, overlooking Santa Monica. Michael, who is a history professor at the California State University in Northridge, specialising in the Third Reich and Richard Wagner, was particularly interested in my theories on Nietzsche and Wagner, owing to his own German-Jewish history (his Jewish mother had survived the Nazi period in Germany).

Cornelius Schnauber, head of the Max Kade Institute and the one who suggested I visit Los Angeles, had organised a series of events on the subject of Nietzsche and Wagner in various cultural institutions in Los Angeles. As there was a large Jewish community and a Wagner Society in Los Angeles, the hall in the Goethe Institute proved too small, and half those who came had to be turned away. During my talk the faces of the Wagnerians close to Bayreuth became stony, although subsequent discussion was begun by a young man who apparently mistook me for a relative of Adolf Hitler and became quite abusive. After I corrected him, there followed an objective discussion on Wagner's and Nietzsche's conflicts with Judaism between various groups among the audience, many of whom were German or Austrian emigrants. This subject made the Wagnerians uncomfortable and at first they kept quiet, many of them having only come to stare at me as a museum piece. Not very diplomatically, I cut short the pro-Wagner eulogising *à la* Bayreuth, which the Wagnerians misinterpreted as a "typically powerful Wagnerian character trait". What would now await me in Japan?

Finally setting off at the end of November 1988, I was pleased to be met at Tokyo airport by two representatives of the Japanese Wagner Society: the Germanist Tomoyoshi Takatsuji and Mrs Yasuko Miyake. Yasuko's husband is a musicologist and had provided an analysis of the form of Wagner's *Tristan und Isolde* for the Bayreuth *Festspiele*. Using the efficient public transport system, we reached the centre of Tokyo by evening.

I had scarcely put down my bags in the guest room of the Goethe Institute, when the first reception of the Wagner Society took place in my honour. There I finally met Tatsuji Ivanbuchi, with whom I had already corresponded and who had translated my book on Weill and Brecht. This professor of German at the Gakushuin University is an internationally recognised authority on Brecht and Weill, translator of German literature and much else besides. He is also one of the most cultured people I have ever met. And one of the most modest.

Now he came up to me in person: a frail gentleman in an elegant three-piece suit. With a faint smile, he warmly shook my hand. He immediately offered me the *Du* form of address which, being quite untypical in Japan, pleased me. "Buchi", as I was to call him from now on, is a cosmopolitan nomad in everything he does, thinks and feels. Come what may, his presence served as a shield in a country that, despite all the familiar Western traces, I found rather disconcerting.

My first, well-attended talk for the Wagner Society in the Tokyo Goethe Institute, on Liszt and Wagner, went smoothly, possibly because I refrained from too critical discussion points. Over the following two days I went to see the Meiji-Jingu Shrine and the Sensoji Temple and attended a performance of Noh theatre: its exoticism appealed and I became very aware of my Eurocentric ignorance.

An excursion with the enchanting Yasuko, which began at five in the morning in Tokyo, was unforgettable. In splendid weather we sped to Kyoto by Shinkansen, the famous Japanese high speed train, to see the imperial residence. The beauty of the palace, its gardens, the temple and the shrines fascinated me. Small, irresistibly smiling schoolgirls in black and white uniforms asked if I would have my photograph taken with them and when Yasuko told them something about me, they hummed 'The Ride Of The Valkyrie', beaming. It was not the time to tell them my opinion on the necrophilia of the opera scene, and for Yasuko's sake said "Cheese" like a good European tourist.

At the Gakushuin University on 29 November, in a marathon event, I presented both the talk on Nietzsche and Wagner and the *Ring* video to an Japanese-European academic audience. When I subsequently showed the video at the Keio University too, the reaction of the women students surprised me. They giggled behind their hands at the erotic scenes. This then turned into general amusement. The end, however, where the dropping of the atomic bomb on Hiroshima symbolised the end of the *Götterdämmerung* visibly moved all the students.

In the following days students came in groups to the university director's room, where I answered their questions on the lecture and video. Each group then quietly filed out, making room for the next.

Among those interested was the theatre expert, actress and Japanese teacher Kimijo Sasaki, who, with great sensitivity not only understood my objectives, but also forcefully attacked the Japanese male-dominated society. She opened my ideas to some things which I, in my tourist enthusiasm, had overlooked. In the years following this meeting a warm, frank friendship developed.

Later, Kimijo bravely got a divorce and moved to Los Angeles with her daughter Marina, where she built a new life under extremely difficult conditions. I met her there in 1991 and it was as though we had said goodbye the day before. There can be no greater contrast than that between the rebellious Kimijo, who had been so cruelly suppressed by her husband, and the conservative Yasuko, who submitted totally to her ambitious husband. Equally contrasting was the sight of kimonos next to blue jeans and radical Europe-orientated socialism at a reception of the Japanese Pen Club.

CHAPTER TWENTY

HITLER AND WAGNER?

Early in 1989 preparations began for the centenary of Hitler's birth. Leo Haffner, one of the leading producers of cultural programmes for the Austrian radio channel ORF Vorarlberg, had prerecorded a discussion with Karl Lubomirski and myself back in autumn 1988 on the subject of German culture, tradition and politics, which could not avoid "Hitler and Bayreuth". As Haffner was not one of those Austrians who turn Hitler into a German, he proposed that I give a talk at the beginning of April in the ORF studio on Hitler and Wagner.

Hitler and Wagner?

While I was preparing the talk I became more and more aware of what consequences this subject had for me personally. It is the most painful chapter of my family history, which I tried to face then for the first time. I didn't want to take refuge in the art world, like Father and Uncle Wieland, and separate Wagner the theatre genius from Wagner the ideologist. Enough generations of Wagners before me had been similarly led to such a fateful repression and ultimately to the denial of individual responsibility, so I now asked myself why I hadn't been able to speak more openly to my grandmother and my father on the subject of Hitler and Wagner. After all, if my grandmother had accepted Hitler's proposal of marriage, I could have been called Gottfried Wagner-Hitler! (Historian Robert Wistrich records the proposal in his *Who's Who In Nazi Germany*, 1982.)

Hitler and Wagner are therefore part of my life. Such a connection has created in me a strong identity crisis which I was only able to overcome by doggedly working it through. With strong doubts at that time about my identity as a Wagner, a German and a post-Holocaust Christian – and through a degree of uncertainty about the theme – I settled on a lecture title in the form of a question. "Adolf Hitler And Richard Wagner?"

The lecture was my first, unsuccessful attempt at an interpretation in which I tried to dissociate Wagner's work – in particular *Parsifal* which was open to several interpretations – from his antisemitic writings. In so doing, I applied suppressive methods so typical of New Bayreuth. I quoted a line from Wagner's regenerative article 'Heroism And Christianity' in which he wrote about his *Parsifal*: "The blood of the Saviour, the issue from his head, his wounds upon the cross, – who impiously would ask its race, if white or other?"[32]

Despite the historical connection between quotations from my great-uncle Chamberlain, Grandmother Winifred and Hitler from November 1923 up to his official statement from the "Wolf's lair" in January 1942, I still had not understood or – from a modern viewpoint – wanted to understand the full consequences of the terrible total vision: namely, that Richard Wagner himself had already contributed his part to the inextinguishable link between Bayreuth, Theresienstadt and Auschwitz. At that time I didn't want to regard Richard Wagner as co-responsible for the big "and" with Hitler.

A year later I disproved this opinion to a large extent during my preparations for my lecture tour of Israel in 1990 and addressed the subject yet again. Today I must acknowledge that I cannot uphold the final sentence of my talk of April 1989 in the Vorarlberg studio of ORF: "Wagner *and* Hitler? I hope the 'and' strikes you as odd...Wagner belongs to art, Hitler to the criminal records file."

In April 1989 I embarked on my first lecture tour of Norway, Iceland, Denmark and Sweden. The animosity towards the subject "Wagner And Nietzsche" and to the *Ring* cycle, which discussion I opened with the video, was noticeable everywhere, for Richard Wagner was still connected with the memory of the Nazi invasion and German occupation in the 1940s. But once people understood that I was neither a member of the master race nor intended to harp on about Wagner's unique greatness, the ice began to melt. Having made it clear that I not only rejected the Wagner cult in Bayreuth from 1872 to 1945, but also the repression of the Nazi period in the New Bayreuth era I was then mostly received with great openness, warmth and interest.

In Iceland in particular I realised that Wagner's use of Nordic mythology only very superficially corresponded to Scandinavian culture. I also learned that Nordic mythology has nothing to do with Hitler's delusion of the Nordic race.

The less conventional the audience, the more open the discussion on the politico-cultural phenomenon of Wagner and the Nazi period. Media interest was high. Only in Arhus and Stockholm did I meet Wagnerians who, in their woolly world view and through their pilgrimages to Bayreuth, did not want to talk critically about their "Master".

On my return flight from Stockholm to Milan I realised how much the Wagner affair is overshadowed in Scandinavia by the fact that they have not yet come to terms with the Nazi past.

While I was preparing for my trip to Israel, in July 1989 I went with Teresina to the premiere of my father's new *Parsifal* in Bayreuth. This time we were the guests of the then managing director of the Upper Franconian Chamber of Industry and Commerce, Helmuth Jungbauer and his wife Helga, who remained unperturbed by the intrigues against me. Jungbauer supported the opposition theatre group Studiobühne Bayreuth, who had made a name for themselves through their refreshingly disrespectful treatment of the Bayreuth Wagner tradition.

On the *Festspielhügel* word had got round about my invitation to Israel to give talks on Wagner, and the usually cool tolerance of our presence now turned icy. With great sensitivity the Jungbauers sensed the atmosphere and their friendly attitude towards us now became warm and open, on public occasions as well in private. As we were escorted by them, even my father's yes men had to accept our presence at official receptions in the opening week of the *Festspiele*. Whereas in previous years Teresina and I had been used to being invited only to the "State reception", we found ourselves at the table of the guests of honour after the *Parsifal* premiere, which all the other invited guests had to pass, including my father and his wife – although they managed not to see us.

I was asked for my opinion of the *Parsifal* and, aware that the tabloid press was within earshot, I answered with careful objectivity. I referred to the end of the opera with the words "redemption for the redeemer", in which, according to Wagner's instructions, Parsifal, as new, Arian Christ, celebrates the last supper as a message of salvation. Contrary to Wagner's conception, father had allowed Kundry to survive in the male Christian temple of the knights of the Grail. And, irrespective of all the writings and directorial instructions of his grandfather, Parsifal had disappeared among the crowd of knights of the Grail. Such misinterpreted democratisation meant that in the Grail there was no individual, but only the knights' collective responsibility – a thought which appalled me. Clearly my audience understood my point, for they kept silent and changed the subject. In 1994 Peter Deeg informed me that Father had altered the end yet again. Kundry, as female Messiah, now offered the goblet to the knights of the Grail as redemption. This was New Bayreuth repression at its most extreme.

After that we saw the *Ring* directed by Harry Kupfer and conducted by Daniel Barenboim. Watching the absurd opening scene where trampling hordes of chorus in a thick mist under a figure which, as insiders later informed me, was supposed to be Wotan – without the *Rheingold* music – I realised that the *Festspiele* could no longer have any meaning for me. The whole *Ring* concept was portrayed as an eco-swindle story of Messrs Wotan and Alberich between two fictional atomic world wars. Not surprisingly the end of this most absurd interpretation was in keeping with the rest of the production: to the "redemption through love" motif, drunks and drug-addicts burped in a sort of East German railway restaurant.

I bumped into Barenboim, after the *Götterdämmerung*, in the Bürgerreuth Restaurant: he expected a compliment for his brilliant production, but I had to tell him I had never seen such nonsense. He feigned interest in my opinion and promised a meeting in the following days. Unfortunately, he didn't keep his word.

CHAPTER TWENTY-ONE

ISRAEL

My first meeting with Professor Herzl Shmueli on 3 August 1989 in Zurich was a complete contrast to that last visit to the *Festspielhügel*. This musicologist had dared hold seminars in Tel Aviv on Wagner as far back as the 1970s, arousing great public interest, and we had first started corresponding in May 1988. The early Romantic period was one of his main areas of study, so he could not avoid the "Wagner case".

Shmueli had grown up in Istanbul, in a traditional Jewish family, and had attended the German school there. At the beginning of the 1930s he emigrated to Israel. He studied mathematics and then from 1950 to 1952 musicology in Zurich. Why Zurich? "Despite all my love for German culture, instilled in me by my education in Istanbul, it was impossible for me to study in Germany after Hitler," he explained.

At our first meeting in August he asked me about my life: "Doctoral thesis on Kurt Weill in Vienna – that doesn't seem to me to be a typical choice for a Wagner after Hitler?" With that our critical, intimate dialogue began, culminating in an invitation for me to give four lectures in Israel in January 1990.

At the beginning of September 1989, I accepted an invitation from the International Music Festival of Montreal to a multimedia talk on "Faust – Goethe – Wagner – Liszt: Poetry And Music". I informed my cousin Winifred Arminjon-Lafferentz of my arrival. Winifred, named after my grandmother, was the second daughter of my father's younger sister, Verena Lafferentz. We had only met each other briefly as children, after which my family had made any further contact impossible; my father spoke of Aunt Verena's family in Nussdorf on Lake Constance as negatively as he did of Aunt Friedelind's. He had told me on one of our walks at the beginning of the sixties in Arosa that Aunt Verena had been "a favourite of the Führer" and her husband, Bodo Lafferentz, had organised the wartime *Festspiele* as assistant of the Labour Front chief Robert Ley. I never quite believed this version of history, in which he represented himself as victim of the Nazis, and saviour of the Wagner archive.

And so we met again, weighed down by the family burden and encumbered by a web of lies and intrigues from our time as children and teenagers, and just before my trip to Israel, of all things!

After a general chat about my talk on *Faust* we finally came round to the crucial subject: the family's past. I could speak openly with Winnie. The humiliations she and her family had had to suffer on visits to Bayreuth made me feel ashamed. We both knew that *Festspielhügel* politics had made human intercourse, even within our generation, impossible since the Wagner Foundation had been set up and the public war of succession connected with this. The wilfully contrived "discussion" on succession was one subject we steered clear of.

Like me, Winnie suffers from the Nazi past. As a painter, she deliberately goes her own professional way. We both view a critical handling of family tradition and a search for one's own identity through one's own work as a constructive alternative and also as a chance for dialogue between the two of us in the future. Just how sensitively Winnie reacts to the shadow of the Nazi past, became clear to me later, in February 1994, during an event in the Tifereth Beth David Jerusalem synagogue, where I had been talking about my work in the Post Holocaust Dialogue Group since 1991. For Winnie, who herself had studied Jewish history because of our family's past, this was her first trip to a synagogue and was a further important step in our joint emancipation from our fateful legacy.

After returning from Montreal I continued working on my Wagner lectures. I had applied to the Ministry for Foreign Affairs and the Goethe Institute for financial support for the project, but had still not received an answer. In fact, after much to-ing and fro-ing, nothing came of it: evidently neither body found my work towards reconciliation in Israel worthy of support.

At the beginning of October 1989 I presented to Herzl Shmueli my proposed topics for the University of Tel Aviv lectures: the video *The Ring Of The Nibelung or The Consequences Of The Misuse Of Power*, "The Fall Of The Gods or *Epatez le Bourgeois* – The Anti-Wagnerian Musical Contemporary Theatre Of Weill And Brecht", "The Cases Of Nietzsche And Wagner" and finally "The Wagner I'm Talking About – An Approach To Wagner's Personality And Work". Explaining this choice I wrote among other things: "My intention remains, calmly and patiently, to make my contribution to a continuing dialogue in small steps on the subject 'Wagner and German culture'. I am fully aware of my responsibility and cannot understand why the West German institutions in Israel (Goethe Institute and West German Embassy) do not support my conciliatory work, in which I have been engaged now for two decades."

Fortunately I received committed help from the head of the music department of the University of Tel Aviv, Shai Burstyn who I fully informed of the contents of the lectures, as I didn't want to give offence to my host country. I also asked him a question which, for me, was critical: "Would it be very tactless to present a few – small – musical examples from Wagner's music at the University?" He agreed to it, although anticipated protests.

Finally everything was ready and on 2 January 1990 Teresina and I flew to Tel Aviv. In the crowded plane there was a confusion of tongues in which modern Hebrew predominated. We listened fascinated, unable to understand, but secure in the knowledge that we could always have made ourselves understood in English or some other language. Travelling at the invitation of the university I did not feel like a tourist, but rather privileged. Reading through the questions on the Israeli landing card for German visitors, I came upon the following question: "Were you a member of a party in the period from 1933 to 1945?" which I interpreted as: "If German, were you a Nazi, or not?" A perfectly justified question, I felt, as guilt and shame flashed through my head. When the pilot announced that we would soon be landing at Ben Gurion Airport I became uneasy. Despite all the trust so prevalent in my correspondence with our hosts Shai Burstyn and Herzl Shmueli – Shai's retired predecessor – I was still a descendant of the antisemitic Wagner family from Bayreuth. What people would I meet? How would they react to my grandmother's, my father's and my uncle's Nazism? Would they regard me as a Nazi Wagner?

Herzl and Shai greeted us with a friendly "*shalom*" and from the outset, showed us nothing but solidarity and readiness for dialogue, which took away a lot of my fear of behaving wrongly. They talked about the itinerary – "our coming Wagner events" – which Shai and his colleagues had planned down to the smallest detail for every day of our stay.

We agreed that I would not touch immediately on critical subjects in my talks – such as Wagner's antisemitism, Hitler, Bayreuth and the Holocaust – since Herzl and Shai knew the audience would address these subjects without our help. I was to understand my talks more as a starting point for subsequent discussion. Added to this was the fact that my appearance in Tel Aviv and Jerusalem was taking place only two months after the fall of the Berlin Wall. My lectures, with their music history base, changed through that moment of world history into a discussion on the politico-cultural phenomenon of Richard Wagner.

All discussion at the luggage carousel of Ben Gurion Airport stopped however when a customs officer informed us that our suitcases had been left behind in Rome. Fortunately my lecture material was in my hand luggage, so I remained relaxed, although I usually do lose my temper on such occasions. Things were just different in Israel!

In a good-natured rush Shai and Herzl took us to the Grand Beach Hotel in Tel Aviv, where, immediately after my arrival I gave an interview to Hanoch Ron from the main evening newspaper *Yediot Acharonot*. Hanoch Ron was well prepared for the discussion: he set the tone and the content, which were then, with variations, followed by other interviews and audience discussions until I flew back on 14 January. For him, his colleagues and the audiences, my opinions on 'The Jews In Music', on Hitler and my family, on my upbringing in Bayreuth as a Wagner after the Holocaust, and on whether Wagner should or should not be performed in Israel, were important. While I was answering I became aware of the responsibility which, from now on, I had publicly to bear in this country. I was no longer prepared to show any consideration for the opinions of my father, who had viewed my trip to Israel with grave misgivings: I had told him about my intended lectures, suspecting that they would have repercussions both for our relationship and for me personally.

The interview with Hanoch Ron opened the floodgate. The journalists were mostly understanding about my desire for dialogue, sympathetic even, which helped me answer difficult questions in a more relaxed and balanced way.

But I still found it difficult to answer the question of whether Wagner's works should be performed in Israel: I had no right to interfere in Israeli domestic policy, but people were not convinced by this, so I suggested that there should be a democratic vote on it in the music institutions. I also expressed an understanding for the victims of the Nazi terror, who no longer wanted to hear Wagner, Hitler's favourite composer. I also criticised the undemocratic action of the conductor Zubin Mehta, who in 1981 had wanted to perform Wagner during a concert, against the wishes of the majority of the audience.

During all the discussions in Israel my exhaustive work on Weill was considered sympathetically, as it had been in New York. The significance of such an explosive mixture – Weill and Wagner – was grasped. It even amused people. Weill's dismantling of the Bayreuth Wagner cult had much in common with my attempts to knock my great-grandfather off his pedestal.

The fact that I grew less afraid to face the Israeli media was due most of all to Teresina, who supported me with devotion and believed fully in the purpose behind my trip to Israel. Her solidarity seemed to carry over to the other members of the audience and even to the interviewers.

People often addressed her in Hebrew because it was assumed that she was Jewish. She then said smiling: "I am 'only' an Italian from a Catholic family." When I told this to Herzl later, he said: "Your story is so extreme people assume you could only be married to a Jewess." Just as important as Teresina's help was that of the few friends and acquaintances who gave me their open support both during and after this decisive time; mainly people with a Jewish history, or with a lot of sympathy for it.

The intensity of the discussions in the first afternoon and evening increased over the following days; my actual series of talks didn't begin until 7 January. The idea that we could quietly tour Israel beforehand proved wishful thinking:. even during our two day visit to a kibbutz, Cesarea, Massada and Arab villages with Herzl and Shai, we talked constantly about my lecture subjects. As Herzl, an expert on this area, convinced me, in Israel Richard Wagner was inseparably linked to Hitler and Nazi Germany. But emotion would not prevent him implementing seminars and lectures at the University of Tel Aviv on this "aberration" in music history.

During these discussions I began to realise how much I had changed. In order to rescue the antisemite Richard Wagner, I had tried to ascribe the blame only to his children and grandchildren. Now I understood that this repression of reality would not hold water. Meanwhile, I have learned that I was in a similarly contradictory situation to my Jewish friends who are Wagnerians. But today I also know it is not possible to split Wagner into the genius composer on the one hand, and the leading ideologist on the other, as his *Weltanschauung* [philosophy of life] belongs inextricably to his work and his life.

A discussion of my experiences and responsibility developed imperceptibly: in Israel I realised I could no longer just articulate my political and moral position indirectly, by grappling with Jewish-German culture. My time in the ivory tower of liberal-left thought was over. I demanded greater personal credibility through deeds. In Israel there were limitless opportunities for undertaking this seriously, as time and again we came to talk about individual fates, about people who had been driven out of Germany by persecution and suffering to Israel and elsewhere. While my hosts, their friends and lecture audiences described their life stories, I became more and more open. Out of the dark, vague yet frightening gigantic shadows of six million victims, individual stories emerged. The desire grew in me to take up a clearer position on our shared history and on our joint responsibility for the present and future. I now started to see Israel as a central motif in the mosaic of my life. I remembered again my time in New York in the Kurt Weill Foundation; the connections between German history, the chronicle of my family and my contrary lifestyle finally became clear to me. I wanted to translate the trust and understanding so constructively offered, by canvassing in future among my own countrymen too, for German-Jewish dialogue. My fears, my insecurity and anxiety dissolved as my insight increased.

One of my first important public appearances took me to Jerusalem where I had been asked by Israeli radio for an interview. The producer Danny Or'Stav gave me a warm welcome and told me he would first introduce me to the listeners in Hebrew. The introduction centred, as Shai told me later, on my life and the lectures. He commented with obvious sympathy on my book on Weill too and the time I had been working at the Kurt Weill Foundation in New York. The only thing I understood of the introduction was the repetition of my grandfather's first name Siegfried, which Danny had obviously confused with my name. When he asked me how I liked it in Israel I answered: "I like it here very much, but my name is not Siegfried. It's Gottfried! I am the great-grandson, not the son of Richard Wagner!" I did not want to be identified right at the outset either with my grandfather Siegfried or with the blond beast and mad heroic figure from the opera of the same name. My reaction caused general amusement and was possibly the reason my first radio interview in Israel went so well.

I was very pleased to hear later, that only two months after this interview, Wagner's music was played again on Israeli radio. Unfortunately, it was 'The Ride Of The Valkyrie', which I rank among the most sinister and questionable of compositions. And yet, our mission proved effective: Wagner was no longer just a taboo subject, laden with emotion. Now a differentiated politico-cultural discussion developed. This was probably the best thing that one could achieve for Wagner's music in Israel.

Four days later I was interviewed in Jerusalem by Ram Evron for

Israeli television. Before recording, he told me that he was in favour of Wagner's works being performed in Israel. I disagreed, which amused him and prompted him during recording to ask more about my rebellion against my family. Via Weill and Grandmother Winifred we came finally to the question of how to deal with Wagner's essay 'The Jews In Music'. I categorically condemned the work and advocated a more discriminating historical approach.

The effect of the television interview was immediately noticeable: the next day total strangers came up and spoke to me in Tel Aviv. When I reacted to this with surprise in an optician's, the optician said in perfect German: "Herr Wagner, don't you know how small our country is? We show our guests Israel in the morning, and in the afternoon we wonder what on earth we can do with them. So don't be surprised that we saw you on television yesterday. Your coming here is important not just for the 'Jeckes', the German Jews. Keep up the good work!"

My first lecture also took an unusual course. My introduction to the video *The Ring Of The Nibelung or The Consequences Of The Misuse Of Power* had been planned to take place at noon at the university. However, a university employee informed me discreetly that there had been protest telephone calls from fanatics opposed to my visit, so they were considering giving me a bullet-proof jacket or protecting me behind bullet-proof glass. I refused. Teresina asked me to do something for my safety. "I am not Eichmann. I have confidence in my hosts," I reasoned. It didn't make Teresina any calmer but she accepted my decision.

Instead of an audience of eighty, as planned, 400 turned up and we had to move to a larger hall. Furthermore, security measures were increased: the audience were searched, and two young Israeli soldiers were posted with guns in the larger, but still crowded hall.

Despite the demand, though, the first row remained unoccupied: fear of contact with a Wagner descendant. I remembered a book with the title *Who's Afraid Of Richard Wagner* that I had been given shortly before the talk began. Without really thinking about it, I said: "There are still some empty seats down here. Who's afraid of Gottfried Wagner?" Liberating laughter broke out, which I joined in with. Laughter continued during the video, even at those parts where, at previous talks across four continents, I had been the only one to be amused! Shai's introduction in Hebrew had seen to that. He presented my text on the history of Wagner's tetralogy faithfully: as a story of the criminals Wotan and Alberich in a struggle for power.

My lecture on Weill and Brecht the following day went quite differently. The fact that someone with my family background had the *chutzpah* to talk at the biggest university in Israel on Weill's contemporary musical theatre as a counter-model to Wagner's *Gesamtkunstwerk*, or total art work, filled the hall. The well-known Israeli singer Adi Etzion, accompanied by her husband Jonathan at the piano, sang Weill songs at the end of the evening – very reminiscent of Berlin in the 1920s. An elderly lady from Berlin, who introduced herself only by her first name, Isolde, asked me: "Herr Wagner, why don't you give your talks in our beautiful German language?" Rather confused, I answered: "Because the majority here in Israel speak English."

Isolde soon came up to me again and said: "You can imagine why I'm called Isolde? Yes, my family loved Wagner's music, and I love Wagner too. I still remember the wonderful productions in the Kroll Opera under Otto Klemperer. And Bruno Walter's *Walküre*." Isolde turned out to be an accomplished Wagnerian, such as I have only seldom encountered. She beamed at me like a kindly grandmother and said finally: "You can't imagine what your visit means to us Berlin Jews." We hugged one another in silence and unsuccessfully fought back tears.

A crucial test for me was the last lecture with the subjective title "The Wagner I'm Talking About". Like the other events it was recorded. Following Herzl's advice I tried to explain Wagner's significance for European music theatre and music history. As the lecture was intended not just for a specialist audience I decided to use colour slides and taped musical examples.

I preceded this with an attempt to come to terms with my own past in Bayreuth. Today I can see that it reflects my insecurity of that time, when I was trying to come to terms with the family history and my own development which were inextricably bound. I had started to understand the course my life had taken, but still separated Wagner's ideology and life from his stage works. What I said at that time on Wagner no longer has anything to do with my present state of mind.

I am still surprised today by the generosity and good will of my audiences. Anyone casting a critical eye over what I said at that time, reading nervously from my notes, could quite rightly have accused me of not having considered Wagner's antisemitism carefully enough. In particular, my statements on "the purely human, the myth" and "redemption and pity" I regard today as the result of my own repression, as an unsuccessful attempt to relativise Wagner's antisemitism, in order to make my own family's past more bearable for myself. It was probably also the last, unsuccessful attempt at self-repudiation, in an attempt to comprehend my father's position.

At the end of my lecture I quoted from Richard Wagner's floridly dishonest letter in diary form of 1 October 1858 to his friend Mathilde Wesendonck. In the letter, based on an imperfect understanding of Arthur Schopenhauer's philosophy, he presents himself as the saint of universal pity, writing among other things: "After all, we know what exists around us only inasmuch as we picture it in our imagination, and as I imagine it, so it is for me. If I ennoble it, it is because I myself am noble, if I feel the other man's suffering to be deep, it is because I myself feel deeply when I imagine his suffering, and whoever, by contrast, imagines it to be insignificant reveals in doing so that he is himself insignificant. Thus my fellow-suffering makes the other person's suffering a reality, and the more insignificant the being with which I can suffer, the wider and more embracing is the circle which suggests itself to my feelings.

"But here lies an aspect of my nature which others may see as a weakness. I admit that unilateral actions are much impeded by it; but I am certain that when I do act, I act in accordance with my essential nature, and certainly never cause pain to anyone intentionally. This consideration alone can influence me in all my actions: to cause others as little suffering as possible. On this point I am totally at one with myself, for only in this way can I hope to give others joy, as well: for the only true, genuine joy, is to be found in the conformity of fellow-suffering."[33]

Wagner has here repressed his own, pitiless antisemitism, which was later to culminate in the demand for a Jew-free Germany.

I declared then: "Here [ie in Wagner's egocentric definition of pity] lies too the key to the final artistic message, which we find in the closing bars of *Parsifal*. This statement represents for me the distinct possibility to interpret Wagner's work responsibly, which of necessity contradicts his existence as an artist in a 'human, all too human' theatre world. Mixing up biography and work means, in Wagner's case, to manipulate the interpretation of his stage works, as well as falsifying his personality. This happened in the past when his work was abused for ideological-political reasons and Wagner's artistic aims were disregarded. I regard it as my duty, as a music journalist, opera director and also as Wagner's great-grandson to refute this.By upholding this point of view, I shall always fall between two stools in Bayreuth. So let us always approach Wagner as the man he was: as a genius of opera in the nineteenth century, without whom the cultural history of Europe is unthinkable."

On reading my text of January 1990 today, I can only shake my head at such repression and inability to judge the Wagnerian legacy as a whole. I was still rooted in the family tradition. I had to liberate myself from it, that much I already knew and it became clearer to me in Israel during discussions. At the time it was more a matter of demonstrating through my talks that I was interested in an ongoing dialogue: that I wanted to escape my isolation and learn. Most of the audiences understood this hidden message and accepted me without mistrust, in spite of the lack of clarity in my remarks. With the trip to Israel, I began once again to try to come to terms with Wagner's antisemitism. I had to gauge his effect on the Bayreuth *Festspiele* as well, and acknowledge that I could no longer uphold my position. Regardless of personal experiences, various publications also spoke against this, such as those by Hartmut Zelinsky, Ulrich Drüner, Paul Lawrence Rose, Marc Weiner and others.

During this painful reexamination of my own knowledge and

conscience I distanced myself from essential landmarks in my youth and student years. I felt removed from the interpretations of Ernst Bloch, Hans Mayer and Claude Lévi-Strauss – in other words those prominent Jewish authors who had been misused in New Bayreuth, in order to repress and distort the past and responsibility.

But back to Israel and January 1990. More important than the lectures were the countless discussions with members of the audience, which through lack of time I unfortunately could not tape. But important episodes remain in my memory, like the meeting with Alfred and Ester Frankenstein in their beautiful house in Ramat-Gan. I also owe to them the initial contact with Herzl Shmueli. Not even my pointing out my great-grandfather's antisemitism could reduce Frankenstein's passionate veneration for Wagner, which takes him back again and again to Bayreuth for the *Festspiele*. And yet, surrounded by the classics of German literature, with coffee and cake and music and discussions on German culture, I felt so at home at the Frankensteins'. It was a shame that this discussion took place in Ramat-Gan and not in Berlin. What a loss Germany had suffered, when it drove out or murdered people like Alfred Frankenstein!

How differently the meetings went with the Wagnerian Harry Riss from the USA, who only told me years later that there had been Nazi victims in his family. He had emigrated to Israel in the mid fifties as a Zionist. He believed he had discovered in me, as great-grandson, several things that had nothing to do with me and little with the "genius Richard". Today Harry accepts my rebellion against the Wagnerian legacy in Bayreuth.

Far more discriminating and complex were my discussions with the musicologist Peter Gradenwitz. My mother had given me a copy of his book, *Musical History Of Israel* written at a time when he shared my criticism of Wagner and was very interested in the tensions within my family – a subject I was only willing to comment on up to a certain point.

Another important meeting for me during my stay in Israel was with Ira Marom, who was working then as an artist in wall projects. The wall and its cracks became the subject of archaeological reevaluation. Ira, who is directly related to Weill and Kafka, was living in Cologne in his studio, a former garage, with his wife Tovi and their daughter. He pursued his projects with admirable energy and lived totally for the future, for which I envied him; he made me see how much I still had to overcome before accepting my own family history and how this constantly cast its shadow on my present. I like to think back on our walks along the beach in Tel Aviv when we would speculate on what would have happened, for example, if Hitler had not come to power and we had perhaps met in Berlin.

On our only free evening in Israel we were invited to a concert given by the famous Israel Philharmonic Orchestra, founded in 1936 by the violinist Bronislaw Huberman. The programme included works by Edvard Grieg, Luigi Boccherini, Franz Danzi and Mozart. Mika Eichenholz conducted. But the evening was by no means relaxing: shortly before we went into the big concert hall, there was a bomb scare, and we all had to evacuate into a side street.

After the all clear, I went to the box office to pick up our tickets. We were warmly received there by the head of the PR department and taken to our places. The young lady then went onto the stage, where some of the musicians were already tuning up, spoke to the first cellist and pointed at us. He stood up and beckoned to us. Rather shyly we went up to him. He gave us his hand from the stage and said in English: "I'm all in favour of performing Wagner in Israel. We are very glad you are here. Thank you." I answered: "But under the right conditions and with broad agreement." He agreed smiling and invited me to come backstage after the concert to meet Mika Eichenholz and cellist Lynn Harrell, the soloist that evening.

Even more touching was an invitation from the Tel Aviv Central Music Library, which also contains the Bronislaw Huberman archive. Nehama Lischitz, director of the library at the time, and her colleagues showed me with justifiable pride the treasures of the book collection, among them a picture of Arturo Toscanini and Huberman on the beach at Haifa in 1938, only half a year before the *Reichskristallnacht*. What was then the Palestine Symphony Orchestra, now the Israel Philharmonic Orchestra, also played Wagner's works until that night of pogroms, such as the 'Prelude' to the first and third acts of *Lohengrin*. I spoke about the collaboration of Toscanini with my grandfather Siegfried in the new production of *Tannhäuser* in Bayreuth in 1930, and about Toscanini's resignation: after the Nazis seized power in January 1933 he refused to perform in Germany any more, although Hitler had personally asked him to conduct again in Bayreuth. With great cordiality Nehama gave me a copy of the book *An Orchestra Is Born*, a unique collection of documents on Jewish musical and cultural history in what was then Palestine and is now Israel. The book, with its friendly dedication, is one of the most beautiful mementos of my first, short trip to Israel.

In spite of the hectic rush of events, interviews and long discussions with members of the audience at my talks, we did not want to miss out on a visit to the Diaspora Museum in Tel Aviv. Teresina and I had the privilege of being shown around by Judith Etzion and the composer and music journalist Benjamin Bar-Am. The clarity of the display through texts, photos and films of Jewish culture and history impressed us, as also did Judith Etzion's explanations. The connection between Jewish and German history and my own family's part in that history, was brought vividly to mind there. The Diaspora Museum has among other things an extraordinarily detailed and extensive data bank available to any visitor to the museum. I keyed in the headword "Wagner" and received four printed sheets of interesting information. I learned, for example, that there were also Jewish families with the name Wagner, who were first recorded in the seventeenth century in Leipzig and Frankfurt am Main, among other places.

I also learned that there had been a Jewish community in Bayreuth since the beginning of the thirteenth century. In 1933 261 Jews were resident there, which meant 0.7 per cent of the population of Bayreuth. On 10 November 1938 – *Kristallnacht* – the beautiful synagogue, built in 1760, was destroyed and the homes and shops of Jewish citizens were plundered and devastated by the SA. The following day the population of Bayreuth attacked their Jewish compatriot and desecrated and destroyed the Jewish cemetery. On 27 November 1941 fifty Jews were deported to Riga and on 12 January 1942 the last eleven

Jewish citizens of Bayreuth were taken to Theresienstadt.

Angrily, I thought again of how I had been deceived as a child by my family and most teachers. Where were the good burghers of Bayreuth and my family on 10 and 11 November 1938? We left the Diaspora Museum in silence.

Our encounter with Holocaust survivor Moshe Hoch, the head of the Institute For The Preservation And Study Of Jewish Museum Of The Holocaust, in Yad Letslilei, was also distressing. The description of his persecution as a child by the Nazis rekindled images of the National Socialist past in all its cruelty. The old question nagged at me of how it was possible for such a highly developed nation to turn into criminals.

The attitude of the German media during and after my stay in Israel was peculiar. Most of them knew very little about Wagner's antisemitism, as was evident in their reporting. Their main concern was sensational headlines, presenting me as Siegfried in the fight against Fafner. This didn't help me in my efforts to achieve a more discriminating image of Wagner in Germany and Israel, nor to come to terms with the family history. The German reports from Israel only served to increase my isolation.

Looking back, there is little left for me to report of the Germans I met in Israel. Hans-Heinrich von Stackelberg, the West German cultural attaché was, not just in my opinion, the wrong man in the wrong place. Despite the success of my lectures he could not be persuaded to change his mind about me.

The Israeli media made much more effort to understand me and my concerns. The journalist Hanna Yaddor, for example, summed up my visit in the evening newspaper *Ma'ariv*, under the heading "Thank You For Your Courage", on 16 January 1990: "The talk of the music world in Israel in the last ten days has been the visit by Dr Gottfried Wagner, the great-grandson of the German composer Richard Wagner...He did not meet with any hostility, but with affection and friendship...People recognised him from the media in the street and gave him gifts. In a letter someone wrote to him: 'Thank you for your courage'...He hopes very much to come back to Israel for a longer period. Here he has already gone through his baptism of fire. Now all that remains for him perhaps

is to counter a few hateful remarks from members of his family."
Hanna Yaddor's prediction was to prove correct, especially with
regard to the expected confrontation with my father.

CHAPTER TWENTY-TWO

FATHER'S LAST LETTER

After my return from Israel in mid January 1990 I found it difficult to concentrate. I kept thinking of the possible consequences of my trip and knew that Bayreuth would react after the first wave of reports in the German and international newspapers.

At the end of January the president of the Richard Wagner Society, Josef Lienhart, called me up from Freiburg wanting to know more about my trip. I described the positive results and experiences, the great interest of the Israeli media and audiences. Finally, I declared confidently, a new stage had begun in the discussion about Wagner in Israel. I noted down the themes of our conversation in main outline and sent a summary by fax to my father:

"Dear Papa, this evening Herr Lienhart rang me and informed me of the following, 'to his regret and stressing his appreciation of my work and his kind regard for me': that you had, on the basis of a one-sided selection from various West German newspaper articles on my Israel trip and on the basis of your right as head of the *Festspiele*, demanded that either all existing invitations from Richard Wagner Societies to me are withdrawn and ruled out for the future, or you would publicly distance yourself from those societies. He also says your boycott of the Richard Wagner Societies, if they should choose not to observe your demand, would take effect from the next plenary assembly of the Richard Wagner Societies [on 25 May 1990]. Furthermore, you have been sending Herr Lienhart the said articles highlighted in yellow and with your comments against me since mid January by express registered post. I cannot believe that you would have given such instructions. I ask you, as my father, to act in this instance, especially as your instructions affect firm offers from Richard Wagner Societies now and in the future. I request thar you respond before the end of the week by fax, in view of the very slow postal service. Awaiting your reply, I remain with kind regards, your son Gottfried."

The official reply came two days later. Father wrote to the effect that he had informed the Richard Wagner Society and its local sections that he would not take part in any of their events if it remained possible for me to give talks under the auspices of the Society, as his participation could be construed as sanctioning my views on the development and the artistic standard of the Bayreuth *Festspiele*, which he found unacceptable. He referred among other things here to an article of 11 January 1990 in *Die Welt*, in which I had stated that since Wieland's death the Bayreuth *Festspiele* had become a cross between a stock exchange and a scrap metal market. Furthermore I had emphasised that politics and commerce predominated, to the detriment of music, drama and poetry. Of course, Father did not want his threat to boycott Richard Wagner Society events to be understood as an "instruction", for which, in fact, there was no legitimate right, but rather as an expression of his own personal "preference". None of this, Father maintained, had anything at all to do with my lecture tour in Israel.

What I had said on the possible consequences of the Foundation document for the further participation of the Wagner family in the administration of the *Festspiele* (in the *Süddeutsche Zeitung* of 17 January 1990), Father dismissed with the remark that I obviously lacked thorough knowledge of the sense and content of this document. He also said that in 1981, if I really did have such critical thoughts about my grandmother, as I had asserted in various statements, I should have declined my share of her financial legacy as "dirty money".

At the end of his letter, referring to his overall responsibility for the Bayreuth *Festspiele*, he drew a hard and fast line of separation between father and son.

To avoid later accusations that I was simply trying to provoke my father out of petulance, I attempted to explain my position to him after receiving this letter, but to no avail. I sent copies to friends and others who I assumed were interested in resolving what was now a public conflict. Even looking at it today, the letter spells out to me that he was never interested in a genuine exposition of his own past and responsibility as father and as head of the *Festspiele*. The quotations from the newspapers mentioned, which by no means always corresponded to my statements, were taken out of context, incomplete and based on an arbitrary selection of articles. An objective assessment of international press reports produces quite a different picture. But neither on the *Festspielhügel* nor among the majority of the German media is there any desire to acknowledge this.

One need only look at the press in Israel in the period from December 1989 to January 1990 or the *Wall Street Journal* of 7 January, the *Repubblica* of 15 January, the *Aftenposten* of 18 January or the objective report of my Israel trip in the *Neue Zürcher Zeitung* of 8 February 1990 with the title "Richard Wagner In Israel, Signs Of A Rapprochement": "Potential access to Wagner and his work will certainly continue to improve for future generations and consequently opportunities will increase for the performance of Wagner's works again in Israel. That real steps have already been taken in this direction, is illustrated by the invitation at the beginning of this year to Richard Wagner's great-grandson Gottfried Wagner (son of the grandson Wolfgang), by the University of Tel Aviv. In four lectures, this Wagner descendant was able, as doctor of musicology and director, to talk about his personal approach to his ancestor's works and about his conflicts with those works: Gottfried Wagner was born in Bayreuth shortly after the war (1947). He was confronted early on with the problems surrounding the political and cultural position of his family. Of course, it was neither his nor his hosts' brief to resolve here and now questions about Wagner or the performance or non-performance of his music in Israel. On the part of the university it was the musical interest, keeping discussion alive on this important composer, which was clearly in the foreground, and on Gottfried Wagner's part there was a serious attempt at rapprochment, as he expressed it in radio and television interviews. Without these premises the encounter could scarcely have taken place in such a generally positive atmosphere. It should be noted in particular that this encounter with Wagner's great-grandson took place in a much broader framework than the university milieu had originally planned; interviews on Israeli radio and television, reports by the national and international press, confirm the necessity and the significance of such steps. In Israel too in those days the word *glasnost* was used when referring to the reception given to Wagner."

At the same time I received an official statement from Shai Burstyn in his capacity as head of the music department of the University of Tel Aviv. He wrote among other things:

"I should like to thank you for your efforts in ensuring your visit to Tel Aviv University was so successful. The capacity crowds which your lectures drew, as well as the interest shown by the press, are clear indications that the topics of your lectures are of great interest to the Israeli academic public and, indeed, to a large part of the Israeli population...[The series of lectures] was a project well prepared and well delivered. I wish you success in the future development of the ideas you conveyed in your lectures here."

Comparing the international reactions and those of my father and his friends, I realised it was pointless to expect constructive discussion. I had to continue the course I had begun in Israel in spite of all resistance. Amidst all the personal, cultural, political and ethical differences, I still longed that he would be prepared one day to meet me, just as a father.

But as he showed no inclination to listen to my opinion, and his instruction to the Wagner Societies led to the cancellation of previously agreed contracts, I felt I had no option but to respond. In mid February, 1990, with the aid of my lawyer and constant friend Inge Lehmbruck I wrote:

"Dear Papa...So I must acknowledge that, using the most severe pressure, namely the threat to boycott any events of the Richard Wagner Society, you have prevailed on the president, Herr Lienhart, to cancel any events in which I am involved – three lectures in Freiburg, Baden-Baden and Karsruhe. In other words, you have thought it right not to discuss with me personally what I have actually said and why, but instead to take a course of action via third parties which has had repercussions on my material existence. I must emphatically deny your remark that I accepted 'dirty money' (not my expression) as inheritance from my grandmother. What I received from the inheritance at the beginning of the 1980s was approximately eighty-five per cent (exactly DM83,509.27 before tax) of my grandfather Siegfried Wagner's legacy, and the remaining fifteen per cent (DM12,500.00 before tax) – the figures can easily be verified by the executor Thorwart – from Grandmother's legacy, which I have always regarded as only a part of the Wagnerian property coming from great-grandfather Richard. Gottfried."

As this registered letter was returned to me unopened, Inge Lehmbruck wrote to my father: "I have to draw your attention in due form to the fact that my client, who is economically largely dependent on his lecturing activities, in order to earn a livelihood, would not hesitate to defend himself with all legal means, including court action, if attacks on your part on his professional career should be repeated."

My father's secretary acknowledged receipt of this letter without comment.

Breaking off the relationship with his own son did not stop my father from using his influence to make life in the music world difficult for me. Via his countless contacts and connections he brought about precisely what Inge Lehmbruck had warned him of: always acting via third parties, formulating and justifying his position coherently in his 1994 autobiography *Acts*. Such action has inadvertently helped my position, as people have become interested in my version of events. In the blurb of the German edition my father writes: "In the vast amount of literature on every conceivable subject relating to Wagner and Bayreuth, there persist, in particular where the twentieth century is concerned, so many clichés, tenacious prejudices, half-truths and quite infamous lies. There are as many blatantly uncritical voices in favour just as there are unobjective voices against. Rage, violent emotions of love and hatred explode, all on a relentless scale, so that often enough an adequately sober view is obscured or at least clouded. It seems to me it is high time finally to bury the legends and end the empty talk. My autobiography is intended in the widest sense to offer testimony of greatness experienced and pain suffered, of course from my quite subjective viewpoint, but at the same time substantiated by documentary evidence and accurate records, which have until now largely remained unpublished. The unusual, outrageous, not to say sensational is no figment of my imagination, but lies in the established facts themselves."

I read this text several times, as I didn't understand it. Father emphasises that he is writing from his "quite subjective viewpoint" – in other words he is not aiming at an objective autobiography – its credibility reinforced by documentary evidence. But the choice of documents and their source remain open to criticism, as they are arbitrary and vague. His "subjective viewpoint" apparently includes a selection of "documentary evidence and accurate records", largely unpublished until today. *Acts* serves not even as a subjective account, but as what could be called an arbitrary interpretation of Father's own life.

I grasped this on a first reading. On a second reading I placed the blurb like a pattern over the sections which for me were crucial, in the professional and personal areas, where our differences of opinion were concerned: his interpretation of the antisemitism of Richard Wagner and the Wagner family; his interpretation of Hitler and the Holocaust and the consequences of these for our relationship today. I wanted to know why he represses his own past and the past of his own family – as head of the Bayreuth *Festspiele*, as a Wagner and as my father.

Acts demonstrated to me how he had succumbed to the contemporary mood in repressing his own past by dealing far too arbitrarily with his grandfather's romantic philosophising. It became clear to me, too, how in judging Father's romantically written autobiography, I orientated myself towards rationalism and knowledge of the Enlightenment. I share the opinion of the philosopher Karl Popper, who in his essay 'On The Subject Of Freedom' of 1967 writes in his understanding of rationalism and Enlightenment against the philosophising of the Romantics: "As one of the last stragglers of rationalism and Enlightenment, I believe in the self-liberation of man by knowledge…For in my backwardness I can see in the philosophy of the Romantics and in particular in the philosophy of the three great leaders of German idealism, Fichte, Schelling and Hegel, nothing but an intellectual and moral catastrophe – the greatest intellectual and moral catastrophe that has ever befallen the German and European intelligentsia. This catastrophe, this intellectual and moral chain reaction had, I believe, a disastrous and stultifying effect, which like an atomic cloud is still expanding. It provoked what Konrad Heiden in his book on Hitler, years ago called 'the age of intellectual and moral dishonesty'…What I mean, when I talk about reason or rationalism, is nothing more than the conviction that we can *learn* by criticism of our faults and mistakes and in particular by the criticism of others and ultimately by self-criticism."[34]

Father refuses to acknowledge that only critical discussion allows us to see our own ideas from different angles and judge them objectively. For him, give and take as basis of critical discussion has no meaning. He will not recognise that, as Popper describes it: "the sensible, the critical approach can only be the result of the criticism of others and one can only achieve self-criticism through the criticism of others." Instead, Father wants to impress, forgetting that in art Richard Wagner is not the only "guiding light of mankind".

His language is vague and complicated. In his attempt to legitimise his own power – the thread running through his life history – he inadvertently refers to the third, secret instructor, to the Mephisto of the Nazi opera world, Heinz Tietjen. In the Führer's Bayreuth and Berlin he learned as Tietjen's assistant to recognise every means for holding on to power which was then, in reconstructing the economic miracle that is New Bayreuth, to smooth his path to becoming intendant of the *Festspiele* for life. For the great organiser there was no zero hour.

The behaviour patterns of someone who represses his past constantly recur in his book. He trampled on the dignity of those who could not protect themselves and who refuse to be wholly subjected to his will. One need only read the pages on which he passes judgment on his brother Wieland, my mother (who, when all is said and done, was a supportive wife for thirty-three years), his sister Friedelind, his sister-in-law Gertrud and the "unqualified" fourth generation. Here he applies the phrase "do as you would be done by" only to himself, when he talks of "pain suffered" and presents himself as a victim. One moment he dons the martyr's mask, another the victor's. Like a conjuror, he makes the mass murderer Hitler vanish into the mythological fog. Thus "Uncle Wolf" remains the "kindly human being" that Winifred believed him to be – Winifred, with whom he steamrollered the Foundation statutes as the greatest coup of his life.

He says nothing about the historical connection between his grandfather's antisemitism and Hitler, despite the copious material explicitly documenting the inner relationship between the Wagner family and the Führer. So where is this important part among the "accurate records"? Nor has my father included in his book the correspondence with Wieland. That would have been important for an understanding of what "New Bayreuth" was.

Central scenes are missing in *Acts*, although all those concerned know about them. In this way my Father has thrown away a great and unique opportunity of being credible to himself and to the world. Does he care nothing for the solidarity of the honest, valuing instead the applause of those who simply follow fashion?

I stick to Democritus' aphorism: "I prefer an austere life in a democracy to wealth under a tyrant." This knowledge also gives me the freedom to leave a door open to him. Why should we not be "able to learn through our faults and mistakes and in particular by the criticism of others and ultimately by self-criticism"? In this way my father could discover himself.

CHAPTER TWENTY-THREE

THE BAN FROM BAYREUTH

My father's personal and professional attacks on me had negative and positive consequences. One positive result has been my focusing no longer just on Wagner and Jews, but on the history of Christianity and Judaism. The cultural and spiritual enrichment this has entailed has had a significant effect on my personal and professional development.

On the negative side, opportunities for me in Germany dwindled. Word of our rift spread quickly – and precisely in those places where I had previously had prospects. Everyone in the music world who wanted to offer me work now knew that doing so would attract my father's enmity. Why spoil things with the *Festspielhügel*? However, many circles found my father's attitude towards me excessive and implausible, and I found the international reaction to his autobiography encouraging.

Set against the peculiar relationship Germans have with Richard Wagner, however, my position turned out to be complicated. Wagner is for them pregnant with meaning, his works heavyweight and earnest. Irony and self-irony have never been a forte of the Germans. For them Wagner is either a sacred national relic or a Nazi monster. He is always taken seriously, and he arouses more emotion than any other composer on earth. The reason for this lies in those conflicts contained within the works, life and jumbled *Weltanschauung* of Wagner himself, who misused music as a vehicle of propaganda; he plays with the German soul,

255

which is constantly taken in by idealistic concepts of world improvement. As long as fundamental discussion on Wagner's attitude to the Jews is avoided in Germany, every aspect of the *Zeitgeist* can be accommodated in him. But anyone who, as a post-Holocaust German, finds this wild mixture of theatrical "redemption", racism, antifeminism and Teutomania in Germany not only outdated as a cultural model, but also dangerous, will meet with violent resistance – not only among the Bayreuth Wagner cult community.

Where arguments about Wagner are concerned, Germans very quickly lose their sense of humour. With Wagner the German soul becomes exalted. Woe betide anyone who questions Wagner, especially if he comes from Wagner's family and thus commits the most infamous form of fouling one's nest.

My father and Lienhart succeeded in curtailing any discussion of my trip to Israel at the Federal Congress of the Richard Wagner Society in Mannheim at the end of May 1990, although some local sections wanted to talk about it. However, the majority of those present followed Father's and Lienhart's line and in fear of losing their ticket quota for the *Festspiele*, moved quickly on to the next item on the agenda.

Typical of this attitude was a letter from the chairwoman of the Saarbrücken Wagner Society, Otti Maurer, once a close friend of my grandmother. On 6 June 1991 Frau Maurer informed me, presumably having had the okay from Bayreuth, that on the basis of the – for her – shocking newspaper reports over the last year, she had made the application to the working session of the Richard Wagner Society in Hanover that the main assembly discuss whether it was still appropriate, after my "derogatory remarks" on the Bayreuth *Festspiele*, my father and my grandmother, whom she had loved very much, still to invite me as a speaker at events of the Richard Wagner Society. One must ask oneself, she wrote, whether it was worth jeopardising the friendship of the head of the *Festspiele* and of his sister, Frau Verena Lafferentz, for the sake of one young man, even if he was a member of the Wagner family. Frau Maurer, did not participate in the session however.

The final sentence of her letter is revealing, and reflects

Father's accusation. Here too I am reproached (in the form of a question) for having profited from the inheritance that Winifred Wagner had held together.

To be fair, the attitude of most chairpersons of the German Richard Wagner Societies was mixed. They regarded my critique of Richard Wagner in Israel and its consequences with some understanding. But if it was a matter of the opinions expressed to me in private being voiced in their own local society or even to President Lienhart, they lacked the courage of their convictions. Hence the breakdown of negotiations to give lectures to the Cologne and Düsseldorf Wagner Societies.

A commendable exception and example of steadfastness came from the Munich Wagner Society. Its then president Jürgen Dreher wrote to me, among other things, that the very announcement in the annual programme had led to renewed threats from Gudrun and Wolfgang Wagner, which would certainly have thrown the Federal chairman and the local chairwoman in Hanover into a state of some panic. In spite of this they were looking forward to my "rapprochement with Richard Wagner" and were not going to let themselves be pressurised by the head of the *Festspiele*, but were resolved to stand up to him.

After the lecture in Munich in January 1991 a man was waiting for me outside in the street dressed in leather trousers, green Loden coat and Bavarian hat, with an enormous Alsatian dog. He had put in an appearance once before, many years ago. When I got into my car he shouted at me, pointing to his dog: "My Wolfi will get you yet, you Wagner swine!"

One of the audience in Munich later wrote me a letter which revealed the dilemma one section of the Wagnerians found themselves in. The Jewish Wagnerian Heinrich Frank advised me, with reference to the fourth Commandment, to stop criticising members of my family, especially Winifred Wagner and Chamberlain. People knew of my views on the matter, and no one would assume that I had moved away from my criticism of the woman who had run the *Festspiele* from 1933 to 1944, were I to avoid the subject in future.

Part of my answer to Heinrich Frank included the following: "My statements, always based on public documents and facts, correspond to my understanding of tradition...and my conscience and knowledge as a Wagner after Auschwitz, who will never be prepared to remain silent for reasons of professional expediency out of blind obedience to a questionable family tradition...I have known since my childhood that in so doing I find myself outside the norms of the 'morals and tolerance' of a 'certain German establishment', which represses its own past in self-alienation...

"You speak of the fourth Commandment in connection with my grandmother...Anyone who claims to have been honoured as father and mother, must have acted convincingly through a correspondingly responsible former life and firm actions as a private and public person in the interests of the future of the children... Why do you think I get no answer from Bayreuth to my letters and have been declared *persona non grata* there?...The reconciliation with a certain establishment cannot and may not rest on repression, as occurred in the case of the exhibition *Wagner And The Jews* in 1984 in Villa Wahnfried...You could play a part in mediating my mission to a different, open German establishment which, thank God, exists."

Unfortunately my position and Heinrich Frank's remained irreconcilable. It is impossible for me to remain silent on the deeds of my grandmother and Chamberlain.

One thing I did learn from my correspondence with Frank was to use the word "mission" less in connection with my activities. Even then I did not understand my work as a mission, but as a contribution to finding out the truth about Richard Wagner.

Another interesting episode took place in mid-August, at a conference in Weimar on the subject "The Case Of Richard Wagner In Israel And Germany" in mid August 1991. Herzl Shmueli also took part, and before the start of the discussion in the Autonomous Cultural Centre the chairman of the Richard Wagner Society in Weimar, Eberhard Lüdde, asked me: "What line should we take? All the Wagner Societies at home and abroad have been instructed not to invite you to functions."

I answered: "Thank you for the hint. Whether you or other Wagner Societies want to invite me or not must surely depend on you yourselves."

Lüdde came to all my Weimar talks and to the premiere of my *Lohengrin* in Dessau. He repeated how he did not approve of the Bayreuth policy against me, but as in general he went no further than non-binding promises, I wasn't convinced. Maybe historians should look into the repressed Nazi past of the Wagner Societies some day.

Other representatives from Wagner Societies turned up to my *Lohengrin* Dessau premiere in May 1995. Here again, the picture was not uniform. The Berlin Society obviously toed the Bayreuth line. The *Neue Zürcher Zeitung*, which applauded my concept of a critical reading of the text, then poked fun at the organised booing against me. Two soloists fell in with the anti-Gottfried mood, after having made out for months during rehearsals that they agreed with my concept. Subsequently they were reluctant to be named in the documentary film *Herr Hitler's Religion*. This film, which was televised from September 1995 in various countries, shows scenes from my *Lohengrin* in which Wagner's "New Christianity in the direction of *Parsifal*" is clarified, to the horror of the Bayreuth faithful. The administration and the majority of the ensemble of the Dessau theatre shared my opinion.

I had a particularly difficult time in Bayreuth, not least regarding my correspondence with the mayor, Dieter Mronz. In December 1989 I had sent him, for his information, the introductory texts to my lectures on Wagner at the Tel Aviv University. On 26 March 1990, after having heard nothing from him for three months, I wrote again:

"Dear Dr Mronz, In our talks during the opening week of the Bayreuth *Festspiele* at the end of July 1989 you expressed definite interest in my desire for reconciliation in Israel (cf also the interview of 18.8.89 in the *Nordbayerischer Kurier*) and promised to send me your views on the 'case of the Chamberlain-Furtwängler Strasse'. For that reason in my letter of 21.12.89 I referred, among other things, yet again, to my forthcoming trip to Israel and enclosed the summaries of my three lectures and of my *Ring* video presentation with the intention of evoking some reaction from you...Your continuing silence on the matter...which surely also concerns the citizens of Bayreuth, gives me cause for concern. With kind regards, your Gottfried H Wagner."

One month later I received a four-page letter from Mayor Mronz, in which he congratulated me on the success of my journey to Israel. His remarks on the Chamberlain affair, however, are indicative of the intellectual climate in Bayreuth. With reference to the municipal council member of the Greens, Werner Kolb, who in 1989 had courageously pleaded for a renaming of the Chamberlain Strasse, Mronz came to his position towards the Bayreuth municipal council: on the basis of the fact that the present generation must also be suffering under the heavy burden of the Nazi dictatorship, he pointed out that in Bayreuth a new, more profound sensitivity towards this had developed, which has finally led among other things to confidently freeing themselves from such burdens as the disputed street name, instead of encumbering themselves with new guilt complexes and burdens, through stubbornly clinging on to it.

In July I replied to Mronz: "I find it not only regrettable, but in every respect scandalous, that it has taken twenty-three years to change the name of the Chamberlain Strasse. The example of the Chamberlain Strasse shows that we are not capable of 'confidently freeing ourselves of such burdens as this street name'. The words 'confidently freeing' in this connection make me feel uneasy. Whoever 'stubbornly clings on' to names like Chamberlain in Bayreuth and elsewhere shows what sort of person he is. 'New guilt complexes and burdens' will certainly continue to exist if these antidemocratic powers are not publicly opposed with personal courage and pluralistic-democratic means and people are still not prepared, especially in the period of German reunification, for a thorough acceptance of the past and genuine mourning through firm action – without remembrance ceremonies which often function as rather dubious alibis. The city of Bayreuth could, for example, find a twin city in Israel. After discussions with people there you would certainly, as I did, alter your opinion and attitude to this fundamental subject of German history. I regret that, on the basis of my knowledge and conscience, I am forced to acknowledge that in this sense neither the commemorative text on the *Reichskristallnacht* [in Bayreuth] nor the volume *Wagner und die Juden* [Wagner And The Jews] correspond to my ideas. With thoughtful regards and constant readiness for dialogue I remain, Your Gottfried Wagner.

"PS On the basis of my objective critical statements at the University of Tel Aviv, among other things on the style of leadership of my grandmother as head of the *Festspiele* in the Nazi period, I have been declared *persona non grata* by circles close to the *Festspiele* (letter of 2.2.90) including the federal president Lienhart, black-listed in Germany and my work has been slandered as a 'settling of private scores'. The international professional world and the press, particularly in Israel, has still to deal with this. This will certainly not be awkward for me, as among other things the manipulated selection of press quotations against me will probably have to be aired. *As persona non grata* I no longer have access to the *Festspielhügel*, it is true, but surely I do still to the archives of the city of Bayreuth? Can I, if I am hindered in my researches, apply to you? Also on this subject: 'Can we confidently free ourselves from such burdens?' On the basis of my experiences I fear not."

Mronz never answered this letter. I was not surprised that I was unwelcome at that time in the Richard Wagner Archive and that my work was not encouraged.

Just as revealing is another instance concerning the Bayreuth University, which I naively believed was independent of *Festspielhügel* politics. Professor Walter Gebhard of the German Department wrote to me in June 1993 in connection with a "possible lecture", that he considered the time (before the granting of a doctorate by the university to my father) as inappropriate, not least because the reaction of the *Festspiele* administration to a critical lecture was difficult to predict.

I did well to cancel the lecture. The university's attitude was clear, not only in fact that they had granted an honorary doctorate to my father, but also in the content of the ceremonial speech which Walter Jens had given in January 1994 on the occasion of the 800th centenary of Bayreuth.

Jens rejected the findings of independent research into Wagner's antisemitism and told the representatives of the city of Bayreuth and of the *Festspielhügel* at some length what they wanted to hear. He performed what the Wagner scholar Hartmut Zelinsky aptly termed a "flight into vagueness".

Yet another icon of the German cultural scene joined the Bayreuth game: August Everding, Germany's most powerful intendant. In April 1990 I had written to him and hoped he would support my discussion of Wagner in Germany after my trip to Israel. Typically, the cultural politician Everding reacted noncommittally. But things did not stop there. He managed, in opposition to the head of the Richard Strauss Institute in Munich, Stephan Kohler, and the then chairmen Dr Manfred Frei and Christian Lange of the patrons circle of the Richard Strauss *Festspiele* in Garmisch Partenkirchen, to see to it that my invitation was cancelled to a symposium on the subject "Richard Strauss, An (Un)heroic Life" in July 1991. Word was spread around that I was "difficult, verbose and dangerous".

A planned lecture on "The Case Of Wagner In Israel And Germany" at the Academy of Fine Arts in Munich in 1991, which the composer Günter Bialas had championed, also came to nothing. I had written to Bialas in May, enclosing numerous documents on my trip to Israel. He had been very interested in the subject, but at the end of June 1991 wrote to say that he found himself unable to invite me to give a lecture at the Bavarian Academy of Fine Arts without the consent of my father, as the latter was a member of the music department. According to Dr Bauer, secretary of the Academy, the tensions between me and my father were (still) too great.

My experiences with the media were not much better, whatever the individual reasons. In autumn 1991 Tilman Jens, Walter Jens' son, rang me and asked for an interview in my home in Cerro Maggiore on the subject "My Israel Journey In 1990 And Wagner's Antisemitism". The interview was then broadcast under the sensationalist title "The Inheritance War – Trouble In The House Of Wagner: Wolfgang Wagner Is Angry" in November, on the culture programme *titel, thesen, temperamente*. My cousin Nike deputised as spokesperson for the fourth Wagner generation, although Nike's opinions and mine diverged where Bayreuth was concerned.

Shortly after the broadcast I wrote Nike a letter, to initiate dialogue again after a silence of several years. Unfortunately she did not reply. For years she has reinforced her claim to the succession by criticising the *Festspiele* as run by my father. In an interview in the summer of 1995 she stated: "As in every institution a period of government should not go on too long. There is an urgent need for new ideas, a new artistic will, a new vision. The future of Wagner is at stake. That is what I stand for, and I am ready to take it on." But she did not present a programme for dealing with Wagner's ideology and his antisemitism in his work and theories.

Until then she had avoided being involved in the Bayreuth politicking against me, and in that respect, she differed agreeably from the other two women in the family – Eva and Gudrun – who have ambitions of inheritance. Both worked closely with Father and were tarred by the brush of his power-politics. Two principles of my father rule his pupils almost as much as their master: one can be described as "control from the rear"; the other that "in dealing with the public, leave your sentiments ambiguous". Neither Eva nor Gudrun have the will or the ability to come to terms with Bayreuth's Nazi past, something Eva has already prove by allegedly losing the copies of the films from the motor cycle sidecar that I had entrusted to her.

Tilman Jens should have reported this in his programme. Of course, he also gave my father the chance to make a statement: "I can't turn the Bayreuth *Festspiele* into a playground for Richard Wagner's great-grandchildren. I can only appoint someone here who in my view has something to offer Bayreuth. We are not a training centre for the Wagner great-grandchildren."

Jens: "Does that mean that you are sort of the last representative of the great Wagner family?"

Father: "No."

Jens: "You are the last Wagner?"

Father: "No, I have never maintained that. And I can't understand why I am blamed because my nieces and nephews can't read and understand that."

Jens: "Okay, but if you say that at the moment nothing will come after..."

Father: "I'm sorry, what I was trying to say was that, there is no one from within the family who, based on achievement so far, is any better placed than an outsider...with respect to what they could contribute to Wagner's work."

Jens: "Do you see something like a generation conflict in the great Wagner family?"

Father: "I can only say the following: from the outset my brother maintained that older and younger generations don't work well together."

Talking about me, and the fact that I no longer receive *Festspiele* tickets, he said: "In many of the public talks he has given on tour, my son has made very negative comments about the present structure of the *Festspiele.* Among other things he has claimed that my colleagues are just alibi Jews and that I have been indulging in negative nationalist tendencies. That is an arrogant and terribly false accusation, and furthermore a degradation of this circle of colleagues. That is totally unacceptable."

Jens: "So he doesn't get tickets any more?"

Wolfgang Wagner: "As I have said, I can't receive him here because of my colleagues. If he says such things, attacks everyone, including myself, and acts so negatively, he should not be allowed in the house."

Jens: "How do you feel, playing the role of wicked father, or wicked uncle?"

Father: "Excuse me, I am not wicked! It is only ever one of a very small group..."

Jens: "...your family..."

Father: "What do you mean, my family? Excuse me. Family is a haphazardly compiled community...which happens to have originated from the same root. At some stage one's own personality emerges, one develops and then one makes up one's own mind about things."

Jens: "Herr Wagner, you are now seventy-two. People usually retire at sixty-five. Why haven't you retired yet? Do you have any idea when you intend to do so?"

Father: "Adenauer started to rule Germany at seventy-five and voluntarily retired fourteen years later."

Jens: "Is that some indication of your plans?"

Father: "You will see. You are young. One day you will read it in the newspaper and I presume television will report on it too."

In conclusion, Jens remarked: "The patriarch will decide on his successor jointly with a commission. One may assume that none from the circle of his children, nephews and nieces will feature among the candidates. So, a family tradition is coming to an end. Wouldn't that be a very typical Wagner story. Fifteen years ago Wolfgang Wagner married for the second time. Now there is Frau Gudrun and Katherina, their daughter. In a few years she will have reached her majority and would not be the first female chief in Bayreuth. Nothing changes. Rejoice! Wagner without end!"[35]

I would like to quote two reactions which I encountered in German radio stations after my trip to Israel.

Judging from interviews in January and August 1990, I had the impression that critical discussion of Richard Wagner's antisemitism might be possible on Bavarian Radio. A statement I had made during the August interview – "Post-Wieland Bayreuth has nothing to do with [Richard Wagner's] idea of the *Festspiele*" – was then used as grounds to cancel all collaboration on the planned project. The harmony, in other words the long-term business association, between the local radio station and the Bayreuth *Festspiele* was not to be jeopardised.

In February 1996, the Vienna-based journalist Hellfried Brandl managed to arrange a broadcast with me, without the knowledge of those at the radio station who were close to Bayreuth, on the subject of Wagner, Bayreuth and antisemitism as part of the Bavarian Radio family programme.

An interview with Wolfgang Seifert, a former employee of West German Radio and Free Berlin Radio, went off less favourably. I knew of Seifert through his exculpatory article 'Hour Zero Of New Bayreuth' for the West German Radio, which had appeared in printed form after it was broadcast in February 1970. Research documentation for this had been provided by Father's former assistant director and house dramaturg of the Bayreuth *Festspiele,* Dietrich Mack.

At the end of October 1993 a programme was broadcast on four decades of the "Bayreuth Workshop". In it my statements were distorted and taken out of context. Seifert also dismissed my comments on the "multicultural future of Bayreuth" simply by using my father's words: "That is not suitable for Bayreuth."[36] And, with servility, drew attention to Father's influence in the Foundation Council of the Bayreuth *Festspiele*.

My experiences with a number of leading German newspapers were similarly negative. In particular the London correspondent of the *Frankfurter Allgemeine Zeitung*, Gina Thomas, who stirred up feeling against me in an article of mid April 1995. Thomas was taking her revenge as a German for remarks I had made on the programme *Wagner Versus Wagner*, televised at the beginning of April 1995 by the UK's Channel Four. She did this without any knowledge either of my work or of modern research into Wagner's antisemitic writings, which I quoted. As opposed to objective discussion, she gave free rein to her resentment and kept deliberately silent about the fact that other critical experts, such as Barry Millington, the editor of the *Wagner Compendium*, Paul Lawrence Rose and Dan Bar On had also been interviewed in this programme. But it was the following remarks in particular that caused greatest astonishment: "*The Times* devoted half a page to Gottfried Wagner's childish objections and left his assertions uncontradicted. Other newspapers gave him, someone who likes to present himself as the victim of persecution, a lot of space...Not even the faintest doubt is expressed on his exaggerated assertions. His English interviewers blindly believe him. Full of sympathy, the opera critic of *The Times* describes how far Bayreuth's influence extends: Gottfried Wagner, whom the keepers of the Grail wrongly described as a nest-fouler, is even largely denied access to the German media...Abroad the ignorance of those giving him commissions works in his favour, and they are only too happy to have their own clichéd ideas confirmed."[37]

The German reviews, influenced by Bayreuth, of my *Lohengrin* production in May 1995 were of a similar tone. Since May 1977, in other words since the reviews of my first production, *Fidelio*, nothing has changed. Most of the reviewers aligned themselves with

Bayreuth and wrote in a style devoid of all objectivity: unfortunately, often of any competence in the field either. I will always listen to valid, quality criticism and I shall come to examples of those in time.

Something far more ominous now came to my attention. The American conductor John Edward Niles, with whom I have been in contact since 1990 regarding various projects on Jewish composers murdered during the Nazi period, informed me at the beginning of October 1992 that his brother Thomas, a high-ranking official in the American diplomatic service, had received hints that my Italian family and I were on some international Nazi organisation "black list": "I am very concerned [for] your personal safety. My brother and some of his colleagues were informed that there are people who want to bump you and your family off. I'm not someone who easily gets alarmist, but I must beg you to be very careful." He said we would be in danger if I continued my critical lectures on Wagner's antisemitism, particularly in Germany. This information scarcely surprised me: since my trip to Israel I had been constantly pestered by phone calls at night and death threats.

At that time I was preparing a lecture which the German Council of Industry and Commerce had invited me to deliver in Bonn, introduced, at my request, by Ralph Giordano. Concerned about my family, especially as the activities of Neo-Nazis in Germany at this time had greatly increased, I asked John Edward Niles to get detailed information for me on the various Neo-Nazi groups. I also asked Minister of State Helmut Schäfer from the German Ministry Of Foreign Affairs for help. The list of reasons I supplied, at the beginning of December 1992, included the following: "Since my lecture tour to Israel on Wagner in January 1990 I have regularly received anonymous telephone calls from Germany, in which, among other things, I am abused as 'Jew-lover'." After the publication of a magazine article on my trip to Israel I was viciously attacked by the *Nationalzeitung*. In March 1992 I received death threats in the USA from skinheads, so that I had to give one lecture under police protection. Niles told me of a discussion he had had in the USA with an extreme right-wing German lawyer who apparently lives in Switzerland. He learned from this dubious gentleman that "people in Germany are very angry with me, as I get involved in matters concerning the Holocaust and Wagner". Minister Schäfer ensured my safety. But it left a bitter aftertaste when, in December 1992, we were driven around Bonn and Cologne in an armoured limousine with guards.

Unfortunately, such safety measures were also necessary later, at subsequent lectures on Wagner's antisemitism.

CHAPTER TWENTY-FOUR

ANTISEMITISM AND OPERA BUSINESS

Since January 1990 Wagner's antisemitism had been the focus of my investigative research and the main subject of my lectures. Although demand for my talks in Germany was rather meagre, there was lively interest abroad, especially in Jewish communities and so I increasingly distanced myself, even intellectually, from Germany.

Abroad, where repressive mechanisms are not all powerful, one could discuss Wagner more freely. And discussion was most objective where hosts and audience had nothing to do with Bayreuth. If they did, there was renewed confrontation, but that seldom happened. Yet I must describe a few exceptions, which illustrate how deeply antisemitism has penetrated elsewhere.

For example, a US Nazi called Max Orlando wrote to me a few days after my Israel journey: "'The era of the American Weimar Republic' is coming to an end…Who needs Washington DC and Moscow? Us, Biopolitics USA – our triumvirate E Mullins, R Kuttner and myself – welcome in the twenty-first century. Wagner music is of no consequence…Wagner's anti-Jewish position was instinctive, as the host to the parasite, ie the 'biological Jew' [written by] E Mullins, published in 1968." Orlando enclosed with his letter the "research results" of the McArdle Laboratory For Cancer Research at the University of Wisconsin. I had strong doubts about the authenticity of these documents.

Other fanatics tried to bring me back to the "right path" of Wagnerian hatred of Jews, or just simply threatened me. Being called a "dirty traitor and friend of the Jews" in night-time phone calls has become part of life for me ever since.

In March 1992 I gave a talk in Dallas on "The Case Of Wagner In Israel And Germany". My hosts were the Southern Methodist University, the Goethe Centre and the local Richard Wagner Society. Two ladies on the committee of the Society, both keen Bayreuth visitors, were eager to tell me, in private, what I should and shouldn't say: no politics, not a word on Wolf and Winnie, and lots of enthusiasm for the neo-Christian case of the redeemer Richard Wagner. I thanked them and delivered my lecture against Wagner's antisemitism with even more passion. One of the two ladies exploded and ran shrieking from the hall. Before slamming the door behind her she shouted: "Scandal! Scandal!" But the majority of the audience were on my side and one member of the Wagner Society apologised for the incident. At the end of the lecture, my hosts immediately invited me to give another talk.

My experiences with the conductors James Levine and Daniel Barenboim show what the all-reaching Bayreuth connections are capable of. After a lecture on "The Case Of Wagner In Israel And Germany" at the City University of New York at the end of February 1992, the music historian George Jellinek, who also worked for the *New York Times* radio station WQXR, invited me for an interview. He asked me in particular about *Parsifal*, as the programme containing my interview was to be broadcast in the intervals of a radio transmission of a live stage performance conducted by James Levine on 28 March 1992. The interview went smoothly, and he was "very happy".

I subsequently told friends about the interview – among them Pierre Béique, founder of the Montreal Symphony Orchestra, and Larry Mass, doctor and contributor to the magazine *Opera Monthly* in New York – and that the North American media reported on the broadcast and my part in it.

Pierre, however, informed me on 28 March, that the interview with me had not been broadcast, because I had apparently been "ill". Larry looked further into the matter and wrote in *Opera Monthly* in October 1992, under the title "Met Cancels Gottfried Wagner": "*Opera Monthly* has learned that Richard Mohr, producer of the Texaco-Metropolitan Opera Radio Station, cancelled an interview with Gottfried Wagner, the great-grandson of the composer and outspoken critic of Bayreuth. The interview was scheduled to have run during the 28 March 1992 broadcast of *Parsifal*. George Jellinek, who had interviewed Dr Wagner for his WQXR radio programme and who had additionally conducted the pre-recorded interview for the broadcast, confirmed that the decision to cancel was made because Dr Wagner was judged to be 'too controversial'. While Jellinek did not want to be quoted as opposing the cancellation, he referred *Opera Monthly* to Mohr who gave the following explanation: 'It was a defective tape. You can interpret that as you wish.'"[38]

Jellinek informed me in May 1992 that the interview had been regarded as too controversial, and the decision to cancel had apparently had something to do with the Met-Bayreuth connection.

However, he enclosed a list of radio stations in the USA and Canada who *had* broadcast the interview – thirty-three stations in the USA and a few in Canada – which confirmed yet again how strong North American democracy is. It is not impressed by connections.

Following well-meant advice, I desisted from writing a letter of protest to Mohr. But I couldn't accept his and Levine's attitude lying down. When I received a cheque by way of compensation for a sum which was six times higher than the agreed fee, I wrote to Jellinek: "I shall send the cheque from Texaco-Metropolitan Opera International Radio Network to Unicef and try in that way to turn something bad into something good. I hope you can understand my reaction."

Despite my "too controversial" contribution, only three days after recording the radio interviews I gave a long talk on *Parsifal* in the renowned music conservatory of the University of Cincinnati. My arguments were no different from those in the interview with Jellinek, but not one member of the audience felt provoked, nor could anyone have had a reason to. Afterwards, I received a friendly thank-you letter from the conservatory.

A visit by the eminent violinist and former member of the La Salle String Quartet, Henry Meyer, was very welcome. On this occasion he presented me with a copy of his autobiographical sketches with his best regards. Henry, a Jewish survivor of the Holocaust, had been

James Levine's teacher.

The case of Daniel Barenboim, the one-time *Wunderkind* pianist and protégé of Otto Klemperer, is much more complex, however. There have been several critical studies of his brilliant career, such as Norman Lebrecht's *The Maestro Myth*, Klaus Umbach's *Geldscheinsonate* and Stephen J Petit's *History Of The London Philharmonic Orchestra*. In an interview with the Israeli newspaper *Yediot Acharonot*, published in summer 1992, Barenboim took issue with my exposition of Wagner, the Bayreuth *Festspiele* and Judaism. He had told the Spanish newspaper *El Pais* in June 1993, regarding the Neo-Nazi and xenophobic violence in Germany, that "if the Nazi phenomenon becomes widespread", he did not want to "stay a day longer [in Germany]". I would have had some sympathy for this statement, were not for the fact that one year earlier, German Neo-Nazis had been very prominent during the *Festspiele* in Bayreuth. Until today I have not heard of any statement by Barenboim on this, nor on the historically distortive exhibition in 1984, *Wagner And The Jews* in the Villa Wahnfried. And would he really leave Germany where, in Bayreuth and Berlin they lie at his feet?

In an interview with the newspaper *La Repubblica* in November 1993, entitled "Daniel Barenboim Rejoices And Is King Of Berlin", he said: "But I, as a Jew, defend Germany."

To compound this, in an interview with *Opera Monthly* (May/June 1993) he made every effort, in quite the Bayreuth style, to understate Richard Wagner's antisemitism: "We must remember that Wagner's antisemitism was intellectually *à la mode* in the nineteenth century and he cannot be held responsible for the actual atrocities committed half a century later by those who misused his ideas."[39]

Leonard Bernstein, whom I had met in April 1990 just a few months before his death, would never have said such a thing. On the contrary, he openly stressed his deep aversion to conducting at the Bayreuth *Festspiele* under my father's administration and never compromised Wagner's antisemitism or accepted New Bayreuth's policy of repression, but enthusiastically supported my trip to Israel. We even planned a film project together on the subject of "Wagner And The Jews". Unfortunately, Lenny died shortly after our conversation.

But back to Barenboim: I decided to defend myself against his attacks. In a "Letter to the editor" published in the July/August issue of *Opera Monthly*, 1993 I proved once again Wagner's antisemitic attitude, in which he was not simply *à la mode*. I described the ultimately catastrophic effects of this fanaticism in Germany, criticised the Bayreuth *Festspiele* and even talked about the neo-Nazi gatherings in Bayreuth in 1991. I declared that Richard Wagner, through his antisemitic inflammatory writings, was co-responsible for the transition from Bayreuth to Auschwitz. Moreover, I supported Elie Wiesel, who, in the *New York Times* of 12 January 1992, had criticised the way Barenboim excused Richard Wagner from guilt "because of the tragic thought connection of Wagner's music for survivors of the Holocaust".

In the end Franklin Littell, president of the Holocaust, Genocide And Human Rights Institute in Philadelphia and co-founder of the universally recognised organisation The Holocaust And The Churches, joined the argument. In an article which was printed in various American newspapers, he wrote among other things: "But what happened at Bayreuth, that major fortress of cultural revisionism? Gottfried Wagner, the great-grandson of the famous composer, has a letter in the July/August issue of *Opera Monthly* that probes some of the deeper issues in this centre of revisionism. He is responding to an article in an earlier issue of *Opera Monthly*, in which the vaguely Jewish Daniel Barenboim has attempted to lift the burden of wilful and wicked antisemitism from Richard Wagner's record...Gottfried Wagner will have none of it. He knows the bitter antisemitism of his great-grandfather as a personal burden. He knows the correspondence of Winifred Wagner and Hitler (from 1923 to 1944). He knows the bitterly antisemitic passages in his great-grandfather's letters and in Cosima Wagner's diaries. He asks why, if his antisemitism was so harmless, the skinheads chose Bayreuth for their major rally in August of 1991...We know about Bayreuth's past, and we can be thankful that Gottfried Wagner and his allies won't let that record be hidden for commercial and political purposes. There is a great deal going on in and around 'Bayreuth' today."[40]

No wonder that what happened with Radio WQXR and my letter to the editor were to have repercussions.

Among the reactions were the articles in the *New York Times* of mid August 1993 and in the English magazine *Opera Now* of January 1994. In a long letter to James R Oesterreicher, the music editor of the *New York Times*, I criticised what was a very inaccurately researched article by John Rockwell on the *Festspiele* and the family – published 15 August 1993 – with the title, "The Gods Sit There And Wait For Another Ugly Twilight". Rockwell asserted among other things: "Relations seem to be most bitter between Wolfgang and his son. Gottfried has taken to denouncing his family's history of antisemitism, most prominently on a visit to Israel, the first by a family member – this despite the fact that the two most prominent conductors at Bayreuth today are James Levine and Daniel Barenboim. Wolfgang, calling it shameful to stigmatise the conductors as 'alibi Jews', banned Gottfried from Bayreuth in 1990. 'Henceforth, both in Bayreuth and elsewhere,' he wrote by fax, 'an absolute distance between you and me must be maintained.' Now Gottfried says, his letters to his father are returned unopened."

Part of my letter to Oesterreicher read: "Mr Rockwell does not appear to have seen my recent letter published in the July/August edition of *Opera Monthly*. In this letter I express my opinion of the roles of Daniel Barenboim and James Levine and the hypocrisy of their involvement. Your report only quotes my father's statement, ie that my criticisms constitute 'a shameful stigmatisation of Barenboim and Levine as alibi Jews', but fails to let me respond. The Wagners have profited twice in my grandmother's and now in my father's time by denying any personal responsibility in the Nazi era as well as after the Holocaust. The former victimisers have become the new falsely pro-semitic heralds of today, thanks to people like Barenboim and Levine, the children of the victims, and to the common big business enterprise – the 'Redemption' Bayreuth *Festspiele*. The article also fails to mention my twenty-year struggle to help create better German-Jewish relations, as well as my co-founding of the Post Holocaust Dialogue Group. I have dedicated my life to fighting the evil of the Wagner legacy, attempting to give the public a better understanding and reconciling the important issues that still pull us toward my great-grandfather's art...None of these events, nor my father's intrigues over the 'royal' succession to the Bayreuth *Festspiele* can hide one brutal truth: a reunified Germany has a responsibility not to falsify its past, to face up to the Wagner family's important cultural role in the Nazi tyranny and to fight discrimination against those who, like me, are not willing to engage in a profitable music enterprise."

This letter was not published.

The article in *Opera Now* of January 1994 was false and slanderous. Robert Hartford wrote in connection with my father's seventy-fifth birthday and as promotion for the latter's book *Acts*, under the heading "House Of Cards": "…it is Bayreuth's heir apparent, Gottfried, who is making the most mischief. Gottfried has adopted a fashionable theme: his family's attitude towards Jews and, on the profitable principle of telling people what they want to hear, he has been lecturing his way around America – and Israel too, the first Wagner to set foot there – denouncing Bayreuth as still in the thrall of Nazi ideals and antisemitism. He has made especially vicious attacks on conductors Levine and Barenboim, both Jews, alleging 'Uncle Tom' compliance in working at Bayreuth."

At the end of January 1994 I sent my reaction to *Opera Now*: "Mr Hartford's comments on me and my work are mostly wrong, slanderous and reflect his lack of knowledge of the subjects involved. Here are a few examples of false statements made about me: 1. The issue of Judaism and Wagner has been troubling me for more than twenty years and I am, among others, a co-founder of the 'Post Holocaust Dialogue Group': as such this issue neither constitutes 'a fashionable theme' nor 'a profitable principle'. 2. The author is not informed about the places where I have spoken or will speak on these topics, for example, this year at the United States Holocaust Memorial Museum and Ben Gurion University. Are the distinguished institutions which invite me not able to select their speakers, or are they just inviting me to tell them 'what they want to hear'? 3. I have never said that Bayreuth is 'still in the thrall of Nazi ideals and antisemitism'. My critique is on quite another level. 4. With regard to Messrs Levine and Barenboim, the author is apparently ignorant of my comments, eg in my letter to the editor of *Opera Monthly* (July 1993) or in my August 1993 interview with *Musica* Nr 4 (Kassel). I do not stand alone in my criticism of either Barenboim or Levine: see, for example, Elie Wiesel's criticism of Barenboim in the *New York Times* (Jan 12, 1992). Finally, I will repeat, patiently, again and again, to journalists who are either unwilling or unable to understand me: I do not claim any aspirations to be my father's heir at the Bayreuth Festival."

My letter was printed in full in the March 1994 issue of *Opera Now*. Owing to pressure of work, I had to postpone to January 1996 the firm invitation mentioned under point two to present a seminar on "Richard Wagner's Antisemitism: Consequences For German Culture And Politics Until Today" at the Ben Gurion University.

CHAPTER TWENTY-FIVE

EUGENIO, MY SON

It was while I was preparing for my trip to Israel at the end of December 1989 that, Teresina, Mamma Antonietta and I saw television coverage of the arrest and execution of the Romanian dictator Nicolae Ceausescu and his wife Elena. The feature was followed by the first reports on the ill-treatment of children in Romanian orphanages. We could scarcely believe that, post-Hitler and Post-Stalin, a European state could have committed such crimes for two decades, with the knowledge of Western and Eastern politicians and humanitarian organisations, without provoking a storm of indignation. Not until 1991, in a book by the child psychotherapist Alice Miller, *Breaking Down The Wall Of Silence,* did I find an explanation of the reasons behind such a barbaric development.

She writes: "Ceausescu's deeds and his political career right from the outset, were ruled by the idea of redemption through destruction. Without having had similar motivation in childhood, one will not become a dictator. Just like Hitler, Stalin and others before him, Ceausescu must constantly have heard that it was for his own good that he was being beaten, tortured, and spied on and his soul destroyed. As a child he could never have been able to see through the lie. These unexposed lies later become the fundamental principles of the tyrant." Miller comes to the conclusion: "A mistreated child must repress all doubt in order to survive. If it were to doubt the benevolent purpose of what it suffered, it would place itself in mortal danger. But where does such repression lead an adult who refuses to give it up? As we can learn by the example of all dictators, the belief forms and takes hold that if they do to the people what their parents once did to them – humiliate and dominate, enslave, exploit, mock, and silence them – they will be redeeming them…Both the dictator and his wife were convinced that they were being the best of parents as they tortured 'the people'…It can be seen in the last words uttered by Elena Ceausescu before her execution. As the soldiers attempted to tie her up, she shouted: 'Children! Remember! I have been like a mother to you these last twenty years. Don't forget everything I have done for you!'"

What the Ceausescus did as "loving parents" to their people, who were living in indescribable hardship, is well known today. But during his lifetime Ceausescu, expected grateful homage, as Miller wrote: "Whatever he did, though, was too little to satisfy the child's natural, though previously repressed, needs – its need to be seen and recognised, to be acknowledged and taken seriously; its need for its name and its existence to never again be forgotten in the fundamental, damaging and harmful way that it had been by its parents. A mistreated child has no chance of maintaining this need at the level of consciousness. If the need remains unsatisfied, the child must repress it. As adults we can relieve that repression by no longer denying what happened to us, and we can attempt to satisfy this primal need in legitimate, nondestructive ways.

"If the psychodynamics of child abuse were universally acknowledged today, a man like Nicolae Ceausescu could not succeed in plundering and humiliating an entire nation for twenty years in the guise of national salvation, with the goal of raising a whole nation as his applauding slaves. But his regime is a blueprint of the generally accepted tyranny imposed throughout the world with impunity on children in the name of 'childrearing' and redemption 'for your own good' – dispossession, exploitation, total control, torture, humiliation, disrespect, mistreatment, misuse, persecution, seduction, lies, terror, the deformation of the truth, and pitiless psychological cruelty. All carried out, thank you very much, with a smile and the promise of salvation."[41]

All the important events in my life of recent years have somehow had to do with my journey to Israel. Even the way I found my son.

In early January 1990, we read in the *Jerusalem Post* that, since the execution of the Ceausescus, it was possible to adopt children in Romania. After much discussion, Teresina and I decided to apply to adopt a child from Romania as soon as we got home in mid January. After bureaucratic procedures which went on for months, we flew to Bucharest at the beginning of June 1990 with the necessary documents. It was just a few days before the miners' revolt.

The squalor of the people and the city took our breath away. The depression of the post-"revolution" days – which was unfortunately nothing but a *putsch* by one-time Ceausescu vassal Iliescu and his thugs – also had its effect on us. Damp, stinking soot even penetrated the shops, where we couldn't even find mineral water or milk to buy. Hordes of neglected children ran after us begging, as they had seen by our clothes that we came from the West.

We spent the first night in the Intercontinental Hotel, right on University Square, where the students were camping out in protest against Iliescu. As we didn't speak the local language, we were constantly being swindled and when the hotel tried to charge us higher prices than those quoted by the official travel agency, we decided to move to a simpler, cheaper hotel on the street leading to the university. The first floor was given over to child prostitution and from our room we witnessed a group of militant Iliescu thugs setting about former members of the secret service Securitate. The police arrived too late to prevent a murder.

Finally the moment came. On 6 June we drove with the wily Romanian lawyer George Alexandru, who had been procured for us by the Italian embassy, to Orphanage Four in the workers' district of Bucharest. The Ceausescu regime had left total desolation there too. The orphanage was a prison, surrounded by high fences and barricades. In the filthy dark interior of the concrete building there was a stench of urine and ammonia. There was not a single picture hanging on the walls. No toy to be seen. No children's voices to be heard.

Equally cheerless was the office of the director, who, in her contempt for "her" orphans, was typical of the still omnipresent spirit of Ceausescu. She made it clear to us that if we didn't want any problems in getting a child there would be "little extras".

The door opened, and three children were introduced to us one after the other. Elena, then Christoph and finally Eugenio. Eugenio was in a pitiful condition. He was emaciated and his belly was very distended. His skin was pallid, raw and dirty. His pale blond hair was thin in patches and his teeth were covered with a black coating. His muscles were so under developed, that he had to keep sitting down out of exhaustion: he reminded me of Jackie Coogan in Chaplin's film *The Kid*. As clothes he had on a pair of underpants several sizes too large, and a shirt of synthetic material which was full of holes. His shoes were enormous, so big in fact he could not walk properly. But Eugenio gave me a faint smile which lit up our first moments as future father and son.

The reality of the orphanage was brought back to us by the harsh voice of the director, who said: "As you are already forty-three, you could have Eugenio, he's one of our oldest children."

What had Eugenio had to endure! His mother had given him up immediately after birth. The Ceausescu state classified him as a delicate child, of the "second" category. The more robust children in the "first" category were later destined to enter the service of the Securitate, while the delicate children, who did not appear up to this "heroic" task, were shunted off to squalid orphanages.

We yielded to the director's blackmailing in order to liberate Eugenio from this hell. At that moment he noticed Teresina, who was sitting on a chair in the cramped room. They looked curiously at one another. Teresina gave him some chocolate – for him a really special present! With difficulty, he climbed on to Teresina's lap and smiling, tucked into what were probably the first sweets of his life.

After an odyssey through a Bucharest court, where we had to sign further adoption documents, we finally visited Eugenio two days later as his new parents. He had suspected something was happening and called both Teresina and me "Mama": having only been brought up by women, he didn't know what a father was. We gave him a little plastic truck, which he hugged, beaming, although at the same time scared that someone could take the toy away from him.

Then we went for a little excursion outside the orphanage. He had clearly never been out of his prison: everything was new for him. He reacted with a mixture of joy and fear to a cock, a bus, a crane and the crowds who scurried silently past us with impassive faces.

The first time I tried to pick Eugenio up, he trembled with fear. I put him down again carefully and later he told me that he had only ever been picked up by the nurses when he was being taken to a dark room after having been beaten.

We had to take him back to the orphanage that June, because the documentation was not yet complete, and naturally we were afraid we would never see him again. Iliescu's mob of miners were beginning to "cleanse" the streets of students, and foreigners were unpopular, despite their coveted dollar bills. At one point, we were afraid we wouldn't make it to the airport and had to bribe a taxi driver to take us there.

It wasn't until 30 August 1990, that Eugenio became our son, by decree of a Bucharest court. It was also my father's birthday. So Eugenio became a Wagner on his grandfather's birthday. He was baptised in December of the same year.

I sent Father a photo of Eugenio, which was sent back without comment.

Even before our second trip to Romania, in September 1990 I interpreted the strange coincidence of significant dates in the lives of grandfather and grandchild as a point of departure for a new chapter in my life. On the basis of my own childhood, I knew that I should never allow the shadow of Ceausescu to become all-powerful for Eugenio, as the shadow of Hitler had been for me.

The day we collected Eugenio from the orphanage will remain unforgettable. He clutched our hands tightly and left without a word to anyone, without looking back once. Thanks to the wife of the Italian Ambassador, Giovanna Amaduzzi, and their excellent colleagues, we were able to fly back to Rome immediately.

A new period began in our life, to which we began gradually to accustom ourselves. Whenever Eugenio spoke of his past in the first year of our life together, he always started his story with the words: "And then I flew home with Papa and Mama." It was difficult for him to find his own identity. In everything he did he lacked the life experience of a child who had grown up under humane conditions. For the first five and a half years of his life, he had had no family and had never experienced any kind of love.

Child therapists such as Jean Piaget, Alice Miller, Hans Aebli, Ashley

Montagu, Alfred Adler, David Kirk and many others, whose works I had read before Eugenio's arrival, did describe fascinating theories and models, it is true. But day to day life proved just how difficult it is to realise good intentions. I had a lot to learn as a father, and it was not just to come from wise books.

Eugenio had not learned any language and in fighting to survive in the orphanage he had assumed several anti-social behavioural habits. He had to learn first how to live in a family. Here his new cousin Alberto, who was the same age, helped him; in fact, they grew up like brothers. We tried to teach Eugenio what good and evil, right and wrong were, which also meant that we had to test our own standard of values.

It was particularly difficult to get Eugenio out of the habit of cringing, proto-military obedience, which he had been broken into and which was now increased by his fear of being sent back to the orphanage. His servile eagerness to obey was replaced by the need to learn how to cope with freedom. And for me this whole period felt like a daily tightrope walk between liberating knowledge and bitter experiences from my own childhood.

Following my own experiences, I also wanted to avoid any repressive teaching methods. The hazards of a wrong attitude and of over-reaction were always present for me: I had constantly to remember that Eugenio was experiencing out of phase everything that had been missing from his early life. This also affected the way he played, the way he learned and his need for love. In this way, we were able to experience things we otherwise would not have with another child.

I also tried to satisfy his very personal needs with bedtime stories. But Eugenio was not interested in Grimm's fairy tales. Instead he wanted me to tell him his own life story again and again, but only from the moment he had called us Papa and Mama, and each time he heard this wonderful "fairy tale", he wanted lots of fresh details. He was probably satisfying his backlog need for warmth – although he got plenty of this in our Italian household.

Eugenio's integration into the family took place with the high drama and alternating hot and cold emotions that are only possible in Italy. I envy him that: I would like to have grown up in a *famiglia italiana* too.

In raising my son, a new process of integration began for me too. My thinking, feeling and acting all changed greatly. Eugenio confronted me with the real responsibilities of planning a common present and future. A lot that once seemed important to me, including the Bayreuth past, was put into context or simply lost all significance. Above all, I had to learn to be patient, which is certainly not one of my virtues!

Outside the family the process of integration didn't always go smoothly. A positive start in the family and kindergarten group were followed, once he started school, with phases of isolation, caused by his former enforced passivity and lack of motivation. In everything he did, Eugenio had to activate all his energies, in order not only to absorb what was new in any school day, but also to fill the gaps and the deficit in experience from the past. As his teachers did not know how to help Eugenio by motivating him as an individual, his five years at primary school often proved an endurance test.

Neither the teachers, nuns nor parents of the other children showed us much solidarity: any deviation from the prescribed syllabus or discussions on more liberal educational methods were rejected and hidden resentments came out into the open. For example it was maintained that I, as "foreigner and intellectual" with my family background, could not understand the people of Cerro Maggiore. Fortunately my Italian family didn't let this upset them.

This climate was hardly conducive for Eugenio's development, which could only really take place at home. He immediately understood my criticism of what was happening in the school and would ask: "And what is your opinion of the story I heard today in school?" He also understood the somewhat alienated position we found ourselves in and whenever I had differences of opinion with the teachers, before going into the consultation room, he would plead with me: "Please, Papa, *piano, piano!*" – he was obviously worried I would tell the teachers too plainly what I thought of them. He had every reason to fear this: I got very annoyed when they kept trying to tell me my son was at the bottom of the class. "We'll see how Eugenio will turn out! My teachers too always wanted me to believe I was untalented. Eugenio's horizons are already opening up today beyond the signpost marking the end of Cerro Maggiore."

Teresina and I were not prepared to take such nonsense from

teachers we believed to be inadequate and a close friend of ours, the pediatric neuropsychotherapist Anna Maria Carugo, arranged for us to visit one of the leading pediatric clinics in Milan. The result of the test by a colleague of Anna Maria's was very reassuring and gave every cause for optimism.

The more Eugenio was integrated in our family, the more clearly he articulated his interest in his own past and in my family. We had certainly expected the questions he asked us, but were still moved when they came. He gradually understood that before the time with us he had not had any family life. We could only soften the pain of the loss of an essential part of his childhood by pointing out that he was after all now living in our family. Although he showed amazing understanding, his reaction made it clear just how much he needs me and how much I still have to learn to be a steady and balanced father.

The need to develop my paternal qualities was emphasised further when Eugenio started asking questions about my own father. I had avoided the subject up to then – I still hadn't found any balanced answers to his questions about his grandfather. One day, as we were visiting Papa Antonio's grave, he suddenly asked where his other grandfather was buried.

I answered: "Your Grandfather Wolfgang isn't dead. He's living in Germany."

He wanted to know why this grandfather didn't come and visit us. I became nervous: I didn't want to paint a gloomy picture of my father in this, the first discussion. So I said: "Grandfather sees lots of things differently from us. His theatre, his friends and his new family keep him very busy, so he hasn't any time left for us."

Eugenio didn't say any more and then disappeared up to his room for some time. When he came down he declared hotly: "If Grandfather Wolfgang doesn't have any time for us, then I don't want to see him, his theatre or his new family either!"

His reaction moved me very much. I picked Eugenio up and said to him: "Who knows, maybe Grandfather will talk to us one day."

He didn't believe me.

On that October evening my work on this book faltered. I felt like giving up and wrote to Ralph Giordano that evening: "I ask myself more and more often, for whom am I actually writing my obituary –

this book – in my isolation in Italy, that prevents me from living. In one thing you have perhaps deluded yourself: that I could write my book as well as do other things. I find working on it such a strain that I scarcely have any energy left for anything else. I have severely overestimated my inner strength for this constant overcoming and breaking through of inner walls…I stare into the past of a family that was never mine, and to my horror this too often isolates from the present in my own family who love me, and I see no opportunity of building up a future for myself that corresponds to my needs…It all seems more and more uncertain to me, and my isolation is increasing. For a long time, my concern is not for myself, but for the future of my Eugenio, for whom I would like at least to ensure an education. For his sake I shall continue to hold on. On him I project my hopes for a better tomorrow, and he will always be confident of my love."

Ralph Giordano answered me at once by fax: "I have been aware of your growing despair…You are indeed right to 'take stock'. You are running up against brick walls and only injuring yourself by doing so. That is one thing. The other is the social, financial situation, and that is depressing enough. The worst thing is that your gifts are lying fallow, as it were, not getting established – that there apparently exists here in Germany no demand for what you are, do and want. You yourself have already distanced yourself very much from it, and I don't know whether you would be up to the constant fight, or rather guerrilla warfare, you would have to wage here. I've been born into it, so to speak and so I'm used to these conflicts with the outrageous, albeit only up to a certain point. I too sometimes consider flight, to a different, less problematic place, to jobs that give pleasure too. At the same time I know that I am 'nailed' to this country and will never get away from it. The same holds for you too, even if you are not living geographically in Germany, nevertheless the whole weight of it is squatting on top of you, as it were. And that is not going to alter either…

"I too was only able to 'stop the wheel of fate' at forty-one, so I lived long enough 'on the outskirts'. Yet, without the period up to that point nothing would have turned out well afterwards. Life's just like that – it's the blows of fate that form us, and not the strokes of good luck. That doesn't mean of course you have to be stuck in difficulties all the time. But it does mean drawing useful lessons from it, in overcoming it. Don't see things as too black or too rosy – but think that your book could achieve something! Keep at it, there you can achieve something real, purposeful, a crucial stage in your life. I know how difficult it is when you're oppressed and harassed by so many other things. But I also know how a degree of fatalism can save one...Once you've finished it, you will no longer be the same person, the *status quo ante* will be biography, life story, and you will continue to hang on to the threads of that, but in a new stage...To try is the essence of life – if you know why you tried. All these components apply to you and what you are capable of. You can do it. Don't give up. Fight. Use the time. For Eugenio's sake, yes. But also for your own!"

The final sentences in particular strengthened me in my conviction that we can learn from criticism of our faults and mistakes, in particular through the criticism of others and ultimately too by self-criticism, as Karl Popper says.

I thought of the grandfatherly letter Ralph Giordano had written to Eugenio on his eighth birthday, on 30 April 1993. In it he wrote: "I wish you all the best for your birthday today – presents and a lot of happiness, the greatest and most precious of which is, as I know very well, the love of your mother and your father...Their greatest happiness is to know that you love them back with your whole heart...While I'm sitting here in my home in Cologne and writing to you for your birthday, I look over my shoulder and what do you think I see? You! On lots of photos that all have a place of honour and that I look at several times every day. I can see Eugenio laughing, I can see Eugenio alone, but then together with his father and mother too, and all three of you are a wonderful sight! And that is the way it should continue to be."

The idyl of a "happy family" has to be constantly worked at, as Eugenio and I both know: for us, as father and son, there is no other way but that of dialogue.

CHAPTER TWENTY-SIX

ON TOUR WITH RICHARD WAGNER'S ANTISEMITISM

T he trip to Israel and its repercussions had a marked influence on my work, evident from simply looking through the lecture subjects and articles I have written since 1990. The essential themes were: "As A Wagner In Israel", "The Case Of Wagner In Israel And Germany", "Richard Wagner's Antisemitism: Contradictions And Consequences For German Politics And Culture" and "Wagner And Antifeminism". All closely interconnected, they document a constant process of development, which is both complex and almost inexhaustible. The three basic themes formed the basis for lectures on the reception of Wagner in and around Bayreuth. Complementary themes such as "Does Wagner's *Gesamtkunstwerk* [total art work] idea still have a future?", "Lamas And Kundry's Images Of Genius – Notes On Elisabeth Förster – Nietzsche's And Cosima Wagner's Falsifications And Their Consequences Up To The Present Time", "Toscanini, Wagner, Hitler", "Redemption For The Redeemer – Thoughts On Wagner's *Parsifal*" and "Wagner's Bayreuth – Bayreuth's Liszt: Art As Ideology And Art As Liberation", as well as theoretical thoughts on Wagner's *Lohengrin* during my Dessau production of that opera.

In contrast, although still closely connected, are the other main subjects: my contributions on the subject of Kurt Weill and Viktor Ullmann, who was murdered in Auschwitz in October 1944 and whose epoch-making compositions I have been intensively researching since 1990.

In my lecture at the 1995 Bruckner festival, entitled "The Destruction Of Creativity In The Arts: Conformist Music: Nazi Ideology And Music As Political Propaganda", I pointed out in particular the historical connection between Wagner's antisemitic writings, Hitler's racist lunacy and culture, right up to Joseph Goebbels' guidelines on music.

Purely "aesthetic" subjects with psychological aspects such as a lecture on Mozart, or on Goethe's *Faust* in compositions by Liszt, Schumann and Wagner, served to keep me financially above water and open doors for the subjects I was really interested in. The tension of Wagner, on the one hand, and Weill and Ullmann on the other, was central to my interests. For me it meant ultimately the exposition of the two thousand-year-old conflict between Judaism and Christianity and the Bayreuth temple cult as an expression of romantico-religious redemption mania, according to Richard Wagner; and with all its consequences up to Auschwitz. I understood the whole development more and more as the consequence of a perverted Christian antisemitism, which had reached a climax with Wagner in Bayreuth.

The historian Friedrich Heer, whose works I have recently reread after many years, opened my eyes to this painful knowledge. Rereading his words ended my being torn between repression and critically coming to terms with the antisemitic past of my family. Heer's much-discussed standard work, *God's First Love. Christians And Jews Over Two Thousand Years*, was rightly called by *Spiegel* editor Rudolf Augstein "an atomic bomb between book covers". In this book Heer, an Austrian Catholic, proves, fascinatingly, that "the concepts of Jew-hating and Jew-killing were based on Christian theology, taught by the most eminent fathers of the church".[42] Heer comes to the conclusion "that Auschwitz and Hiroshima are based on a thousand-year-old theological tradition".[43]

One outcome of my new insight was renewed relentless critical questioning of history and my family history in a process which left no stone of my former world of ideas unturned. The more knowledge I gained through ever more enthusiastic historical study, and in discussions on human experiences, the more firmly I distanced myself from the bogus Christian traditions of my family in Bayreuth. Traditions which had lost all credibility after the Holocaust.

1953: Gottfried posing with papier-mâché swan, a prop used in his father's debut production, *Lohengrin*

Gottfried with his father and sister Eva. Gottfried deduced as a young child that a show of admiration for all things Wagnerian could render him acceptable to Wolfgang and by this means he would avoid being sent to children's homes whenever the festival organisation loomed. His older sister Eva lacked her brother's rebellious nature, although she too was sent away

Gottfried aged four with his black Scottish terrier, Pupsi. Taken in the grounds of Villa Wahnfried in 1953

Gottfried, aged nine, 1956: the year he was confronted with a documentary on Nazi Germany and his family's past

Gottfried (left) and Wolf-Siegfried (Wieland's son, nicknamed Wummi) with Hera, their Newfoundland puppy, at the main entrance of Villa Wahnfried in 1953. Although reality was to prove quite different, this fourth generation of Wagners was intended as *Festspiele* directors of the future

Villa Wahnfried, badly damaged by the RAF in April 1945. On the right is Siegfried Wagner House, where Hitler lived in the 1930s. From 1947 onwards it was used as a base for US counter espionage

1952. Herbert von Karajan (centre) twice became a member of the Nazi Party in Germany and Austria, then later created the Salzburg Festival, producing and conducting special performances of Richard Wagner's operas

Friedelind, Winifred and Verena in 1954, the year Friedelind returned to the *Festspiele* for the first time after her escape from Nazi Germany

Wolfgang (right) with Wilhelm Furtwängler (centre) in 1951

Ellen and Wolfgang after the *Lohengrin* premiere in 1953

Eva and
Gottfried
amongst their
mother's
friends, 1955

Wolfgang and Ellen at a Society Of Friends Of Bayreuth dinner in 1956 (Wieland standing). So wide
was the gulf between the brothers that they wouldn't share the same dinner table after productions

Wieland and Winifred
in the early 1960s

Winifred and Wolfgang at the stage entrance of the *Festspielhaus*, 1957. They were always in agreement on essential business decisions, usually against Wieland

Ellen and Wolfgang, 1957

Gottfried with Lotte Lenya, 1978: Gottfried was contacted by Lenya to work on the Kurt Weill archives, Weill having been the subject of his doctoral thesis

During a rehearsal of *Arlecchino* by F Busoni with the ensemble of the Trier Theatre in 1978

Gottfried next to Ralph Giordano and Hanna Jordan, a famous German-Jewish set designer who lost part of her family in Theresienstadt

Gottfried and his wife Teresina in front of the oldest synagogue in the world, in Massada, 1990. The invitation to lecture at Tel Aviv University was a turning point in his life

With Herzl Shmueli, the well-known Israeli musicologist and Gottfried's host at Tel Aviv University. Taken in August 1992, Zürich

Abraham Peck, the Post Holocaust Dialogue Group co-founder, with Gottfried in March 1994, Berlin

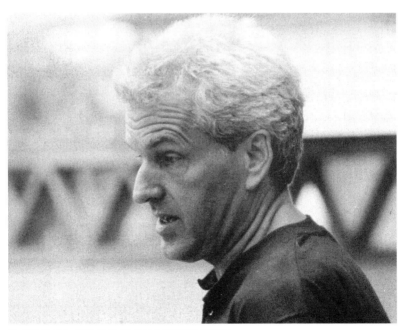

Gottfried in July 1996, photographed by Riccardo Bremer

Eberhard Wagner

Gottfried's farewell to Bayreuth and its Wagner cult on 29 July 1997 with his son Eugenio, wife Teresina and his nephew Alberto, following a passionate debate after publication of the German edition of *He Who Does Not Howl With The Wolf*. The reaction it caused surprised even Gottfried. Photograph by Fabio Tosca

Gottfried in 1997, photographed by Riccardo Bremer

Gottfried with Teresina, Eugenio and mother-in-law Antonietta Malacrida, photographed in 1997 by Fabio Tosca

The break also prompted in me a search for new ethical guidelines. Any form of religion claiming sole powers of redemption, any fundamentalist ideology became intolerable to me. My question, based on knowledge and experience, was and is: how can I achieve universal understanding with other ways of thinking, feeling and acting that are alien to me? I think it is through knowledge, by which mankind liberates itself, as Popper has said. My view of the world broadened and I accepted that there are many paths to paradise on earth and in heaven. They should, however, be based on active sympathy with all those deprived of their rights, irrespective of sex, nation, colour of skin and belief. The word race disappeared for ever from my thinking.

Heer says: "Christianity today is rather like a tree, or a forest if you will, on a mountaintop: uprooted by a storm...The reason for this alarming fact is that Christianity is not rooted in the soil from which it stems – from Jewish piety, the Jewish fear of God, love of humanity, love of earthly pleasures, joy in the present and hope for the future...a true revival, a rebirth of Jewish piety, could possibly depend on whether the synagogue would assume the role of mother in the Mother Church and elder sister of the younger daughter churches. The return of Jesus the Jew to the community of His brothers who have borne His cross as crusaders from the fourth century to the twentieth century – this could be an event of extraordinary and vital importance."[44]

In my study of Judaism I found new ethical impulses in Reform Judaism, which interestingly enough arose in Germany, in the wisdom of the Psalms, as it arose out of Jewish historical experience and deep piety. For example, Psalm 142 of the Jewish Bible, an instruction from David, when he was in the cave: "I cried unto the Lord with my voice; with my voice unto the Lord did I make my supplication. I poured out my complaint before him; I shewed before him my trouble. When my spirit was overwhelmed within me, then thou knewest my path. In the way wherein I walked have they privily laid a snare for me. I looked on my right hand, and beheld, but there was no man that would know me; refuge failed me; no man cared for my soul. I cried unto thee, O Lord: I said, Thou art my refuge and my portion in the land of the living. Attend unto my cry; for I am brought very low: deliver me from my persecutors; for they are stronger than I. Bring my soul out of prison, that I may praise thy name: the righteous shall compass me about; for thou shalt deal bountifully with me."[45]

Belief in God contains disbelief. This is expressed, for example, in a passage from Psalm 139, in the Jewish version: "Surely the darkness shall cover me; even the night shall be light about me. Yea, the darkness hideth not from thee; but the night shineth as the day...How precious also are thy thoughts unto me, O God! How great is the sum of them! If I should count them, they are more in number than the sand: when I awake, I am still with thee."[46]

The poem 'Prayer' by Ilse Blumenthal-Weiss, that she wrote in 1945 after her time in the concentration camps of Westerbork and Theresienstadt, is inconceivable without Jewish piety. It summarises my thinking:

> I cannot hate.
> They strike me. They kick me with their feet.
> I cannot hate. I can but pray
> For you and me.
> I cannot hate.
> They throttle me. They pelt me with stones.
> I cannot hate. I can but weep.
> Bitterly.[47]

Ilse Weiss's husband and son were murdered in Nazi concentration camps.

My spiritual development is closely connected with my Jewish friends, active with me since 1991-2 in the Post Holocaust Dialogue Group. I shall come back to them and our organisation later.

My quarrel with Christian antisemitism includes that of Richard Wagner and his descendants. What sparked further investigation into the subject was a letter from Marcel Silberstein of Basle, who wrote to my host Shai Burstyn at the Tel Aviv University in mid January 1990, only a few days after my lecture tour in Israel: "Wagner's antisemitism can be segregated neither from his general personality nor from his music." He added this statement to Hartmut Zelinsky's article in *Musik-Konzepten* of 1978 with the title "Richard Wagner's 'Fire Cure'

Or The 'New Religion' Of 'Redemption By Annihilation'". Zelinsky's assertion that Wagner was partly responsible for the rise of Hitler and National Socialism in Germany, I neither could nor would yet believe in 1990. My hesitation and the unease that Zelinsky provoked in me with his revolutionary thesis, first formulated in 1975, I can only interpret today after years of painstaking preoccupation with the subject. It was my fear of an irrevocable break with my own family – above all with my father – but fear too of the end of a repressed childhood dream, to go back to Bayreuth and take part in a critical appraisal of Wagner in Bayreuth. Fear of a loss of identity. And fear of the international opera business, with all the Bayreuth connections on which I would be dependent as opera director.

By 1992 – after my own lengthy investigations into the connection between Bayreuth and Auschwitz – I became painfully aware that there was no way past Zelinsky's findings.

I do not share Zelinsky's philosophical understanding of the historical link with Hegel in the politico-cultural phenomenon of Richard Wagner: Wagner had no solid philosophical basis and thus remains a dangerous, self-appointed pseudo-philosopher. But otherwise Zelinsky's work represents a turning point in international Wagner scholarship. His pioneering work is the courageous act of an ostracised loner who has my sympathy and respect.

As he writes: "Present-day Wagner admirers deceive themselves on Wagner's antisemitism – either they ignore it totally, in order not to sully their image of the genius…or they treat it as a sort of whim of genius, which is rather embarrassing and curious, but certainly not to be taken seriously."[48]

The self-deception of most Wagnerians was repeatedly confirmed on my travels in recent years. But since the publication of Zelinsky's article in 1978, Ulrich Drüner's doctoral thesis 'Richard Wagner's Artistic Creation Between Ideology And Myth', the painstaking historical study *Race And Revolution* by Paul Lawrence Rose (1992) and above all the interdisciplinary standard work *Richard Wagner And The Antisemitic Imagination* by Marc Weiner (1995), a slow change has come about in a minority of Wagnerians and a majority of those critically interested in the man. The subject is being taken more and more seriously, as Weiner illustrates in detail the close connection between biography, theoretical writings and the stage works through thorough analyses of the music scores. The antisemitic writings as an essential part of the politico-cultural phenomenon of Wagner in their unique effect, cannot and should not be overlooked any longer after Auschwitz.

My personal summing up, from experience and knowledge of the causes of the conflict, comes to this: Wagner's *Festspiele* idea and its realisation in Bayreuth signify a loss of reality and humanity. In this sense I, as a great-grandson of Wagner, have become an anti-Wagnerian. I became aware of the difficulty of presenting my knowledge on Wagner objectively, as a descendant of Wagner. At the beginning of my lectures I described my special situation to my audiences. The following, not very academic introduction to one of my lectures reflects this:

"Anyone addressing Richard Wagner's antisemitism finds himself confronted by complex problems. Wide-ranging, interdisciplinary knowledge and a passion for individual responsibility are required, that must be put to the test in the selection and presentation of documents. Equally important is looking to the personal motives in dealing with the subject, as here one is touching on deep layers of human experience and suffering."

About myself as a speaker: "I am aware that I am speaking to you as a great-grandson of Richard Wagner, who was Hitler's cultural model. So I am speaking here not only as a music historian. Richard Wagner's antisemitic writings cast their shadow over my life. The subject contains fundamental questions such as repression, 'not wanting to talk about it', denial and the falsification of real links between German culture and politics in which Richard Wagner plays a decisive and inglorious role. Whether I like it or not: the subject is part of my existence. It is linked to something I consider typical of the German mentality, namely the separation of the private and the public sphere in the discussion and translation of fundamental ethical positions. I refuse to condone such separation and consider it dangerous on the basis of historical experience and knowledge, and as a Wagner after the Holocaust; we are dealing here with humanitarian values and individual responsibility. Anyone demanding open, unbiased discussion on this theme and humane dealings with those of different opinion, will not only run up against resistance and rejection. He will also find himself exposed to slander, existential problems and threats, which are a mask for all kinds of intolerance."

Equally unacademic was my practice in the lectures of projecting texts, showing films and weaving in musical examples. Often the lectures were followed by lively debate, but sometimes too by an icy silence.

Between 1990 to 1995 I toured as the anti-Wagnerian great-grandson of Wagner giving lectures in Germany, Switzerland, Austria, England, Italy, the USA and Canada. Critical thoughts which required critical comment from the listener on basic ethical questions in art and politics, polarised audiences. Their reaction varied: they were either polarised, quietly, indirectly or in open criticism of Richard Wagner, or of my interpretation of his work and personality. Many were disturbed in particular by the fact that I, as a descendant of Wagner, was so critical of him.

The various national, historical, political and cultural backgrounds and personal histories of my audiences influenced their reaction, as did the religious make-up of the group – whether they were mainly Jewish, Christian or mixed – the age range, or whether they were experts or opera fans. From the wide variety of reactions, I learned to beware of crude generalisations and I slowly began to adjust for each particular audience. But one thing did not alter: a Wagner descendant talking critically about Wagner can always expect surprises. It's never boring.

Sometimes the reaction was extremely emotional, which stemmed from the Nazi past: repression, denial, silence, falsification. The example of Wagner, his antisemitism and the Nazi involvement of my family in Bayreuth clearly illustrates that each individual bears personal responsibility. Anyone talking about Wagner and the Germans, of necessity questions the self-confidence of many Germans.

Frequently Wagnerians, who only endured my criticism because I am a great-grandson, retreated into personal anecdote and experiences of Wagner and the *Festspielhügel*. In this way they didn't have to question their image of the composer. Instead they tried like missionaries to bring me onto the "right" path for the "Bayreuth case". I always tried to stay polite and didn't see much point in intense discussion.

The minority of German anti-Wagnerians behaved quite differently towards me. Despite their ideological aversion they were interested in the composer, and seemed surprised to meet an atypical Wagner. Consequently we had some very intense and stimulating discussions.

The evenings with Ralph Giordano in Wuppertal and Bonn in 1992 will remain a particular memory. Before both lectures Ralph gave an introduction to my work and me personally, which I saw not only as an important aid, but also as an obligation for continuing along the stony path of my conflict with Bayreuth and its form of Wagner worship.

The invitation to give a lecture on "Wagner's Antisemitism: Contradictions And Consequences For German Politics And Culture" in mid December 1992 at the German Congress of Industry and Commerce had a political motive: Germany's international reputation had dropped to zero that year through the crimes committed by Neo-Nazis (the arson attack in Solingen and other violent actions), and leaders in business, politics and culture wanted to create a liberal image. A critical Wagner who spoke against his great-grandfather's racism, presented by Ralph Giordano, one of the most important German-Jewish voices, seemed to fit the bill perfectly.

All my conditions for these events were agreed to. The audience was confronted before the lecture with pictures from my travelling exhibition *From Bayreuth To Theresienstadt-Terzin* to the sounds of the music of Viktor Ullmann. This was followed by a visual analysis of a colour slide of Arno Breker's Bayreuth Wagner bust, to the sound of the 'Ride Of The Valkyrie'. Ralph Giordano then gave his opinion on Bayreuth and the connections of the *Festspielhügel* and their negative influence on my work before introducing me. The lecture mainly concentrated on Wagner's antisemitism, illustrated using quotations from his inflammatory writings, and on the repression and falsification of the Nazi period in New Bayreuth.

The reaction: discomfort, smattered with a few polite, but certainly not unfamiliar objections. As usual, people congratulated me in private and promised to support me "indirectly", because, as I heard many times that evening, one must take into account the sponsors in Bayreuth, Father, Barenboim and Levine. The press reacted kindly to the lecture, although in a garbled manner. Here again there was no clear statement on my criticism of New Bayreuth.

The reaction of Ernst Dieter Lueg – who at the time was responsible for the important *Report From Bonn* on WDR-Fernsehen – was typical. At the reception for me and Ralph Giordano after the lecture he said he was pleased with my efforts and promised to do what he could for me in WDR. Empty words. Is it coincidence that Lueg is occasionally given the job of presenter at the opening of the *Festspiele*?

It became clearer to me that discussion about Wagner meant the end of any meaningful professional future in Germany. When I mentioned this to Ralph Giordano, he said: "Criticism of German politics and culture can only be expressed in Germany, and in the case of Wagner, only by a Jew. As an oppositional Wagner, you have no chance here at the moment. But I hope that will change one day."

I answered: "So German antisemitic philosemitism *à la* Bayreuth connections?"

He nodded.

To my surprise, an ongoing interest in my work has developed in Austria since 1989, first in the form of discussions with the literary scholar Leo Haffner, which came about with the aid of Karl Lubomirski, and then with features on Hitler and Wagner, Weill and my biography on ORF (Austrian Radio) in Vorarlberg and Vienna. Since 1992 I have also regularly given interviews on Austrian television. I have known Gaby Flossmann, who works for the cultural division of ORF 2, since 1968. Our firm friendship has had a common theme: German-speaking Jewry and coming to terms with the consequences of National Socialism in Germany and Austria. Wherever she could – and that is by no means always easy where my subjects are concerned – she has managed report in detail on essential stages of my work round the world.

In Vienna I met the sociologist Michael Ley and his wife, the painter Charlotte Ley-Kohn, with whom I not only discussed the effects of the Holocaust on the next German, Austrian and Jewish generations, but also carried out projects, such as the filming of my Dessau *Lohengrin* production as part of the documentary film *Herr Hitler's Religion*, directed by Petrus van der Let.

In marked contrast to my experiences in Germany, I am met with continuing interest in the themes of my work in Austria. In Vienna, and again at the time of my lecture on "Music And Nazi Ideology" at the Bruckner festival in Linz in 1995, I didn't have to restrain myself in my comments on Hitler, Vienna and the Austrian Nazis. Instead, I encountered the special way in which they were dealing with their own thousand-year-old history: behind the insults – the derisive use of double-edged flattery – a caustic black humour and self-mockery always shines through, something most Germans lack. This attitude is particularly prominent in Austrian Jewish culture. I know today why I wrote my doctoral thesis on Weill and Brecht specifically in Vienna and not in Berlin. The mordant humour of the two iconoclasts of the last days of the Weimar Republic before Hitler's master race twilight – fully comparable with the lack of direction in the period after the fall of communism at the end of the 1980s – makes me prefer Vienna to Berlin even today.

The Swiss – the Zurichers in particular – and their Wagner, to whom in 1849 they so kindly granted nine years of asylum: what do they have to do with Wagner's antisemitism? One thinks of Mathilde Wesendonck and her immortalisation in *Tristan und Isolde*. Swiss antisemitism? Yes, here too there have been painful historical events that people do not like to talk about in Switzerland. In particular in the Nazi period, when Switzerland turned away Jews fleeing from Germany, and money stolen from Jews disappeared into Swiss bank deposits, many Swiss were blameworthy. But one should guard against prejudice.

In Switzerland too, people are prepared to come to terms with the dark chapters of European history as well as their own pasts. Such willingness was demonstrated in October 1992 when I was invited by my patron and friend Albi Rosenthal, the legendary musical antiques collector and patron of the arts, and Walburga Sia Strecker, daughter of the founder of the Nietzsche Colloquium in Sils-Maria in Switzerland, to speak about Cosima Wagner's and Elisabeth Förster-Nietzsche's distortions of history. My target was not only Cosima's and Elisabeth's falsifications while they were still alive. I also spoke of Richard Wagner's autobiographical falsifications, and pointed out the continuity in dealing with German and individual history in my family right up to today. Whether Richard, Cosima, Winifred, Wieland or Wolfgang – they all used and use history in the interests of their power-political and economic aims. Elisabeth Förster-Nietzsche behaved similarly with regard to the Weimar Archive.

After the lecture, several German academics in the audience remained awkwardly silent, but the Swiss philosopher André Bloch, organiser of the Nietzsche Colloquium, presented me with a key to the Nietzsche House in Sils-Maria, as a token of his appreciation, with the words: "No one's forbidden to enter the house here. You are always heartily welcome."

My reception in Zurich was equally generous. As in Sils-Maria, I spoke in the Zurich Paulus Academy, in November 1993, to a group of Swiss with a sensitive awareness of history on the subject of Wagner and antisemitism. Right next to the lectern on a stage was a piece by the artist Thea Weltner, 'Children's Shoes And Breadbins', a reminder of the murdered children of Theresienstadt. The *Israelitisches Wochenblatt* and the *Neue Zürcher Zeitung* reported the event objectively.

After the lecture, an Orthodox Jew invited me to his home, where we discussed my ideas on directing *Lohengrin*. He regarded Lohengrin as a Messianic figure and showed me a painting of a tree in the desert, with a church tower driven into its trunk; Judeo-Christian cultural history with all its dark shadows. This picture and the mysterious discussion inspired me later on in the visual concept for my *Lohengrin* production in Dessau: two pillars of a cathedral are set on two tree trunks.

In Italy there is scarcely any discussion on Wagner and Judaism, and people in the country of the Vatican have shown only detached interest in my lectures, whether they touch directly or indirectly on the subject. Their confusion over Wagner has been fuelled by the influence of Bayreuth and inadequate translations and not much is likely to change this. Media reports are restricted to the occasional account of bomb attacks and violence in Israel, which cannot promote discussion about antisemitism. It is no wonder that I have often had to pack my suitcases in order to exercise my task as "historian with the wrong subject" elsewhere in the world.

It is still a wonder how unconcerned people are in Italy about coming to terms with their own antisemitism: it wasn't until 1994 that the subject became the focus for a discussion within the framework of a travelling exhibition, *The Lie Of Race*. The Catholic Church has been one of the most important bulwarks of European antisemitism since the fourth century, and its role during and after Mussolini was hardly commendable. It took the Vatican forty-three years to grant Israel diplomatic recognition in 1993! Unfortunately, I do not read anything of this in my son's history books.

On my many journeys in North America I encounter great interest in my subject. Anyone who has lived there knows that the cohabitation of many ethnic groups from all over the world is based on the principle of diversity while recognising equal rights for all. In spite of all the criticism levelled, I consider the American model capable of development and improvement. There is still something in the USA of the pioneering spirit, of curiosity, spontaneity and unaffectedness, and something of this mentality was also expressed at my lectures and in discussions afterwards.

The knowledge, quality and quantity of research regarding the subjects I deal with are particularly impressive there: all the important work after Zelinsky and Drüner comes from the USA. The works of Paul Lawrence Rose of Pennsylvania State University and Marc Weiner of Indiana University outshine anything that has been published on the subject in Europe. And in many colleges and universities the liberal spirit prevails in the sense of militant diversity.

Diversity and the integration of Jewish groups into the respective institutions, or at least the recognition of German-Jewish history as a subject, is instrumental in the acceptance of problematic subjects. By generating invitations for me, it was evident that North American German communities are still influential. Because of its Nazi period Germany itself has aroused interest; people like hearing the "rebel against his own clan", not least because it reminds them of TV series like *Dallas* and *Dynasty*. Precisely because of my family background, a lot was expected of me and my performance was fundamental to the judgement cast on my lectures. A fair precondition. I look forward to every trip to North America, as I do to visiting Israel, my elective home, and to returning to Italy.

I also feel at home at the George Washington University in the USA. The director of the musicology department, Professor Roy Guenther, embodies the "liberal American", whom I esteem as a colleague and a private individual. The fact that my lectures "Wagner – Nietzsche", "Weill", and "Wagner In Israel And Germany" took place in the capital of America had positive consequences which I shall come back to.

Furthermore, I was able to appear in numerous universities in Canada and the USA, and I still enjoy a lively exchange of opinions with many academics I have got to know on lecture tours.

In many cities too, the local Goethe Institute and American branches of German firms have supported me. Two Jewish cultural institutions in the USA – the Hebrew Union College in Cincinnati and the United States Holocaust Memorial Museum in Washington DC – played a major role in my trip to Israel and my dispute with Wagner's antisemitism. When I spoke in February 1992 in the Mayerson Hall of the Hebrew Union College, a world-renowned Jewish theological institute, on "The Case Of Wagner In Israel", I knew that there had been resistance to my invitation. That this resistance was discreetly overcome was down to Abraham Peck, lecturer in modern German history and Judaism, administration and programming director of the American Jewish Archive in Cincinnati and author of numerous articles on German-Jewish history of the nineteenth and twentieth centuries. Cincinnati is not only the American twin city of Munich, with a large proportion of Americans of German origin, but also has a significant Jewish community. German and Austrian Holocaust survivors live there, who know the history of the Wagner family very well.

After the lecture these people, who were quite particularly affected by German race mania, came up to me with great openness, even with warmth. The director of the Hebrew Union College, Alfred Gottschalk, was among them and he, for one, now had no more objections to future collaboration and my point of view.

Others had not had to go through the Holocaust, but nevertheless were very sensitive to the subject. The mother of James Levine was introduced to me as a member of this group. To my surprise she asked me if I thought it right that her son was conducting in Bayreuth. I answered: "Only your son can answer this question."

A further landmark was an invitation from the United States Holocaust Memorial Museum in Washington for March 1994. They were already familiar with my work before making contact in autumn 1993, and in particular with a long article in the *Washington Post* at the end of April 1993. This interview, by Judith Weinraub, who had researched her subject thoroughly from November 1992 to April 1993, is for me one of the fairest accounts of my story. Publication coincided with the opening of the Holocaust Memorial Museum and was presented as an alternative German voice.

The lecture evening itself further demonstrated the spirit of mutual trust and interest. Despite a snowstorm, the hall was well filled, and the discussion was of a high calibre, not least due to the presence of Paul Lawrence Rose, investigator of Wagner antisemitism. Here, as in other Jewish institutions in North America, I found sympathy and a desire for ongoing dialogue, which actually gave me the energy to continue my work in Germany too and find it meaningful.

CHAPTER TWENTY-SEVEN

THE POST HOLOCAUST DIALOGUE GROUP: AND IN THE BEGINNING WAS AUSCHWITZ

Founding the Post Holocaust Dialogue Group was also connected with my trip to Israel. Franklin Littell had heard of my lectures on Wagner in Tel Aviv through the media and in summer 1990 he invited me to the twenty-first annual congress of his organisation, The Holocaust And The Churches, in Stockton College, New Jersey, which was to take place in March 1991. He asked me to speak on my experiences in Israel, the story of the Wagner family and German history in relation to Wagner as a politico-cultural phenomenon.

I was only vaguely aware of the provocative nature of the organisation and the other guest speakers, having gathered some knowledge of it since the end of the sixties through descriptions of friends and acquaintances and read a lot on the subject of the Holocaust. Until my trip to Israel, though, I had not met any experts on the subject.

I began to understand the intellectual ambiance of the meeting from the opening session on 3 March, 1991. The organisers' openmindedness was evident in their choice of vice-president: Hubert Locke, professor of political science and sociology, is an Afro-American Christian. But Locke by no means suppressed the problems of his own group. He is the author of numerous works such as *The Detroit Riot Of 1967* (1969) and *The Care And Feeding Of White Liberals* (1970). When I asked him why he, as a black, had become vice-president of the organisation, he answered: "The Holocaust is the culmination of experience with totalitarian systems, which can always be repeated if we don't watch out. As such it is independent of categories such as skin colour, nation, religion and ideology."

At this first meeting in 1991 I took part in all the discussions I could, and my own lecture met with great interest. Right at the start I had an unforgettable encounter with the respected liberal senator Paul Simon who, under Richard Nixon, had been seen as one of the most promising Democrat presidential candidates. We were introduced after his impressive opening speech on contemporary human rights, which he illustrated by reference to the American educational system. He shook my hand warmly and said: "Hey, Gottfried, I have a photo of you at home that I took in Wahnfried Park in 1951 when I was an officer in the US Army. I lived in the Siegfried Wagner House for a few weeks as a kid and you were always hanging around. But how come you're talking here about your lecture tour on Wagner in Israel, with your family history?"

I answered: "I think it's high time we talked about the effects of the Nazi period in Bayreuth after 1945."

We subsequently continued our frank discussion by letter.

In those three days in March I met a lot of people with whom I either developed a warm friendship, or have since occasionally exchanged opinions. I became friendly immediately with Franklin Littell, his wife, the historian Marcia Littell-Sachs, and the host and organiser of the event, Jan G Colijn, director of general studies at Stockton College, and Henry Knight, professor of religion at Tulsa University. They introduced me into the various groups and to two participants who interested me in particular and gave me a warm welcome. One of these was Abraham Peck, the other, the Reform rabbi Steven Jacobs from Huntsville in Alabama, who has published a considerable number of quite revolutionary works on Jewish faith and history, most notably his book *Rethinking Jewish Faith After The Holocaust*, published in 1992, which opened my eyes to the Jewish suffering during the Second World War.

My lecture on the evening of 4 March to a full hall was another baptism by fire after Israel. Afterwards, Abraham and Steven approached me and we talked until early in the morning, and decided to organise ourselves as children of Nazi victims and Nazi criminals. What unites us even now is summarised in the six points of the statutes of our Post Holocaust Dialogue Group. As our slogan we took the words of the Jewish judge and Holocaust survivor Samuel Gringauz in 1947: "Our tragedy must become the starting point of a new humanity."

We presented our six-point programme at the twenty-third scientific congress of The Holocaust And The Churches in Tulsa, in March 1993. It was then prepared by another board member, the composer Michael Shapiro, for future official registration as a non-profit-making organisation. The text of the statutes reads:

1. We, the children of the victims and the children of the victimisers, see the Shoah/Holocaust as a unique rift in Western and world civilisation and the starting point of a new morality in terms of thoughts, feelings and actions.

2. We stand opposed to the repressing and silencing of any and all discussion of the Shoah/Holocaust and the continuation of any and all prejudices and hatreds resulting from the activities of our parents and grandparents both now and in the future and directly attributable to the trauma of the Shoah/Holocaust.

3. We fully believe that the sharing of our own unique burden of this tragic past in a continuing present and future dialogue is of vital concern, independently of any religious, ideological, and/or political group. With our dialogue we give concrete evidence how our generation, and those after us, will confront the challenges presented by the Shoah/Holocaust and its ever present influences.

4. We begin our dialogue with tolerance, respect and self-critical awareness as the children of the victims and the children of the victimisers. Our mutual willingness to share our burden is coupled with our unhesitating commitment to overcome our present ignorance, prejudices, and misconceptions, and to present to those who are open and receptive a model for present and future trust and understanding.

5. We see ourselves as an international activist organisation

whose avowed purpose is not only to inform others of the Shoah/Holocaust through scholarly conferences and publications, but to fight both theoretically and practically against any kind of totalitarian dogmatism religiously, politically, and ideologically. We stand for the adoption of human rights for all human beings, fully believing that we are responsible for our own actions, ever mindful of the "different other".

6. We hope by our humanitarian actions and our scholarly work to influence governments and nation states, thus lessening fear of present or future repetitions of the Shoah/Holocaust, striving at all times to realise our goal of a world living together in peaceful tolerance and appreciative of all diverse humanity.

Words were followed by deeds. After establishing the group in Seattle, March 1992 there were not only annual meetings with the aid of Franklin Littell's organisation, but conventions with other internationally recognised organisations: Remembering For The Future, Christianity And The Holocaust, National Workshop On Christian-Jewish Relations, The Evangelical Academy near Frankfurt am Main and the international institute Au Coeur De La Communication (ACC). The international media – except that in Germany – has also shown great interest in recent years. Unfortunately the percentage of Germans of my generation in our group is still very small in comparison with that of members with a Jewish background, but overall our organisation is growing and membership spans three continents.

One of the reasons for its international appeal is the fact that we have developed mutual appreciation of the different psychological, historical and family backgrounds. Membership comprises women and men with very different professional, national, religious and political backgrounds, and the choice of themes reflects this. In choosing discussion topics we also examine the statutes of our organisation in a spirit of self-criticism. So that we could talk about our identities as post-Holocaust Germans and Jews, we had to come to terms with our experiences in life and our family chronicles in their historical context.

Abraham and I have been moulded by the liberal political developments at the end of the sixties. As former "sixty-eighters" we had common intellectual orientations, towards such intellectuals as Jews of the Frankfurt school Max Horkheimer, Theodor W Adorno or Hannah Arendt. But in our coming to terms, we by no means nostalgically romanticised our own student years. Rather, we were self-critical and set new targets for responsible actions as the children of Nazi victims and Nazi victimisers. In spite of all the biographical differences, this joint learning process went surprisingly smoothly.

It also became clear to me at this time though that that my idea of a reconciliation between Germans and Jews is not realistic: reconciliation is only possible between perpetrators and victims. No guilt can be bequeathed to us, the children of the victimisers, let alone a direction for reconciliation.

Even so, Abraham and I have been corresponding almost weekly since March 1991. Our exchanges on life and reading matter are very intense and as far as we can, we involve other members or those interested in our organisation. Dan Bar On, for example, whom we met for the first time in March 1993 in Tulsa, has been important in this critical process of self-questioning. He presented us with six questions about the effect of the Holocaust on our lives: when and how were we confronted with the Holocaust? How did we cope with our lack of roots? How do we deal with social alienation and being different? Can we empathise with the role of victims and victimisers? Are we living our own lives without the shadow of the Holocaust? Have we found a middle path between the desire to live and the desire to die, through knowing about the Holocaust?

We needed time to answer such complex questions seriously and finally wrote down our thoughts some months later. While I approached each question individually, Abraham answered Dan Bar On's questions in the form of an article.

It is also instructive how Dan Bar On judges the dialogue between Abraham and me. He describes it as "microcosm of the German-Jewish dialogue" and writes: "Gottfried Wagner and Abraham Peck are brave people. Their parents would never have been able to talk with one another. Only fifty years have passed since the ancestors of one were deeply involved in the atrocious act of attempting to annihilate the ancestors of the other. The survivors gave a solemn commandment to their descendants, never to forget and never to forgive. Why does Abraham try to break this commandment? Why does Gottfried try to break through the silence which came over the German people after the crime became public knowledge: silence that is a mixture of shame and the desire to shrink from responsibility for the murder, to forget and to be forgiven?...For their own sakes, they are looking for a dialogue which, though breaking their fathers' commandments, will help them articulate their internal quest for hope."

He then analyses what the Holocaust has brought about in our lives: being uprooted in our childhood from our environment, isolation and mistrust: "Gottfried found...his intellectual harbour in the post-War Jewish and gentile writers who tried to grapple, genuinely, with questions similar to his own about 'Who is Wagner?'. However, he had to pay a high price for his courage and was ostracised from his family and his homeland. He has a new personal sanctuary [in Italy] which protects him from the storms awaiting him in the open sea...After describing painful childhood memories which have shaped their [Gottfried's and Abraham's] life stories, they quickly disassociate themselves [from these memories].

"Gottfried does it by giving too conclusive answers to questions which have no final answers...Abraham tells us that he believes the future will be good for the next generation, but his last sentences indicate that he cannot really believe that whole-heartedly: 'Can we ever free ourselves of the need to be watchful? We must be ever watchful and not believe there exists a simple answer 'Yes' or 'No'. If we do not succeed, what may our children face?"

And he sums up: "It is quite terrifying! There is no real sanctuary in the world after Auschwitz", and he draws the analogy between our dialogue and building a house: "...unlike building a house, there are many participants in this process. All these watchful eyes and ears of the living and the dead, all with such extreme and conflicting sensibilities that the possibility of failing is endless. The original discourse of yesterday may easily become the pseudo, 'as if', discourse of tomorrow. How can we know? How can we find our path?"[49]

Today my answer to this is clearer than in August 1993. The dialogue between Abraham and me is a continual process of learning and maturing. Looking at the situation at that time, Dan Bar On was correct in his judgment. Today I – and probably Abraham too – would answer Dan Bar On's questions quite differently. Based on my experiences in our group, I would now evaluate more positively the way the problems which have arisen for me through being a descendant of Nazi victimisers have been handled: even the longest path through the darkness eventually leads to light.

In 1995 Abraham wrote an article entitled 'Germans And Jews In Dialogue: Is There Anything To Discuss?'. In it he said: "Yet half a century after Auschwitz an entire generation of Germans and Jews continues to share a legacy and a burden that in the words of Sabine Reichel, born in 1946 in Hamburg, 'is like an historical umbilical cord that can't be cut off and that pulls at the most unlikely moments.'

"At the heart of this cord is family history. It is an obstacle to both Germans and Jews. For Germans it remains the great divide between silence and dialogue. It is a diseased branch on the pages of far too many family trees.

"Every well-meaning German wishing to engage in a frank discussion of German-Jewish relations (and there are quite a number) is nearly always reduced to tears or to silence when the inevitable question is asked: 'What did your father or grandfather do during the Second World War?' To argue that he was in the German Wehrmacht or armed forces is no longer much of a rejoinder: the collaboration of the front-line troops with the racial ideologues of the SS in the murder of the Jews is by now a well-established fact.

"Even more disarming is the question: 'What did your parents or grandparents know about the Final Solution?' – the planned destruction of European Jewish life. Often the answer is one of genuine ignorance. German families in the main did not discuss this particular issue in the years after 1945. But we are beginning to learn that many more knew what was happening to the Jewish family who suddenly disappeared from their apartment building one day and never returned. Many more knew because their fathers, husbands, sons and brothers could not keep a *Reichsgeheimsache*, a state secret, which the Final Solution was always intended to be. In letters from the front, from the concentration camp, or in drunken, sometimes terribly guilt-ridden confessions while home on leave, these men told a great part of the home-front just what was happening in the 'east' to the Jews of Nazi-occupied Europe.

"But family history is also a problem for Jews. Children of Holocaust survivors, such as myself, have grown up in the eye of a hurricane, surrounded by the shadows of the Holocaust. We have grown up knowing that the Holocaust is a part of our being but often do not know why. Many have asked next to nothing about the suffering of our parents during the Holocaust years or the absence of murdered grandparents, uncles and aunts. These children of survivors fear the trauma inherent in their parents' reply."

Perhaps it was my sensitivity to the sufferings of others which increased my need for justice and spurred me on to a greater degree of personal courage. I see Abraham and myself today more and more as witnesses of the second generation, who do not deny or suppress the fact that they are the children of Nazi victims and Nazi criminals. Describing ourselves as "witnesses of the second generation" I see our special responsibility as being part of the present and the future, and that we are making our concrete contribution so that another Holocaust can be prevented.

How much there is still to do is illustrated clearly by events in Bosnia and Ruanda. But with this active, positive approach and commitment we will also be able to better come to terms with our personal fate. Today I no longer find it so terrible that "there is no real sanctuary in the world after Auschwitz". I am at home where people love, understand, or try to understand me. For me this is a release from the tradition of my family in Bayreuth.

Home for me as a cosmopolitan – husband of an Italian and father of a son originating from Romania – is first and foremost with my family in Italy. But as a nomad I can put up my tent anywhere in the world where a mutual acceptance of difference is regarded as enrichment.

Responsible conduct, in respect of others as well, makes my life meaningful. I acknowledge this despite all the uncertainty concerning my future existence and knowing that my thinking seems strange to many and is not necessarily beneficial to my career as freelance director and journalist. Another reason to see the more positive aspects in my destiny, is in how I construe my life. With all my enjoyment of life, I still use as starting point the metaphysical knowledge expressed in the book of Kohelet: "All is merely a breath of air…Whoever increases knowledge, increases suffering."

Discovering that I am constantly making mistakes also influences my life with my son. I am slowly trying to make him understand that my work in the Post Holocaust Dialogue Group is a constructive part of my existence. Through the group, I learn to respect "being different" in a particularly intense way – an experience which I want at all costs to impart to my son. I hope he will understand some day why I refused to become a typical Wagner in Bayreuth, one that would have repressed memories of the Holocaust. This ethical position is obviously linked to my commitments in the Post Holocaust Dialogue Group, and here Abraham and I are always in agreement.

I should like to explain the nature of our group work by using four examples of my activities.

Thanks to Sharon Gutman, a member of our group, the second international congress – "Remembering The Future" – took place in March 1994 at the Humboldt University in Berlin. We met after years of hospitality and superb organisation in the USA. For Abraham and the other Jewish members the choice of location was anything but problem-free: Berlin was primarily the capital of Hitler's Reich and the nearby Wannsee Villa the place in which, in 1941, the "Final Solution" was agreed for their relatives. Only a few steps from the Humboldt University is the Opernplatz, scene of the book-burning in 1933.

Despite such historical associations, preparations for the Viktor Ullmann memorial concert went well. Ullmann had been murdered fifty years ago in Auschwitz and I chose the following motto for this commemorative event: "Who could not escape, who escaped, who remembers."

The concert itself was preceded by a talk by Abraham and me on the subject "From Monologues To Dialogues". Only a few people came to the round-table discussion in the Auditorium Maximum; yet those who did engaged in intense discussion with us. The hall was only half full for the concert, but we were not discouraged: the Holocaust and Ullmann lacked the media and big-music-business spend and was clearly not an evening of German brotherliness between Christians and Jews. But for those in the hall – who were mainly people with a Jewish history – our efforts had been worthwhile.

The programme contained works by Viktor Ullmann, Kurt Weill and Michael Shapiro. The months of preparation, the discussions on the organisation, financial, historical and linguistic details, and the content, bore fruit. Michael Shapiro, Abraham Peck, Sharon Gutman, Jan Colijn, Franklin and Marcia Littell and all the willing hands behind the scenes created a uniquely intense atmosphere on the evening of 16 March on the stage of the Auditorium Maximum of the Humboldt University, with the soprano Mildred Tyree, pianists Jerome Rose and Michael Shapiro and the cellist Ithau Khen, for our "Zero Hour Of Dialogue" in Germany. It will remain unforgettable for us thanks to its strong emotions and its success. As our work was also mentioned during the closing event of the congress, in front of leading German personalities – including Genscher, Bubis and Giordano – and the media, at least an introduction was made to Germany. Whether our dialogue there can develop further remains to be seen. The difficulties facing a continuation of our work in Germany on a more regular basis are still enormous, but I firmly believe in a future for our group in that country too.

In accordance with the Post Holocaust Dialogue Group statutes, great importance is given to dialogue between the different generations in our group. This constant mutual learning process is very important, as illustrated by my discussion with the New York-based psychiatrist Yehuda Nir.

I met Yehuda briefly in March 1994 at the twenty-fourth international scholars' congress of The Holocaust And the Churches in the Rider University in Lawrenceville, New Jersey. He gave me a copy of his autobiography, *The Lost Childhood*, published in 1989 which had been translated into nine languages. Yehuda's memories were very moving: a Polish Jew, he survived the six years of the Second World War with his mother and sister. I recall especially the sentence: "We were living in times when one had to be grateful to another human being for not exercising his option to kill."[50]

Despite the horror of what he experienced, he tells his story without hatred or prejudice, which particularly impressed me. After I had read the book I kept thinking of the motto of his memoirs, from Samuel Beckett's novel *Malone Dies*: "Let me say before I go any further that I forgive nobody. I wish them all an atrocious life and then the fires and ice of hell and in the execrable generations to come an honoured name."[51] This motto confused me a lot, as at the time I found it in contradiction to the humane tone of the book, our friendly meetings and international events we both attended. So in November 1995 I wrote to Yehuda and asked: "How can you manage to be my friend in spite of the motto of your book…and my family history?"

Yehuda answered: "Yours isn't an easy question to answer, but I'm happy that you asked, because it allows me to gain additional insight into my feelings toward the Germans; the murderers of my father when I was eleven years old. By quoting Beckett, I express what it means to have one's innocent father murdered when one is a child. It did not mean that I don't have hope, that I don't believe in the possibility of creating a better, peaceful world."

Yehuda continued (referring to the Dutch edition of the book, with a special introduction for students): "My book intends to encourage young people not to be passive, to take charge of their lives as I did under German occupation. The Germans took away from me the ability to forgive, but I hope that my book will help young people create a world in which one can forgive. I see you, Gottfried, as a herald of that world. You are the Lohengrin who doesn't hide his past, the Lohengrin who says, 'Please, Yehuda, ask me about what my parents did.' You describe yourself honestly as 'a child of perpetrators', born a 'post-Holocaust German'. You say that you have been crucified on the history of

Germany, and I believe you. You don't even ask for forgiveness – all you want is to engage in dialogue to understand what has happened, how it happened, and to ask whether it is possible to prevent it from happening again. You are a German who can help create a world in which we, the Jews, can contemplate forgiveness." What a responsibility that letter and my friendship with Yehuda puts on me!

A similarly strong effect was wrought on me by Michael Wieck's autobiography *Der Untergang von Königsberg – ein Geltungsjude berichtet* [The Decline Of Königsberg – A German Jew Reports], which, through its humanity became the basis of another important friendship in my life. I corresponded with Michael about many things, among them my relationship with my father. Like Yehuda, as child and teenage survivor, first of the Nazi terror and then of the Red Army terror in the former Königsberg in East Prussia (now Kaliningrad, Russia), he has a unique understanding of family and the historical dimensions of the consequences of the Nazi period. In addition, after an internationally successful professional life as a violinist, this distant relative of Clara Schumann-Wieck is also able to appreciate the politico-cultural conflict arising for me as a Wagner and a German born after Hitler's death. After talks with Yehuda and Michael, who met in 1995 at the premiere of my production of *Lohengrin*, I know exactly why work in the Post Holocaust Dialogue Group is meaningful for me.

During a short journey with the painter Toby Heifetz, niece of the world-famous violinist Jascha Heifetz, in autumn 1992, I learned just how much art can help preserve human dignity in the shadow of death and horror. Toby's special artistic talent, and her interest in the activities of our group, was a useful prerequisite for a joint Theresienstadt project. Originally she and I had planned a performance of the Ullmann opera *Der Kaiser von Atlantis* with the conductor John Edward Niles, but it unfortunately came to nothing due to financial problems. Nevertheless, the journey and confrontation with Theresienstadt were to prove important for us.

Preparations for this began, of course, long beforehand. Toby had already created impressive collages on the subject of last days and death from 1991 on, which were then fully to correspond with the visit to Theresienstadt. The journey together – Toby's first to Germany – began in Nuremberg with a visit to the Dürer House and the site of the Nazi rallies, then moved to Bayreuth and the *Festspielhügel,* with its busts of Richard and Cosima relics of Hitler's favourite sculptor, Arno Breker.

Götterdämmerung was being performed that day, conducted by Barenboim. Toby wanted to see inside the theatre and so, at the beginning of the interval, we went to one of the auditorium doors where we were immediately intercepted. The situation was unbearable, and I said angrily to one of the attendants who would not let us enter the auditorium: "Either you let me briefly show Mrs Heifetz from New York the auditorium, or I'll publish something about the police methods on the *Festspielhügel*." We were granted five minutes.

It was a relief to leave Bayreuth and move on to the next stage of the journey: Prague, the Jewish quarter, and then the citadel and the Theresienstadt (Terezin) ghetto. Historical documentation can only partially reproduce the area's witnessed hells, instead leaving the intensity of the "forecourt to Auschwitz" to the individual feelings of the visitor. For me, the art exhibition in Courtyard Four with copies of drawings and paintings of the condemned Bedrich Fritta, Leo Haas, Karel Fleischmann, Otto Ungar, Malina Schalkova, Hugo Sonnenschein, Sona Spitzova, Petr Kien and in particular the drawings of the Theresienstadt children, was a shocking experience. They were almost unbearably intense in their expression of perversion in the Nazi city of Jewish culture, of the "Spa Theresienstadt For European Jewry" as a terminus or intermediate station on the road to murder. Toby and I each photographed our impressions from these pictures, the music and literature and these were shown with critical commentaries in an exhibition *From Bayreuth To Theresienstadt*, in mid December 1992 at the German Industry and Commerce Congress.

In 1995 the American magazine *German Life* asked Abraham and myself to write about our group as part of the fiftieth anniversary of the liberation of Auschwitz, for their April/May issue. It was also another opportunity to reflect on our objectives. Among other things, Abraham wrote: "Amidst the silence and mistrust shared by Germans and Jews, however, individuals in both communities have sought each other out and have attempted to engage in dialogue. Dr Gottfried Wagner and I, for instance, have been involved in a German-Jewish dialogue since 1991. We have appeared before audiences in New Jersey, Ohio, Washington, Oklahoma, and Berlin. And in the fourth year of our encounter it has become painfully clear to both of us that we have not come as far as we had initially envisioned. As Gottfried has stated, we have yet to reach the kind of 'objectivity' necessary to free us from the shadows of the past. He continues to feel shame at the thought of what happened to my family during the Holocaust, and the role played by his family in its suffering. He feels angry and powerless at his inability to provide his family with the sense of mourning necessary to begin the steps towards understanding. Other Germans born after 1945 share similar feelings: they, too, bemoan how difficult it is for them to be Germans, to suffer under the burden of history and the attendant sense of homelessness and rootlessness...Are we engaged in a dialogue of illusions? Do the eyes and ears of the dead and the living see and hear two Don Quixotes attacking windmills drenched in the blood of millions? And are they covered in the *Verdrängung*, the suppression of a confrontation with the crimes of their nation by those too guilty to speak or too tired of the Auschwitz theme to care? Perhaps. But this I have learned. As they run toward their identity as Jews, post-Holocaust Germans and Jews must meet somewhere in the middle. For the moment, it matters less what we have to say to each other than that we believe in the possibility of dialogue.

"But is this possibility worth the encounter, especially when so many Jewish friends tell me that there is absolutely nothing to say to Germans? I was never certain of this until I met Gottfried Wagner. Gottfried and I have been drawn together because we share a common desire to understand each other's burden as a result of who we are and the consequences of our family history. We are still unsure of what results we want to achieve as individuals and as Germans and Jews. Am I looking for a new kind of reparation? Is Gottfried's generation still responsible for confessional memories of guilt? Is Gottfried secretly longing for a teary hug of reconciliation, even after I have told him it is not mine to give?

"We tremble at the thought of all the shadows that lurk over us. But we also know that our post-Holocaust world has not changed enough to withdraw from the challenge. We see the Holocaust all around us, in the brutalities that occur in national and international conflict, in the apathy with which we can view the victims of war, and in our lack of trust in law, religion, medicine, and technology as important and immutable foundations of our world.

"The Holocaust has shaped us both. But we are responsible for helping to shape the way it is remembered by future generations, starting with our own children. Can we go beyond the hatred, guilt and shame of our generation to leave a different world for them?"

In July, I received a phone call from Lara Nuer, the daughter of Claire Nuer, who founded the Institut au Coeur de la Communication (ACC) in Paris, Montreal and San Francisco. She had heard of my work and the Post Holocaust Dialogue Group through Dan Bar On and was planning an international meeting for August that year in Auschwitz under the slogan "The Turning Point". Auschwitz! A meeting in Auschwitz?

Rather nervously I asked Lara what my contribution could be to this meeting. She answered: "We of the ACC know your articles and the aims of your group. Like you, we want dialogue between perpetrators and victims and their children; not just between Germans and Jews, but between all essential conflict groups of past and present. Your aims are very similar to ours. We beg you and Abraham to come to Auschwitz as speakers at the three seminars."

I accepted without hesitation. Lara sent me the main questions for the discussion: "What created the preconditions for such large-scale destruction in the 1940s? What elements of general human behaviour made the unacceptable possible? How does this type of behaviour affect all sections of society?" Contemporary questions followed: "How can we avoid the large-scale destruction that could result from these conditions? How can we instead construct a healthy, sustainable society, beginning with our individual actions within our families, our own work and in smaller communities? How can our individual actions then be transmitted to all sections of society and gain influence?"[52]

Unfortunately Abraham could not attend the meeting, but another member of our group, Tommaso de Cataldo, went with the ACC colleagues from San Francisco. For my part, I prepared various lectures, texts, sound and video material.

Driving past the watchtowers of Auschwitz-Birkenau, I was shocked by the incredible size of this death factory behind barbed wire. I thought of the words of my friend Harry Guterman from Tulsa, who had survived years in this hell: "It was all a lot worse than you can possibly imagine." Dazed, I entered the garden of the Catholic "Meeting House", which is only a stone's throw from the three concentration camps in Auschwitz. The intensity and diversity of what I experienced in the next twelve days in three seminars, can scarcely be described. The human contacts I owe to this place would fill a book.

In particular I want to recount two episodes. The first involves Bernard Offen, who guided us through the concentration camps Auschwitz One and Auschwitz-Birkenau and with whom I shared a hotel room, furnished in socialist style. Our life together had something of the surreal about it, independent of time and space. A survivor of Auschwitz-Birkenau, Plaszow, Julag and Mauthausen, he had been told of my background, although I never sensed any resentment against me for one moment. Before the start of the harrowing tours of the camps he gave me two tips that I will never forget: "What you're going to see now is difficult to describe in words. It will exceed your powers of imagination. Follow my personal fate in Auschwitz, that I'll be telling to all of you. Then six million murdered people will become conceivable to you again. Don't leave the group, because you should not try to come to terms with what you will see and experience there alone. Share your experiences with those who are near to you." I learned with time to follow his advice. But I had wildly overestimated my psychological strength. I had been convinced I could assist others, but now I myself needed help.

At the railway of death in Birkenau, Bernard told us how, on 24 August 1944, his father had been selected to join a group of new arrivals destined for the gas chambers, while Bernard had been sent to the group who were to survive for the time being. At Crematorium Four in Birkenau, he described how the SS sent around 2,000 people to their deaths at each gassing session. I started to cry. Bernard took my hand and silently we went, after saying a *kaddisch* (prayer for the dead) for his father, to his former hiding place near the latrines. On the way Henry Knight supported me, having noticed that I could no longer cope with the situation.

I had imagined that on further tours I would be able to handle the confrontation better. I was deceiving myself. Every new tour through the two concentration camps became even more unbearable, as each time I realised more of the horror of the place. In the beginning I had hoped to be able to protect myself, by acting as photographer. A vain hope. Bernard, who had lived through this hell, was like a father to me. Through his loving understanding I slowly started to grasp that I had to regard this death factory of the past as part of being human. Only afterwards was I aware that the others were weeping as well.

I was further moved by Irit Weir, a young woman from Israel in her mid thirties, who lives in Napa, near San Francisco. During the third seminar, after the renewed confrontation with Crematorium Four and the murder of Bernard's father, the participants went to sit in the shade of a willow tree in front of the monument to Nazi victims. Suddenly Irit stood up and declared to all those present: "First of all I'd like to thank Gottfried for kindly accepting me. Also, I'd like to tell him that here [in Auschwitz] we have switched roles. He is the victim and I am the criminal. He is the one who is suffering here. If we now want to go beyond not accepting the question of guilt [between us] and everything connected with it, as Claire [Nuer] suggested, then we must be more open with one another."

Claire threw in: "Take your time. Guilt does not stop us from being responsible in the correct way for what we want to create."

To which I responded: "I must point out that we in the Post Holocaust Dialogue Group have been talking about guilt and shame. I am grieving. But guilt cannot automatically be passed on to the next generation, because this would start a tragic and terrible vicious circle. But to be here in Auschwitz means for me to feel deep shame. You have helped me replace the words 'guilt' and 'shame' with the word 'mourning', and since yesterday that has been a new experience for me."

After the walks through the camps there were seminars and discussions with representatives of conflicting groups: Jews and Palestinians, Romanies and Sinti, a Serbian woman, a Croatian woman and a Moslem woman. None of us – and we comprised people from thirty-three nations, all engaging in passionate discussion in a confusion of tongues – was seeking out a main culprit. It was much more a matter of creating, in Auschwitz, a higher degree of sensitivity for the suffering of all mankind.

Regrettably, this message of peace, which Claire and Lara so courageously expressed, provoked protest from several French-Jewish circles. The Germans I met in Auschwitz were people in shock, not ashamed of their tears for the millions of murdered Jews, Christians, Romanies and Sinti and all the others. We kept asking ourselves: "What can I, as an individual, and we as a group, do to fight forms of totalitarian behaviour in and around us?" There was talk of becoming human through the common experience of Auschwitz, but never of absolution and redemption by people for people.

When I landed at the Malpensa airport in Milan, Eugenio leapt into my arms and said relieved: "Papa, thank God they didn't kill you there."

I answered with a smile: "On the contrary: I made lots of new friends. We all just want to learn to live in peace with one another." I hope I can convey to my son in the future, what I experienced in Auschwitz, as a further turning point in my life.

CHAPTER TWENTY-EIGHT

EPILOGUE

When the original German edition of this book appeared, at the end of February 1997, I knew that it was likely to polarise public opinion on the subject of "Richard Wagner in Bayreuth". As it was, I underestimated international media interest and the subsequent knock-on effect, because I mistakenly assumed that my autobiography would be driven into the background by other passionately conducted discussions in the German-speaking countries on repression of the Nazi period. Fierce controversy had broken out yet again, over Daniel Goldhagen's book, *Hitler's Willing Executioners*, and over the exhibition on German Nazi Wehrmacht crimes, in Munich. Even "neutral" Switzerland was forced to face up to the repression of Hitler's barbarism, when overwhelming evidence against the Swiss banks aroused worldwide attention to murky business done with Nazi gold – in other words, with stolen Jewish property. Increased international sensitivity to the subject of repression was to help discussion of my book.

On subsequent reading tours, from March to mid December 1997, in Germany, Switzerland, Austria and Belgium I made myself available not only for discussion with my readers, but also with the media, in interviews, round table discussions and talk shows. At the same time I was confronted by published reviews of my book.

The unusually high pressure generated by a crossfire of opinions and the constant travelling made it impossible for me to come to any coherent conclusions on the reactions at the time. Like other authors whose books arouse public controversy, I was forced to recognise that opinions on my autobiography had assumed their own dynamic, which only seldom had anything to do with my intentions. At first, I found the profusion of reactions confusing, for, apart from objective articles – such as those in the *Neue Zürcher Zeitung, Süddeutsche Zeitung, Deutsche Lehrerzeitung, Liechtensteiner Vaterland, Die Presse* – others with a more conformist tendency appeared, based on vague claims to power, which aimed at preventing constructive criticism of the existing politico-cultural situation within the Bayreuth Redemption Co Inc.

The similarity of damaging tactics used by the various conformists in the media scene was striking; in particular, simplification and banalisation of the subject matter, reminding one of Milan Kundera's phrase, in his *The Book Of Laughter And Forgetting*: "The struggle of man against power is the struggle of the memory against forgetting."[53]

While I was trying to analyse the conformist journalists' opinions, I came across the books *Der Wahnzinn Der Normalität* [The Madness Of Normality] and *Falsche Götter* [False Gods] by the psychoanalyst Arno Gruen.

In *False Gods* Gruen sees "the capacity of man from birth to decide over his life. Either his empathy becomes the kernel of his being, or he will constantly try to escape it." In this sense, for Gruen "human development is always the history of the damage to his abilities". Hence he distinguishes between "the integrated man, who remains in contact with his inner self and acts accordingly, and the man who focuses outward, who has a divided consciousness and a divided perception. His actions will always be directed against the holistic and in spite of technological progress, offend against life."[54] In *Madness Of Normality* Gruen describes the split in the inner life of all conformists – therefore in the media too – when dealing with information, in the following way: "In order to rationalise, they have to separate thinking and feeling from one another. Public power is a means for maintaining the inner split. But such a man does not seek power for its own sake, but to find support in it and in order not to disintegrate. Hence he cannot afford any compromises either. Every increase in control enlarges the inner vacuum and of necessity provokes an intensified need for domination. If such people are treated with respect, they will interpret any compliance as weakness. Because for them there is no equality, for them there is only domination and being dominated."⁵⁵ Hence Gruen comes to the general conclusion that for the man "who has surrendered to power, there can basically be no equality in social relations...Dealings with other people are determined by strength and weakness. Therefore more and more power must be accumulated. The aim here is to become invulnerable and be able to prove invulnerability."⁵⁶

But what do Gruen's perceptions have to do with the would-be "Redemption Co Inc" in Bayreuth, conformist journalists of all shades and my autobiography? Anyone who has studied some of the striking reactions of such groups to my book over the past year, will understand the connection.

On 28 February 1997 my father, Wolfgang Wagner, to the applause of the *Festspiele* sponsors, the Society Of Friends Of Bayreuth, foremost among them President E Hilger and private banker KG Schmidt, described my autobiography as "insulting, defamatory and slanderous". With reference to the Bayreuth *Festspiele* he called the book "a considerable impairment and as yet unassessable injury to its international repute". As in his 1994 autobiography, *Acts*, in his three-page open letter to the international media he ignored the influence of Wagner's and Hitler's antisemitism on the *Festspiele* and hence on himself and his work.

It was clear to me that the city of Bayreuth and the media subservient to the *Festspielhügel* would now have to take up positions against me, as my attack on the institution of the *Festspiele* also applied to them. It came as a pleasant surprise to find that the mighty Redemption Co and its circles could neither dominate the international, independent media world in their usual way, with furtive legal threats, nor proceed with demagogic counter-attacks. On the contrary: hitting out at me helped attract even greater international attention to my book. The reaction it had stirred up catapulted it into the bestseller lists in Germany, Austria and Switzerland, and translations into six different languages have been negotiated.

On 10 March, 1997, the mayors of the city of Bayreuth issued an open letter in which my book was decried as "malicious agitation" and they refused to engage in any serious discussion on the effects of Wagner's antisemitism. But this ploy backfired, as discussion flared up anew and international media pressure on the repressive paradise of Bayreuth grew. The contrast between my father's autobiography and mine became more focused and my wish for a disclosure of the connection between family and German history, and the case of the Wagners in Bayreuth was given more and more respect. The *Neue Zürcher Zeitung* of 12-13 April 1997, acknowledged that "[my] book had rendered a contribution to that critical history of Bayreuth that neither Wieland nor Wolfgang Wagner have provided or provoked".

On the very day of my reading in Bayreuth – 24 April 1997 – I learned from the *Nordbayrischer Kurier*, which is loyal to the *Festspielhügel*, an exhibition about my grandmother, Winifred Wagner, Hitler's intimate friend, had been cancelled by the *Festspiele*. The official reason for the cancellation, as reported by the *Neue Zürcher Zeitung* at the end of April was: "...a still incomplete processing of archive material from all over the world which has only recently become accessible. The in-part surprising new facts would first have to be classified according to their historical background, declared Wolfgang Wagner. Selected documents on that part of *Festspiele* history which is accompanied by manifold prejudices [ie the Nazi period] will be published in this year's *Festspiele* book." The truth was that, as a result of discussions inspired by my book, a German bank had withdrawn its offer to finance the planned pro-Winifred Wagner exhibition.

The international media was not fooled: they recognised the *Festspiele* administration's intention to deceive and expressed quite frankly their doubts about the reasons given for the cancellation.

The deception continued at the opening of the Bayreuth *Festspiele* on 25 July, 1997. The *Festspiele* book tried to hoodwink the world's media into believing that six postcards (from the years 1929 to 1936) from Hitler to Winifred Wagner was the sum total of the correspondence from the Führer to the great lady from 1923 to 1945. The atmosphere during the international press conference on 27 July was suitably charged and there were some hard-hitting attacks from the international press regarding the irresponsible treatment of undesirable, incriminating documents before, during and after the Nazi period.

Despite this situation both sponsors and the *Festspiele* administration kept up the attack against me: on 28 August – at the end of the *Festspiele* – one could read in the *Süddeutsche Zeitung* the official, corrected version of events during the press conference on 27

July: "By 'fascist and racist elements', which Wolfgang Wagner identified among many critics [on 27 July 1997], he meant the book by his son Gottfried, not articles by journalists."

The media offensive continued in September when the chief dramaturg of the Bayreuth *Festspiele*, in close cooperation with some members of the Society Of Friends Of Bayreuth, attempted to bring their massive influence to bear on German and international public opinion (*inter alia* in Austria, Britain, the Netherlands and Finland).

The publication of an article in the *Allgemeine Jüdische Wochenzeitung* (AJWZ) on 2 May 1997, played a decisive part in the slander campaign waged by the Redemption Co and its hangers on. The content of the article – by the non-Jewish author Horst Seferens – corresponded to headlines which are revealing as regards the power games played in and around the *Festspiele*: "What Gottfried Wagner still needed to say to his therapist: Wagner's book is an, at times, painful attempt at that grasping philosemitism, with which a certain type of German tries to effect a sort of change of front – an egoistic clutching at Jewish coat tails." Seferens viewed himself later as a victim of headlines he had not written himself, rejected their connection with his "essay" and thought in this way to escape all responsibility. He went even further: he alleged, with reference to an anonymous editor in the *AJWZ*, that the critical counter-views, which had been voiced in the *AJWZ* on 12 June against his article, had been "ordered". Searching questions to the board of the *AJWZ* and many wilfully blind Jewish Wagnerians both inside and outside Germany remain unanswered.

A similar "psychoanalysis" intended as personal defamation was provided in an article by Frederic Spotts, a faithful follower of Wieland Wagner, New Bayreuth pilgrim since 1957, and author of one of the plethora of conformist books on the history of the Bayreuth *Festspiele*. In his article in the July 1997 issue of the London-based *Opera*, he states: "It is debatable whether such a story is appropriately discussed in a cultural publication or in a journal of clinical psychology." I reacted briefly as follows:

"Frederic Spotts' criticism of my autobiography is based on a wrong assumption with regard to the goals which I follow in the book. Contrary to the reviewer's book on the Bayreuth Wagner Festival, my autobiography does not focus on the aesthetic consequences of the theatrical work in Bayreuth since 1951, but mainly on its socio-political implications. Therefore, most of his review misses the essence of my book.

"The attempt to save 'New Bayreuth' with aesthetic arguments – an attempt Spotts supports – forces him into an historically and scientifically untenable assessment of the political role played by the second and third generations post-Richard Wagner.

"The work of observers such as Köhler, Hein, Naegele, Karbaum, Zelinsky, Schüler, Craig, Prieberg, Wulf, Meyer, Wistrich and Ley (among others) has convincingly demonstrated that Wagner's descendants and the 'Bayreuth Circle' developed Wagner's antisemitism to a level of normative space and politics wherein Hitler found it easy to operate after World War I. In my opinion, playing down the history of Bayreuth is dangerous.

"With regard to the reviewer's suggested factual corrections, I have relied on information given to me by my grandmother, Winifred Wagner. Insofar as she – or I – may have erred, these points have already been considered for the English, American, French, Spanish, Italian and Japanese publication of my book, as well as for the third German edition.

"PS: The allegations which the reviewer makes regarding my inheritance are simply false."[57]

The aforementioned persons wanted neither to deal with my autobiography in its development up to the chapter "Eugenio, My Son" nor with the final chapter, "The Post Holocaust Group: And In The Beginning Was Auschwitz"; they remain angrily silent on Ralph Giordano's charge "against the Bayreuth lies" in his introduction, as they do not want to face up to the consequences of his statements. They feel no responsibility when dealing with personal power and therefore their goal remains, to use Gruen's words, "to become invulnerable and be able to prove invulnerability".[58]

Exploring the reasons for this I leave above all to readers of integrity (Gruen), for whom I wrote my autobiography. Despite everything, I do not condemn those named who have attacked me: I am grateful to them for having furthered my autonomy and my future life beyond Wagner and Hitler.

Gottfried Wagner, 18 January 1998, Cerro Maggiore

NOTES

1. *Selected Letters Of Richard Wagner*, edited and translated by Stewart Spencer and Barry Millington, JM Dent & Sons 1987, p 888.

2. Zdenko von Kraft, 'Genius', in: *Das Bayreuther Festspielbuch*, Bayreuth 1951, p 5.

3. Arnold Zweig, 'Antwort an Béla Balazs', in: *Weltbühne*, No 1/1930, p 618.

4. Dietrich Mack, *Das Trauerspiel der Macht, Miszellen zur Ring-Interpretation (nach Gesprächen mit Wolfgang Wagner, aufgezeichnet von Dietrich Mack)*, *Rheingold* programme of 1970 Bayreuth *Festspiele* 1970, pp 3-12.

5. Richard Wagner, 'The Jews In Music', *Wagner* [magazine], translated by Stewart Spencer, Vol 9, No 1, January 1988.

6. Richard Wagner, *Religion And Art* (Chapter 1, 'Know Thyself'), in: *Richard Wagner's Prose Works*, Vol 6, translated by H Ashton Ellis, University of Nebraska Press 1994, p 274.

7. Friedrich Nietzsche, *Human, All Too Human*, translated by RJ Hollingdale, Cambridge University Press 1986, p 80.

8. *Cosima Wagner's Diaries*, Vol 2 (1878-1883), translated and edited by Geoffrey Skelton, Collins 1980, pp 772-3.

9. Houston Stewart Chamberlain, *Richard Wagner*, translated by G Ainslie Hight, JM Dent 1897, p 176.

10. Houston Steward Chamberlain to Adolf Hitler, 8 October 1923, quoted in: Hartmut Zelinsky (ed), *Richard Wagner. Ein deutsches Thema*, Berlin-Vienna 1983, p 169.

11. Winifred Wagner, "Open Letter", in: *Oberfränkische Zeitung*, 14 November 1923, quoted in: Zelinsky, op cit, p 169.

12. Siegfried Wagner, letter to *Deutsche Zeitung*, Berlin, 6 June 1921.

13. Siegfried Wagner to Rosa Eidam, Christmas 1923, in: Michael Karbaum, *Studien zur Geschichte der Bayreuther Festspiele (1876-1976), Part II, Dokumente und Anmerkungen*, Regensburg 1976, p 65.

14. Adolf Hitler to Siegfried Wagner, 5 May 1924, in: Karbaum, op cit, p 65.

15. *Bayreuther Bund der Deutschen Jugend* (BbdJ), 'Proclamation', in: Karbaum, op cit, p 74.

16. Winifred Wagner, *Meistersinger* programme of wartime *Festspiele* 1943, Bayreuth, p 11.

17. Friedrich Nietzsche, 'The Case Of Wagner' in: *Basic Writings Of Nietzsche*, translated and edited by Walter Kaufmann, Modern Library, New York 1968, pp 638-9.

18. Foundation charter of Richard Wagner Foundation, Bayreuth, pp 8, 10ff, and 4, quoted from: Wolfgang Wagner, *Lebensakte*, München 1994, pp 446-463 [the statutes are omitted from English edition, *Acts*, Weidenfeld & Nicolson 1995].

19. Ibid.

20. Ibid.

21. Winifred Wagner in: *Zeit Magazin*, No 19, 30 April 1976.

22. Ibid.

23. Josef Herbort, 'Vom Junior Keine Konkurrenz', in *Die Zeit*, 3 June 1977.

24. Roy Koch, 'Special' [report on the *Fidelio* premiere], in: *The New York Times*, 30 May 1976.

25. Wolf-Siegfried Wagner, Interview with Karsten Peters, in: German edition of *Harper's Bazaar*, April/May 1985.

26. Immanuel Kant, *Critique Of Pure Reason*, quoted in: *Philosophisches Wörterbuch*, Stuttgart 1969, p 621.

27. Nietzsche, 'The Case Of Wagner', p 647.

28. Franz Liszt, 'Chopins Individualität' in: *Gesammelte Schriften*, Vol 1, Hildesheim-New York 1978, pp 94ff.

29. Uri Toeplitz, quoted in: *Neue Zürcher Zeitung*, 8 February 1990.

30. Karl Lubomirski, *Die Zeitpendel (I Pedali Del Tempo)*, Florence 1990, p 25.

31. Richard Wagner to Ludwig II, 14 October 1868, in Spencer and Millington (eds), *Selected Letters Of Richard Wagner*, p 732.

32. Richard Wagner, 'Hero-dom And Christendom', in *Religion And Art*, in: *Richard Wagner's Prose Works*, Vol 6, p 280.

33. Richard Wagner to Mathilde Wesendonck, 1 October 1858, in: Spencer and Millington (eds), *Selected Letters Of Richard Wagner*, p 423.

34. Karl Popper, *Alles Leben ist Problemlosen*, Munich 1995, pp 158ff.

35. Tilmann Jens, 'Der Erbfolgekrieg [the war of succession]', in: *titel, thesen, temperamente*, televised 10 November 1991.

36. Wolfgang Wagner, quoted in: 'Werkstatt Bayreuth im Wandel [workshop Bayreuth undergoing change]', WDR Radio, 3rd Programme, broadcast 30 October 1993.

37. Gina Thomas, 'Wagner Vs Wagner', in: *Frankfurter Allgemeine Zeitung*, 15 April 1995.

38. Larry Mass, 'Met Cancels Gottfried Wagner', in: *Opera Monthly*, October 1992, p 40.

39. Daniel Barenboim, Interview, in: *Opera Monthly*, May-June 1993, p 4.

40. Franklin Littell, 'Confrontation In Bayreuth', in: *Los Angeles Jewish Times*, 27 July 1993.

41. Alice Miller, *Breaking Down The Wall Of Silence*, Dutton, Toronto Ontario, 1991, pp 105ff.

42. Friedrich Heer, *God's First Love. Christians And Jews Over Two Thousand Years*, translated by Geoffrey Skelton, Weidenfeld & Nicolson 1970, dust jacket text.

43. Ibid.

44. Ibid, pp xiv-xv.

45. Sidur Sesat Emet, Edition B (Jewish Bible), Psalm 142.

46. Ibid, Psalm 139.

47. Ilse Blumenthal-Weiss, quoted in: Heer, op cit, p 2.

48. Hartmut Zelinsky, 'Die "Feuerkur" des Richard Wagner oder die "Neue Religion" der "Erlösung Durch Vernichtung" ['Richard Wagner's "Ordeal By Fire" Or The "New Religion" Of "Redemption By Annihilation"', in: *Musik-Konzepten*, No 5/1978, Munich, p 79.

49. Dan Bar On, Introduction to: Dr Abraham Peck and Dr Gottfried H Wagner (eds), *The Uses And Abuses Of Knowledge*, texts submitted at the twenty-third Annual Scholars' Conference on "The Holocaust And The German Church Struggle", 8 March 1993 in Tulsa, Oklahoma, *Studies In The Shoah*, Vol 17, pp 428-30, University Press of America, Lanham, Maryland, 1993.

50. Yehuda Nir, *The Lost Childhood*, Harcourt, Brace Jovanovich, New York 1989, from text on dust jacket.

51. Samuel Beckett, *Malone Dies*, John Calder, London 1956, p 2.

52. Information leaflet of the ACC, Paris, July 1995.

53. Milan Kundera, *The Book Of Laughter And Forgetting*, trans by Aaron Asher, Faber & Faber, London 1996.

54. Arno Gruen, *Falsche Götter – Über Liebe, Hass und die Schwierigkeit des Friedens*, DTV, Munich 1993, p 11.

55. Arno Gruen, *Der Wahnsinn der Normalität, Realität als Krankheit: Eine Grundlegende Theorie zur Menschlichen Destruktivität*, DTV, Munich 1996, p 189.

56. Ibid, p 139.

57. Gottfried Wagner, letter in *Opera*, November 1997, pp 1282-3.

58. See note 56.

INDEX